Making The Point

Making The Point

J. ALEXANDER SCHARBACH
AND
CARL MARKGRAF

Portland State University

THOMAS Y. CROWELL COMPANY
New York • Established 1834

Library of Congress Cataloging in Publication Data

Scharbach, J. Alexander.
    Making the point.

    Includes index.
    1. English language—Rhetoric.   I. Markgraf, Carl,
joint author.   II. Title.
PE1408.S29   1975   808'.042   75-4863
ISBN 0-690-00764-7

Thomas Y. Crowell Company
666 Fifth Avenue
New York, New York 10019

Typography design by Libra Graphics, Inc.

Manufactured in the United States of America

CONTENTS

A List of Articles According to Writing Principles

PLAIN STYLE

AWARENESS

ANALYSIS

PROBLEM SOLVING

SOCRATIC DIALOGUE

RHETORICAL TONES AND STYLES

ARGUMENT

In the final analysis, writing is an art and a craft and should be treated as such. Like music and painting, it can provide a doorway to the discovery and development of one's inner being. It satisfies the human need to articulate one's deepest thoughts and feelings, and to reach out to communicate with others. It offers fulfillment, and it offers joy. Beyond this, writing is a door to discovery of the world outside. We are all aware of the power of the written word to help order and synthesize the mass of confused information that every day piles in upon us, to create—even if only momentarily—a sense of understanding and control without which life becomes insupportably complicated.

[Regina M. Hoover, "Taps for Freshman English?" *College Composition and Communication* XXV (May 1974); 153].

About This Book

The title—*Making the Point*—bluntly states the practical nature of this book. It speaks to student-writers of whatever condition and of all ethnic backgrounds and shows them not only how to discover and bring into clear focus what they have to say but also how to make their points in language and structures most appropriate to their intended readers.

We have tried to be direct and honest about composition difficulties and problems we all encounter just as we urge students to be in their own writing. In introducing fundamentals of composing and rhetorical strategies, we have tried to be *descriptive* rather than *prescriptive*. Whenever possible, we lead students to discover for themselves what basic features make a composition effective, whether it be a letter-to-the-editor, an essay examination answer, a speech, a business report, or a scientific analysis. We use frequent examples. For this reason all selections, which are listed by rhetorical type following the Table of Contents, are closely interwoven with explanatory text and lead directly from one to the other.

Pedagogically, we agree with psychologists like Peter M. Hall, who maintain that "Development and growth require open, not closed, flexible, not rigid, systems. Development and growth require thinking and consciousness which depend on diversity, heterogeneity, conflict, alternatives, challenges, change. . . . Habit and routine are the consequence of stability and custom and reflect the opposite of development. An individual, to develop and use his potential, must be challenged, must accept ambiguity, must participate in conflict and must seek to grow and develop with the rest of his associates."[1]

As our grateful acknowledgments will show, we share, too, with our colleagues—the many contributors to NCTE journals devoted to better teaching—an awareness of the critical importance today of *ethnic writing*. In the case of Blacks, Chicanos, and American Indians, we not only introduce some of their literary voices but also deal frankly with the issues of Bidialectalism (biloquialism). Who can doubt that the outcome of debate over these controversial matters will help determine both the quality of life of those millions who speak dialects at variance with Standard English and the future character of American civilization and culture?

Over the years in teaching "freshman comp," we have tested whatever new approaches and theories we thought would help student-writers grow and mature while discovering that composition can be learned and, therefore, taught. This book reflects that eclecticism. We have deliberately drawn upon at least eight fields of subject matter, in or out of fashion, that can be made helpful to beginning writers: Grammar, Rhetoric, Literary Criticism, Linguistics, Semantics, Tagmemics, Problem Solving, and Hermeneutics. Also we have taken from the behavioral sciences whatever we judged insightful and helpful.

The order or sequence of chapter material we present need not, of course, be followed. Ours is conventional enough, dealing as it does first with motivation, next the problems of language and dialects, and then the sentence and the paragraph, followed by much emphasis upon "Thinking and Feeling for Writing" and "Rhetoric and Style." These last two sections we have tried to give fresh consideration and treatment.

In the preparation of this book we are especially appreciative, too, of the Portland State University Library staff and particularly of Mr. Edmond Gnoza of the Humanities section.

[1] "Social Factors Limiting the Development of Human Potentialities," in *Explorations in Human Potentialities*, ed. Herbert A. Otto (Springfield: C.C. Thomas 1966), p. 157.

1

College Writing Now and Your Future

No one needs to tell an earnest college student that getting a higher education is demanding and often even exhausting. Going faithfully to classes, meeting assignment deadlines, and finding the energy to concentrate while doing required reading take their toll. And if you also have a part-time job, as many must to eat and to pay for ever-mounting tuition costs and fees, you find that being a student requires real dedication.

Besides these demands, you have to cope with the personal and social changes that always follow going to college. You encounter new problems involving your values and attitudes toward others—especially your family and friends, old as well as new. It is painful to discover that personal growth necessarily means change, and change results in new choices and, frequently, in painful compromises.

If getting a higher education is so trying, why does anyone—why do you?—put up with it?

Polls taken on college campuses provide answers such as these: to enjoy the respect a college education brings, to earn a better living, to learn more about myself and others, and to be a more useful citizen. These desires are at least partly reflected in this list taken from a survey of successful executives. Note what factors they put in the first two places.

SUCCESS ATTAINMENT FACTORS (CONTRIBUTIVE AND CAUSATIVE)

1. *Intelligence* — Having one or more of the abilities of mental acuity, reasoning, comprehension, and common sense

2. *Verbalization Skills* — Having the ability for effective expression, for conveying true meaning

3. *Integrity* — Having high religious, ethical, or moral values, and honesty

4. *Self-concept* — Having belief in self, acceptance of self; may include freedom from shame and anxiety, nondefensive attitudes

5. *Leadership ability* — Having the ability to get things done through others; may include team building and charismatic qualities; may include the ability to work with people

6. *Adaptability* — Having the ability to adapt to changing conditions and requirements, adapting to or coping with adversity; may include continuous pursuit of knowledge and skill attainment, progressiveness

7. *Aspirations* — Having the desire to achieve; ambitious; aspiring to raise oneself above others or to acquire wealth or personal gain

8. *Drive* — Having qualities of determination, persistence, diligence; work oriented, hard worker

9. *Commitment* — Having the characteristic of setting goals; may include risk taking, pledging self to objectives and goals of firm, pledging self to help others

10. *Accidental factors* — Good health, good luck, being at the right place at the right time; being with a growth oriented firm; help from others; educational background, social background, family background, father's influence, inheritance; opportunistic, appropriate, or favorable circumstances[1]

Now it is true that the kind of writing you are asked to do in an English composition class may seldom be related directly to the letters,

[1] Dick Berry, "How Executives Account for Their Success," *Business Horizons* 16 (October 1973): 33.

reports, memorandums, etc., you will be required to write later in your profession or career. But what you are being asked to do is to learn to explore ideas and facts, to enlarge your understanding of people and life, and to mature mentally while learning to express your own judgments and feelings.

You probably do not need to be told that English instructors naturally seek to infuse into their classes the *humanistic* state of mind, which is a way of looking at oneself and life quite alien to many students. For example, in your courses in your major field—business administration, science, education, art, social science—you know you are preparing for a possible future career or a desirable pattern of living dependent upon mastery of concepts and techniques necessary for that world. You are learning useful facts and theories. But what happens in your English composition classes? All of a sudden you find yourself being asked to be creative, to discover and explore sensations and feelings you may not have realized you had. You are asked to deal with ethical and aesthetic values until then never considered. In short, the composition class may become a quite unsettling—if exciting—atmosphere. Then, too, you not unnaturally find yourself trying to please this humanistic-minded instructor, a task calling for potentialities you may not have known you possess.

Yet it is this process of intellectual and personal growth resulting from such assignments, however disturbing and confusing they may be at times, that have made these composition courses required by most colleges. Since writing involves thought and emotion as well as skill in using language, these courses can be most challenging. They call for development of awareness of ideas and the power of the language to express them. They teach you to concentrate upon a train of thought while seeking to gain a desired emotional response from the reader. They encourage you to see clearly the other side of any argument so as to be prepared to counter it. Yet demanding as it may be, any composition course offers the unique excitement of seeing your own personal observations and understanding of people and situations come to life on paper.

And what has often been said is true: frequently a student may seem stupid only because he has not been taught to be bright. Even the average student can learn to become an effective writer if he has the proper motivation. If you would do well in developing yourself as a writer and even as a speaker, you might take advantage of other psychological suggestions:

Find your best time to write; know what distracts you and take it into account; if talking is a substitute for writing, do not talk over your ideas.

1. Take your own temperamental disposition into account.

2. But do not be too anxious. Although anxiety helps in gearing one up to do simple tasks, too much of it hurts.

3. Try to develop states of mind and emotions favorable to whatever assignment you undertake. So do not give up before you start or begin finding good excuses for not going ahead.

4. Try to avoid unfavorable surroundings that hinder you from making a genuine effort. Writing a composition requires concentration, as you well know.

5. Reward yourself every time you receive a favorable response to your work or attain a goal. But do not wholly identify good work with high grades. Some of your failures may be most important to your development in that you have tried to reach out beyond your present ability.

6. Do not put down any opportunity to learn. Regard even painful experiences as part of the process of maturing.

7. Find reassurance in the fact that even professional writers share many of the same problems you face in trying to write.

One of these basic difficulties has been memorably stated by James Baldwin, an outstanding black author who knows what it means to try to write honestly about the facts of life today. Baldwin was asked this question by an editor: "In what way—if any—do you feel that the problem of writing for the Fifties has differed from the problems of writing in other times? Do you believe that this age makes special demands on you as a writer?"

Here is Baldwin's reply:

> I suppose that it has always been difficult to be a writer. Writers tell us so; and so does the history of any given time or place and what one knows of the world's indifference. But I doubt that there could ever have been a time which demanded more of the writer than do these present days. The world has shrunk to the size of several ignorant armies; each of them vociferously demanding allegiance and many of them brutally imposing it. Nor is it easy for me, when I try to examine the world in which

I live, to distinguish the right side from the wrong side. I share, for example, the ideals of the West—freedom, justice, brotherhood—but I cannot say that I have often seen these honored; and the people whose faces are set against us have never seen us honor them at all.

But finally for me the difficulty is to remain in touch with the private life. The private life, his own and that of others, is the writer's subject— his key and ours to his achievement. Nothing, I submit, is more difficult than deciphering what the citizens of this time and place actually feel and think. They do not know themselves; when they talk, they talk to the psychiatrist; on the theory, presumably, that the truth about them is ultimately unspeakable. This thoroughly infantile delusion has its effects: it is contagious. The writer trapped among a speechless people is in danger of becoming speechless himself. For then he has no mirror, no corroborations of his essential reality; and this means that he has no grasp of the reality of the people around him. What the times demand, and in an unprecedented fashion, is that one *be*—not seem—outrageous, independent, anarchical. That one be thoroughly disciplined—as a means of being spontaneous. That one resist at whatever cost the fearful pressures placed on one to lie about one's own experience. For in the same way that the writer scarcely ever had a more uneasy time, he has never been needed more.[2]

In short, to write anything meaningful means, then, to respond to challenges. And "To be challenged—by a person, by God, by a possibility that has been imagined, a problem or crisis—means that an individual *cannot* ignore the situation at hand and devote his attention elsewhere. Challenges, almost by definition, are attention grabbing."[3]

FRESHMAN COMP—WHAT CAN IT DO FOR ME?

Probably no other course receives as much attention and concern from those responsible for it as does good old freshman comp. Perhaps if you have some understanding of the different philosophies regarding this basic course, you may more clearly see its value to you. Here are two statements by outstanding composition instructors who, as you can see, have strong feelings on the subject.

[2] Excerpted from *The Fire Next Time* by James Baldwin. Copyright © 1962, 1963 by James Baldwin. Used with permission of The Dial Press.

[3] Sidney M. Jourard, "Towards a Psychology of Transcendent Behavior" in *Explorations in Human Potentialities*, ed. Herbert A. Otto (Springfield, Ill.: Charles C. Thomas, Publishers, 1966), pp. 369–370.

What is Freshman Composition about? Recently, in *College English*, Robert Russell acknowledged that "The course was not designed to train students to write for English teachers. Its primary object was to develop the student's ability to write coherent, literate, expository prose of the sort that he would be asked to write throughout the other departments of the College."* There is nothing extraordinary about this statement. It is for this purpose that I chose it. A survey of journals would uncover hundreds of similar statements. May I paraphrase? The goal of Freshman Composition is to teach the student to write an acceptable essay in another course. Yes. While I agree that the goal is not and should not be to teach students how to write for English teachers, yet it is a paltry, pitiful goal to ask students to spend a minimum of 3 hours a week, 18 weeks a semester, preparing to write an essay in another class. What has this got to do with their *lives*? (Biblical tone intended.) Oh I know, it prepares them for class which prepares them for the exams, which prepare them for the degree, which prepares them for, which prepares them for, which prepares them for. . . . Bull! What has this to do with life?[4]

* Robert Russell, "The Question of Composition—A Record of Struggle," *College English* XXX (November 1968): 173.

The subject of the course is the students' writing. It is secondarily their thinking, to the extent that their thinking expresses itself in words. The aim of the course is to make the students write better, or to put it another way, to improve their verbal thinking, to extend their ability to capture and create experience with words. . . . We want to help our students transform experience into knowledge, verbalize whatever they have done or undergone, so that they will know what these are. . . . We want, then, to help the students towards exploring, defining, and so in part mastering themselves and the world around them, which is largely a world of words. . . . We should like to lead students towards the means through which they might escape their inarticulateness, no matter how fluent it is, because inarticulateness, as we all know, has political, as well as psychological consequences. All people, including those who, like many of our former students, look daggers from out of their silent, suburban rage, want a "voice." They want to be heard, but first they must learn to speak, and here the teacher of composition can be of use.[5]

Frankly, all English teachers share such views, but we dread one thing more than anything else. What is that? Student apathy.

Student apathy. Its signs are the looks of boredom and reluctance

[4] Deena Metzger, "Relevant 'Relevance,'" *College Composition and Communication* 31 (December 1969): 339.

[5] George Stade, "Hydrants into Elephants," *College English* 31 (November 1969): 149.

too often seen on classroom faces. Its sounds are the repressed groans and hostile—or worse yet, resigned—voices moaning, "What are we expected to write on this time? How long has it got to be?" Its sad results are the lifeless, superficial "essays" some of which bear penciled word-totals in the margins.

To combat that apathy and turn hostility into creative energy, instructors have been urged, at one time or the other, to adopt a wide variety of means and approaches to teaching composition. Obviously, some of these will be considered "good" by some instructors and "bad" by others. Our purpose in presenting them is to suggest how rich and complex are the resources of English when applied to teaching writing.

1. *Grammar.* For too many years it was thought absolutely necessary to make students masters of *syntax* (the ways in which words form phrase and sentence patterns). It could include also *morphology* (word structure) and *phonology* (pronunciation). It is now recognized that a knowledge of grammar does not in itself enable one to write effectively. Its appeal to some composition instructors is that grammar is a subject matter full of specific details.

2. *Literature.* Some departments of English continue to argue that the study of works of English and American literature should be the main subject-matter content of composition courses. The theory is that literature is the English instructor's specialty and provides great models as well as humanistic values as topics. Others, however, favor adopting as models for student writing the kind of professional writing found in current periodicals dealing with controversial issues and viewpoints.

3. *Linguistics.* The study of the nature and structure of human speech has also received much emphasis as an approach. Its close ties with social sciences such as anthropology as well as its impact upon grammar make this approach appealing to many language specialists.

4. *Rhetoric.* For centuries, rhetoric was thought of only in terms of Aristotle's "the art of persuasion." But in recent years it has come to include study of all the possible means whereby speakers and writers try to make audiences or readers "identify" with them and their "messages." The term has of late been much abused as "dressed up lies."

5. *Stylistics.* The examination in literary works of all the features of language, form, and thought that make up the individual style of an author is another way of fostering language awareness.

6. *Seminar.* This approach favors small classes wherein the students are divided into groups engaged in reading and editing one another's work, raising questions about the nature of writing, conferring with the instructor when necessary, participating in conferences with other groups in the class, and even "publishing" their best efforts.

But none of these approaches in itself ensures intense student interest and good writing attempts. And for good reason — almost everyone finds writing unnatural!

SPEECH VERSUS WRITING

Direct speech face to face is the "natural" way of communicating with someone. In fact, many languages are wholly oral ones and have no system of writing. In speech we have the advantage also of the tones of voice, facial expressions, gestures, and body movements of the kind now called "body English." The main advantage of speech over writing is that you can see whether you are being understood, agreed with, or doubted. As a result, if necessary, you can swiftly change your verbal strategies as well as your original purpose. In *Huckleberry Finn*, Mark Twain well illustrated such possibilities. The scene below follows the one in which Huck's conscience made him feel he had done the wrong thing in helping his slave friend, Jim, escape to freedom. Huck is on the verge of turning Jim over to slave hunters on the river when he decides he should go against his "social conscience" and not turn Jim in after all.

Right then along comes a skiff with two men in it with guns, and they stopped and I stopped. One of them says:
"What's that yonder?"
"A piece of a raft," I says.
"Do you belong on it?"
"Yes, sir."
"Any men on it?"
"Only one, sir."

"Well, there's five niggers run off to-night up yonder, above the head of the bend. Is your man white or black?"

I didn't answer up prompt. I tried to, but the words wouldn't come. I tried for a second or two to brace up and out with it, but I warn't man enough—hadn't the spunk of a rabbit. I see I was weakening; so I just give up trying, and up and says:

"He's white."

"I reckon we'll go and see for ourselves."

"I wish you would," says I, "because it's pap that's there, and maybe you'd help me tow the raft ashore where the light is. He's sick—and so is mam and Mary Ann."

"Oh, the devil! we're in a hurry, boy. But I s'pose we've got to. Come, buckle to your paddle, and let's get along."

I buckled to my paddle and they laid to their oars. When we had made a stroke or two, I says:

"Pap'll be might much obleeged to you, I can tell you. Everybody goes away when I want them to help me tow the raft ashore, and I can't do it by myself."

"Well, that's infernal mean. Odd, too. Say, boy, what's the matter with your father?"

"It's the—a—the—well, it ain't anything much."

They stopped pulling. It warn't but a mighty little ways to the raft now. One says:

"Boy, that's a lie. What *is* the matter with your pap? Answer up square now, and it'll be the better for you."

"I will, sir, I will, honest—but don't leave us, please. It's the—the—Gentlemen, if you'll only pull ahead, and let me heave you the headline, you won't have to come a-near the raft—please do."

"Set her back, John, set her back!" says one. They backed water. "Keep away, boy—keep to looard. Confound it, I just expect the wind has blowed it to us. Your pap's got the smallpox and you know it precious well. Why didn't you come out and say so? Do you want to spread it all over?"

"Well," says I, a-blubbering. "I've told everybody before, and they just went away and left us."

"Poor devil, there's something in that. We are right down sorry for you, but we—well, hang it, we don't want the smallpox, you see. Look here, I'll tell you what to do. Don't you try to land by yourself, or you'll smash everything to pieces. You float along down about twenty miles and you'll come to a town on the left-hand side of the river. It will be long after sun-up then, and when you ask for help you tell them your folks are all down with chills and fever. Don't be a fool again and let people guess what is the matter. Now we're trying to do you a kindness; so you just put twenty miles between us, that's a good boy. It wouldn't do any good to land yonder where the light is—it's only a wood-yard. Say, I reckon your father's poor, and I'm bound to say he's in pretty hard luck. Here, I'll put

a twenty-dollar gold piece on this board, and you get it when it floats by.
I feel mighty mean to leave you, but my kingdom! it won't do to fool with
smallpox, don't you see?"

"Hold on, Parker," says the man, "here's a twenty to put on the board
for me. Good-by, boy; you do as Mr. Parker told you, and you'll be all
right."

Thanks to Mark Twain's skill as a writer, this incident "sounds"
like an older but still wily Huck reminiscing about a great moment in
his youth. Twain shows the power of real-life dialogue, of voices bat-
tling with one another for advantage as can be found only in speech.
The scene is a great one in literature because, as he has throughout this
novel, Twain has found the proper "voice" for Huck.

"VOICE" AS SELF-DISCOVERY

Finding your own *voice* as a writer may still be your biggest problem as a beginning student-writer. You may see yourself as already able
to play the role of the kind of career person you hope to become — say a
technician, nurse, teacher, accountant, physician, lawyer, social worker,
scientist, or artist. You may even be able to think and speak with some
confidence about matters in your chosen field. In this sense you have
found your voice, meaning an outlook on life and a personality consistent with your ambitions. But what happens to this confident voice
when you enter a composition class?

If "finding your voice" means speaking or writing on topics you
know something about and have strong feelings and opinions on, then
it is synonymous with *sincerity*. Peter Elbow, an instructor at MIT, has
made this point most effectively.

> Consistent, trustworthy, and solid writing—not dull writing, how-
> ever—comes only when the writer has found his own voice and is thus
> writing sincerely. In fact, it is this location within the self which is a nec-
> essary home base for full utilization of flights of obliquity.
> My main argument for sincerity, however, is simply that a terrific
> liberation occurs when a writer finds his voice. I can only guess at the
> cause of this freeing up process. It seems that except for the rare person
> who is both very talented and very confident, the real sound of one's voice
> is scarey. We shrink at the sound of it. (Just the other day a student wrote
> of how frightening it would be to meet himself alone in a well-lighted
> alley.) Writing, then, is characteristically unclear because it so often con-

sists of *using* one's voice while at the same time shrinking from the use of it and thus disguising it. A person writes consistently and well only when he becomes comfortable with the sound of his true voice.[6]

As it has been for centuries, the test for sincerity remains one of the best means of judging the worth of any piece of writing, and, as you may well know from experience, when you do not believe in what you are trying to say, a writing assignment becomes a torturous ordeal. Sincerity and voice are thus tied in with one's personality, one's basic character, viewpoints, tastes, and self-image. If you are displeased with your present voice, you can change it, improve it, by making changes in your life. In modern existential terms, you are what you do; so change what you do and you change what you are. After all, isn't "growing up" a matter of adopting views and roles consistent with your concept of being "a man" or "a woman" of the kind you would like to be?

Back in 1762, a young Scot by the name of James Boswell went to London in order to find a suitable career and "personality" for himself. Here is how he has expressed his own confusing experience in trying to shape himself and his future and thus find his voice. The marginal notes serve to summarize the various stages he goes through during a short time period.

He wishes to act and be dignified.

He values being proud and regards himself as "a superior animal."

He candidly admits his failure to live up to his ideal of being a serious-minded person.

He confesses that on being forced to return home he hid his low spirits by doing wild things.

I was now upon a plan of studying polite reserved behaviour, which is the only way to keep up dignity of character. And as I have a good share of pride, which I think is very proper and even noble, I am hurt with the taunts of ridicule and am unsatisfied if I do not feel myself something of a superior animal. This has always been my favourite idea in my best moments. Indeed, I have been obliged to deviate from it by a variety of circumstances. After my wild expedition to London in the year 1760, after I got rid of the load of serious reflection which then burthened me, by being always in Lord Eglinton's company, very fond of him, and much caressed by him, I became dissipated and thoughtless. When my father forced me down to Scotland, I was at first low-spirited, although to appearance very high. I afterwards from my natural vivacity en-

[6] Peter Elbow, "Comment and Rebuttal," *College Composition and Communication* 30 (April 1969): 594.

But all the time he secretly knew he was not the "inferior being" his companions thought him to be.

He recalls pretending to laugh off criticism of his clownish behavior.

He wanted to be a man of dignity but excuses his failure on grounds he lacked enough money to play the role.

He wryly admits coming into money did not transform him into the lofty-minded man he wanted to be.

Gradually he faced up to facts about himself but still wished to imitate men he admired.

deavoured to make myself easy; and like a man who takes to drinking to banish care, I threw myself loose as a heedless, dissipated, rattling fellow who might say or do every ridiculous thing. This made me sought after by everybody for the present hour, but I found myself a very inferior being; and I found many people presuming to treat me as such, which notwithstanding of my appearance of undiscerning gaiety, gave me much pain. I was, in short, a character very different from what God intended me and I myself chose. I remember my friend Johnson told me one day after my return from London that I had turned out different from what he imagined, as he thought I would resemble Mr. Addison. I laughed and threw out some loud sally of humour, but the observation struck deep. Indeed, I must do myself the justice to say that I always resolved to be such a man whenever my affairs were made easy and I got upon my own footing. For as I despaired of that, I endeavoured to lower my views and just to be a good-humoured comical being, well liked either as a waiter, a common soldier, a clerk in Jamaica, or some other odd out-of-the-way sphere. Now, when my father at last put me into an independent situation, I felt my mind regain its native dignity. I felt strong dispositions to be a Mr. Addison. Indeed, I had accustomed myself so much to laugh at everything that it required time to render my imagination solid and give me just notions of real life and of religion. But I hoped by degrees to attain to some degree of propriety. Mr. Addison's character in sentiment, mixed with a little of the gaiety of Sir Richard Steele and the manners of Mr. Digges, were the ideas which I aimed to realize.[7]

Like the rest of his *London Journal*, this excerpt shows James Boswell at the age of 22 as an ambitious young man frankly admitting his shortcomings in language that rings with sincerity. He has already found his proper voice by writing about his life in London with honest candor.

[7] From *Boswell's London Journal, 1762–1763*, Frederick A. Pottle, ed. Copyright 1950 by Yale University. Used with permission of McGraw-Hill Book Company.

And also like his later *Life of Johnson*, the *Journal* reveals Boswell's genius for making the story of his daily life at the same time an authentic history of the world of London as it was 200 years ago.

Donald M. Murray, professor of English at the University of New Hampshire, sees that the student-writer has four responsibilities to face up to in trying to find his own original voice. The first of these is the right, or duty, to find his own subject. The instructor may suggest certain general areas of subject matter that possibly may appeal to the student, but even if he wishes to he cannot go much beyond that. Only the student himself knows how he sees the world and really feels about it.

The student's second responsibility is to find for himself the facts and data which will support his beliefs and the views he advances to make his point to the reader. To discover supporting facts, he must make the creative effort of examining his experience, even spending some time in selective reading in a library.

Being aware of the possible criticism to come from his readers and, therefore, taking into account the demands of that reader-audience is the student's third responsibility. If he has a voice, he will have listeners, and he should want to win their respect if not always their agreement with what he has to say.

The fourth charge may be the most difficult one of all, for it involves the student's finding the most suitable *form* for his subject. How can he best make his point? Should he choose just to explain it? Should he make a story of it or couch it in a fable or a drama? He must realize that *how* is almost as important as *what*.[8]

These four areas of responsibility will be taken up in considerable detail throughout this book. Another and perhaps better way of looking at them is to see them as freedoms. They permit and encourage you as a writer to explore your knowledge of the world and your experience in it. Also they make you in many respects your own taskmaster and critic, and in doing that they ensure your personal growth and give maturity to your voice.

It is not easy to accept such responsibility. In trying to avoid it, some will make the excuse: "I'm no genius and I'm no great brain, either." Perhaps the best reply to such an excuse is to say, "Across the country, there are about 1 million freshmen like you taking comp right now. How many of them are geniuses or super brilliant students?"

"Genius" and "talent," words often loosely used, tend to discourage many people from even trying to be original. What a famous English

---

[8] Donald M. Murray, "Finding Your Own Voice," *College Composition and Communication* 20 (May 1969): 119–120.

critic and essayist, William Hazlitt, said in his essay "On Genius and Common Sense" still holds true:

> Genius or originality is, for the most part, some strong quality in the mind, answering to and bringing out some new and striking quality in nature. . . . [An artist like Rembrandt, for example] saw things that everyone had missed before him, and gave others eyes to see them with. . . . Capacity is not the same thing as genius. Capacity may be described to relate to the quantity of knowledge, however acquired; genius to its quality and the mode of acquiring it. Capacity is a power over given ideas or combinations of ideas; genius is the power over those which are not given, and for which no obvious or precise rule can be laid down. Or capacity is power of any sort; genius is power of a different sort from what has yet been shown. A retentive memory, a clear understanding is capacity, but it is not genius.

Hazlitt's insight here deserves further thought. He clearly says any intelligent person having a good memory and some definite ideas about life and people drawn from his memory of past experiences may have the *capacity* to write. And this capacity can be broadened and deepened by thinking through what has been lived and what has been learned by that experience.

So no one has to be a genius to be *original* in thought and expression, but he does have to work to increase his capacity to see common sense facts in the world around him. Anyone who makes the effort can, as Hazlitt said of Rembrandt, give "others eyes to see" the truth as he knows it. And that is the source of all power.

FOCUS POINT: PREWRITING CONSIDERATIONS

1. Try to decide what it is you want from college.

2. Sort out values important to you.

3. Make yourself language conscious.

4. Examine the possibilities freshman comp offers you.

5. Understand just why writing may be "unnatural."

6. Begin discovering your own proper voice.

TOPICS FOR DISCUSSION AND WRITING

1. With honesty and your present best skill, write on one of the following topics. Your instructor may first call for a class discussion of some of these wide-open subjects. If so, make your statement deal with the points raised by your classmates but mainly go into detail on your own views and why you believe them true. As much as possible, draw upon your own experiences to back up what you have to say.

   What I want from college
   What high school did not prepare me to expect
   Working on a job is also educational
   Why a good friend decided against more education
   The kind of writing I did in high school
   Television programs having personalities I like (dislike)

2. Here is a brief statement of a principle and program on which Evergreen College, a new institution, has been established. What do you think of the educational values and system it suggests?

   Synopsized, Evergreen's mission is to create graduates "[who] can, as adults, be undogmatic citizens and uncomplacent individuals in a changing world." To achieve this, the College has adopted a problem-centered learning approach—that is, most credit-bearing academic programs are designed to encourage the student to seek solutions to real or hypothetical problems, bringing to bear on those problems all the knowledge and skill he may already possess as well as any additional knowledge and skill he or his instructor may deem necessary for him to learn in order for him to arrive at a solution.[9]

3. What are the problems you are going to have to cope with if you are to become a more effective writer? Write an analysis listing and discussing these problems.

4. Everyone, no matter what his or her family and social backgrounds are, has keen memories of various experiences that in some way have revealed what "life" is all about. Try to recall some such im-

[9] Kenneth A. Donohue, "Reinvesting Higher Education," *Business Education Forum* 27 (February 1973): 24.

portant moment, and, as best as you can, find words for it. The following are some possible memory aids:

It happened in the store on the corner.
I was standing in line.
They were new neighbors.
We had this car.
He was the kind of person you have to watch out for.
Nobody seemed to want the dog.
The first time it was easy.
He was just another policeman.
No one ever told me.
I wasn't looking for trouble.
My best friend moved away that year.
It was really beautiful.

5. Begin keeping a journal writing down daily experiences and ideas that seem worth recording. This is a practice followed by many professional authors who regard journal entries as good source material.

2

Your Language and Your Readers

WHO IS TALKING?

No one who gives it some thought is likely to deny that we are all shaped by the language we have been brought up to speak and the culture that goes with that language. This being true, what can we learn from the following two pieces of writing? What does the language of each tell us of its author?

They keep on telling us, those welfare ladies, to take better care of our money, and save it away, and buy what's the best in the stores, and do like them for dresses, and keep the children in school, and keep our husbands from leaving us. There isn't nothing they don't have a sermon on. They'll tell you it's bad to spend your money on a smoke or a drink; and it's bad to have your kids sleep alongside you in the bed and you're not supposed to want television because you should be serious with your dollar, and it's wrong for kids, too; and it's bad for you to let them stay out after dark, and they should study their lessons hard and they'll get away ahead and up there.

Well, I'll tell you, they sure don't know what it's about, and they can't know if they come knocking on my door every week until the Lord takes all of us. They have their nice leather shoes, and their smart coats, and they speak the right order of words all right, so I know how many schools they been to. But us? Do they have any idea of what us is about? And let them start at zero the way we do, and see how many big numbers they can become themselves. I mean, if you have got nothing when you're born, and you know you can't get a thing no matter how you tries — well, then you dies with nothing. And no one can deny that arithmetic.

They just don't understand what it's like. You are born in a building where it's cold, and the rats keep you company all day and you are lucky if they don't eat you at night, because they're as hungry as you.

Then the food, it's not always around when you want it, and you don't have money to buy what you do want. Then you go to those schools, and the teachers, they looks down on you, and makes you think you have done something wrong for being born. They shout and make faces, and they treat you like dirt and then tell you to be a doctor or a lawyer; if you just go to the library and stay in school and be neat, that's all it takes. Once in a while lately they want to take you on a trip crosstown, and show you a museum or something. They tell you that you haven't got any pictures at home. So there, take a look and now you own them, and man, you're rich.[1]

  The best way of knowing what it means to be a Negro is to be a Negro. To put it more poignantly, as Baldwin says, "Search, in his shoes, for a job, for a place to live, ride, in his skin, on segregated buses, see with his eyes, the signs saying 'White' and 'Colored' and especially the signs saying 'White Ladies' and 'Colored Women.' "* Griffin, author of *Black Like Me* (New American Library of World Literature), tried this approach by medically darkening his skin to discover what it is like to be black in America. Obviously, there are obstacles inherent in this direct kind of education. Seemingly, the next best approach to obtaining a close inside feeling for what is going on in another man's life is through day-to-day interaction with him and his. Complexities prevent our use of this approach too. So we settle for a third best way. We seek to approximate the Negro's experiences as closely as we can by use of literature (novels, short stories, biographies, autobiographies, diaries, poetry, and drama), in which the author has expressed himself in such a way that we can identify with him and live the experiences, albeit vicariously. Thus literature can give us a closer inside feeling for what is going on in our Negro culture.[2]

  * James Baldwin, *The Fire Next Time* (New York: Dell Publishing Co., 1963), p. 77.

What are the similarities and the differences between these two selections? In both, the "voices" we hear are those of women saying something very important to them, but each has a different social background and is addressing a different audience. The first speaker is a black woman talking out of the depths of her bitter experience of being

[1] From Jack Daniel, "The Poor: Aliens in an Affluent Society," *Today's Speech* 18 (Winter 1970): 18. By permission of the publisher.

[2] Nancy L. Arnez, "Racial Understanding through Literature," *English Journal* 58 (January 1969): 56.

poor, black, and on welfare. She voices her resentment against the "welfare ladies" who "have nice leather shoes, and their smart coats, and they speak the right order of words all right, so I know how many schools they been to."

Listening to her, you know this woman has the right to speak as she does and she has not lost her sense of humor—bitter though it be—and her compassion for others, even for the rats which "keep you company all day and you are lucky if they don't eat you at night, because they're as hungry as you."

In dramatic contrast, the voice of the second speaker is obviously that of a white woman who is very well educated and who is addressing other educators like herself. She is most earnest in proposing that whites, ignorant of what it means physically and emotionally to grow up black in the United States, should read black authors who "can give us a closer inside feeling for what is going on in our Negro culture."

DIALECT: BIDIALECTALISM AND STANDARD ENGLISH

There is, however, an even more important difference between the two voices—that of language. The second speaker uses the kind of English generally considered "correct and proper" that linguistics scholars call *standard English*. The first speaker reveals in her speech characteristics of what the same linguists label *black English* and consider a *dialect*. We must hasten to add that *both standard English and black English are to be considered as dialects of the English language.* So the term "dialect" does not have a bad or pejorative meaning; it simply means a recognizably different kind of English spoken by any group of people—black, Chicano, Puerto Rican, Indian, or any other so-called minority.

The fact that a dialect is different does not mean that it is better or worse than any other dialect! However, it is true that, until recently, standard English—the dialect identified with well-educated speakers and writers as found in publications and television news broadcasts— has been considered the one dialect necessary to master. Anyone who wished to obtain and hold a well-paying job and desirable social position was expected to learn standard English. This has meant that many disadvantaged people have had to learn what is virtually a second language: an ordeal called *bidialectalism* (also called "biloquialism").

Many black and other minority leaders still regard it as essential that their people continue to become proficient in standard English; but some, for various reasons, side with a group of English composition instructors who would put an end to enforced bidialectalism. At the 1974 College Composition and Communication Convention (CCCC), the following highly controversial resolution was voted approval:

STUDENTS' RIGHT TO THEIR OWN LANGUAGE[3]

We affirm the students' right to their own patterns and varieties of language — the dialects of their nurture or whatever dialects in which they find their own identity and style. Language scholars long ago denied that the myth of a standard American dialect has any validity. The claim that any one dialect is unacceptable amounts to an attempt of one social group to exert its dominance over another. Such a claim leads to false advice for speakers and writers, and immoral advice for humans. A nation proud of its diverse heritage and its cultural and racial variety will preserve its heritage of dialects. We affirm strongly that teachers must have the experiences and training that will enable them to respect diversity and uphold the right of students to their own language.

As interpreted by its sponsors, the adoption of this policy would let minorities and anyone else brought up in families and areas where standard English is a "second language" speak and write in whatever dialect was most natural to them. They would no longer be expected to "catch up" with the privileged middle-class students. Presumably, they would be permitted — even encouraged? — to grow up speaking and writing, for example, the kind of black English dialect found in the following piece written by Alice Childress, a distinguished writer, actress, and theater director. A thirteen-year-old black boy, Benjie Johnson, who is well on his way to being hooked for good on heroin, is speaking:

My block ain't no place to be a chile in peace. Somebody gonna cop your money and might knock you down cause you walkin with short bread and didn't even make it worth their while to stop and frisk you over. Ain't no letrit light bulb in my hallway for two three floors and we livin up next to the top floor. You best get over bein seven or eight, right soon, cause

[3] Committee on CCCC Language Statement, *A Proposed Position Statement*, Spring 1974, p. 6.

seven and eight is too big for relatives to be holdin your hand like when you was three, four, and five. No, Jack, you on your own and they got they thing to do, like workin, or going to court, or seein after they gas and letrit bills, and they dispossess—or final notice, bout on-time payments—and like that, you dig?[4]

How widely accepted the CCCC resolution will be remains to be seen. The main question, however, is this one: What do you, as a student-writer, think of this policy to end enforced learning of a standard English dialect? Your answer is important because your development as a writer, a speaker, and a person depend upon your response. The view we adopt in this book is that it is to the advantage of every student, whatever his language backgrounds, to learn to communicate in standard English if he hopes to reach and influence English-speaking people all over the world. Having such knowledge and language skills, he enjoys a freedom of social and economic choices which might otherwise be denied him.

Every dialect is rich in meaning and expression, and skill in its use gives one the power to persuade and move others. So a choice of voice means a choice of language and the vocabulary and grammar that make up that dialect. In the "Topics for Discussion and Writing" section immediately following, you will find further discussions of the issues involved in the choice of dialects, which, it is hoped, will be enlightening and helpful not only in developing your own voice but also in understanding the validity of other voices.

FOCUS POINT

1 Language is a most powerful instrument for preserving or changing social values and institutions.

2. The language one speaks and writes reveals his social backgrounds.

3. Dialect is a variety of language used by some definable group.

4. Bidialectalism means acquiring skill in another dialect in addition to one's own "natural" dialect.

[4] Alice Childress, *A Hero Ain't Nothin' but a Sandwich* (New York: Coward, McCann & Geoghegan, Inc., 1973), p. 9.

TOPICS FOR DISCUSSION AND WRITING

1.   RESPONSE TO GEORGE R. BEISSEL[5]

As a matter of fact, if standard English is defined as the English of those who conduct the important affairs of the community (a definition not unfamiliar in Ann Arbor), then without learning so much as one more consonant cluster black people will automatically speak standard English the moment they get power in their own communities. But the mere words "black power" frightened America as badly as government of, by, and for the people would agitate the heart of Texas; and the American biloquialists (black and white) are still willing to bow and scrape before the prejudice which treats a particular pronunciation as a more important qualification for a career or job than ability or knowledge or integrity. For Mr. Beissel, they are the "educators who are trying to give black people their rightful place in our society." But who can have a "rightful place" in a society that's gone so wrong?

So Mr. Beissel is correct when he says that opposition to biloquialism is political. The opposition is as political as biloquialism itself, for the opposition rests on traditional notions of a just society which our society does not approach. We all know (though the "upwardly mobile" can't admit it and still remain mobile) that if we continue to waste our resources, to barbarize our neighbors, and to pollute earth, air, and water, then we will run the risk of making the planet uninhabitable and wiping out the human race. That is why we should not bring black children or any other children into our "mainstream culture," why we should not make "upward mobility" our motive for teaching or not teaching anything at all. As teachers, we should teach children what they most need to know in order first to survive, second to take some steps toward a really better life for themselves and others. We are foolish and brutal if we condemn them for their dialects. We have far less power to change those dialects than we pretend, and it is grotesque, when there is so much to learn, to pester the children about consonant clusters or *bavin' the baby*. What matters is that the baby should get baved. Besides, we are cheating and swindling if we tell the rejected young that if only they learn standard English the powerful will accept them and the barriers that face them will collapse.

But to speak such obvious truth is not to question the value of literacy. Opposition to literacy exists, so far as I know, only in the imagination of those who equate literacy with biloquialism.

JAMES SLEDD
UNIVERSITY OF TEXAS

[5] "Comment and Rebuttal," *College English* 34 (January 1973): 585–587.

COMMENT ON JAMES SLEDD

While reading Professor Sledd's "Doublespeak: Dialectology in the Service of Big Brother" (*CE*, January '72), I was delighted with his every thrust at bureaucrats and racists, and I felt a warm glow of confidence as he reassured me that what I really ought to be teaching my students is the art of thinking in their own language. Then I put down the article to read a freshman's response to a recent composition assignment I had designed to evoke just such an exercise in thinking. I am hard put to know how to apply Professor Sledd's principles to a specific piece of student writing.

In this particular assignment students were asked to write different answers to the question "who are you?" as asked by five specified people. The completed assignment gives a student a useful reference when he is later asked provoking questions such as whether one's honesty is relative, whether the truth of one's statements can be validly discussed without reference to the social contexts of the statements, whether it is possible or even desirable to integrate all aspects of one's own personality at any one time, etc. The assignment seems to fit Professor Sledd's criteria. Here is one student's response:

WHO ARE YOU?

I. A cop about to arrest you—
    Alright this is the police, what is you name boy, do I look like a boy to you pig. Alright nigger watch you language before I beat you across you head with this jack. Well you'll have to prove that to me, action speaks louder than words, I wasn't doing anything to make you try to arrest me any how my name Martin Roberts. Oh, you are the wrong guy. Next time Be right because I'll shot the snot out of you.

II. Whitey interviewing you for a job—
    Hi whats happening man do you have any job open, I am a very good sales men had 7 years experience in stores carlots and factories anything you name I've had it. What you reason for quiting all these job, see when I get a man I won't one that is responsible of being hear. If you salary is right, you have a responsible cat working for you today, tomorrow, and the next days. Well you is on. Oh my name is Martin Roberts, let go back in my office.

III. Your girl friend—
    Hell-o whats happening baby how are you feeling. Well I am feeling alright, just thinking of what was the mean of being with that Girl last night. Man I dont no what you are talking about, you no I wouldn't nothing like that baby, But, Hell you did, woman I'll take you mine out, and pinch it and see if it will jump if you don't believe me well you can next best thing. Ok honey I'll be right.

IV. Your closest friend of same sex, late at night, as conversation gets very serious—
Hay man I mean brother man I am in some trouble man I got stealing some potato chips, now I have to pay out 100 dollars for just one simple thing. Do you parents no about it yet, man I dont wont them to fine out about that they beat the mess out of me with my cloths on. Well we'll fine it out what we can do.

V. A child whom you have just met—
Hi, man, my name is Martin what is your's Old Blacks the snot catcher I catches any thing you can let loose Well thats go man because I have some Bugger in my nose that is ready to fly. Well I do other things besides that I play sports, now thats whats happening lets see what going down in the park O K man.

My problems come when I try to apply my theoretical sympathies with Professor Sledd to my evaluation of this composition. I believe that I am in tune with Professor Sledd when I contend:

1. Few readers will have serious difficulty in knowing what the student is saying; those who do have difficulty would have to be generally ignorant of writing outside the white middle class.

2. In terms of the imaginative dimensions of the assignment the student has been very successful: he has probed his experience; he has been vividly specific; he has met the varied demands of the different occasions; he has even employed a sense of humor more often missing from "correct" compositions of middle-class freshmen.

3. To effect even minimal mechanical changes in this boy's paper will threaten him with alienation from his peers and family; furthermore, the task of such "correction" would engage so much of my energy that I would seem to damn by adding praise for his "thought."

What then should I say to the student? Even if I take my responsibility as primarily to the student rather than to middle-class standards, how do I meet this responsibility? Should I say, "Right on, man; you got your thing together," and then rap about his ideas and their intriguing exploitation of idiom? Or should I say, "Your paper has many specific merits such as . . ., but . . ." and sneak in all the middle-class professorial objections that his next less "liberated" teacher or employer might raise? Or might I be overestimating the student's ego weakness to think that he will collapse if I tell him the conventional negative responses to his idiom? Has he not clearly elected to challenge his own idiom by attending college? Must (or even "can") an educator guarantee an experience free of the risk of alienation?

Professor Sledd and his adversaries are dealing with language problems at the abstract levels of doublespeak and dialect. I would like some help in solving the same problems at the specific level of student-speak.

I need some help fast because these papers are coming in at the rate of better than one hundred each week.

LOUIE CREW

CLAFLIN COLLEGE

2.   Joe Black, the first black man to win a World Series baseball game, is now a Vice President of the Greyhound Corporation, a former teacher, a Bachelor's from Morgan State and a Master's from Seton Hall. He is quoted in Roger Kahn's book about the old Brooklyn Dodgers, *The Boys of Summer* (Harper, 1971–72):

> He [Joe Black] makes one point to everyone. It is bigotry to exalt the so-called special language of the blacks. "What is our language?" he asked. " 'Foteen' for 'fourteen.' 'Pohleeze' for 'police.' 'Raht back' for 'right back.' 'We is going.' To me any man, white or black, who says whites must learn our language is insulting. What he's saying is that every other ethnic group can migrate to America and master English, but we, who were born here and whose families have all lived here for more than a century, don't have the ability to speak proper English. Wear a dashiki or an African hairdo, but in the name of common sense, learn the English language. It is your own."

SUBMITTED BY MICHAEL W. BARTOS

WILLIAM RAINEY HARPER COLLEGE

PALATINE, ILLINOIS[6]

SEMANTICS: WORDS AS WORLD SHAPERS

No matter what dialect you write in, you are dependent upon words in current usage to name objects, situations, and ideas which affect the thoughts, emotions, and concerns of everyone. How evident this fact is shows up when one begins trying to classify and to relate words commonly heard to real-life problems and situations confronting our society.

Ecology	Drugs
Air pollution	Marijuana
Water pollution	Hashish
Noise pollution	Heroin
Solid-waste disposal	Cocaine
Mercury poisoning	Overdose
DDT	Acid

[6] *College Composition and Communication* 33 (December 1972): 372.

Ecology
Atomic fallout
Oil spills
Sewage contamination
Littering
Mass transportation
Energy crisis

Drugs
Uppers
Downers
Speed
Reds and whites
Methadone
The Man

Law and Crime
Mugging
Purse snatching
Burglary
Juvenile delinquent
Felony
Fence
Police (fuzz, cops)
Murder
Bugging
Prostitution

Society
Minority
Poverty
Welfare
Ghetto
WASP
Civil rights
Bussing
Integration
Watergate
Pornography

The name for anything is, of course, not the thing itself; it is a word, and a word is only a *symbol*—something that represents something else. The symbol-letters spelling the word "shoplifting" make that word itself a symbol, but it is the stealthy act to which that word refers that is the real thing: the act punishable by law. The special study of language that deals with the way words and other symbols (such as the flag, the cross, and soft drink signs) have the power to influence our thinking and actions is called *general semantics*.

Semantics is concerned mainly with the *connotation* of words, the ability they may have to arouse emotions and serve as incentives or inhibitors of action. It recognizes that words have *denotative* meaning—the kind found in dictionary definitions—but goes on to examine how certain words can affect nervous systems and influence the way we "size up" the world and relate to it.

Take that word "shoplifting." To most people it probably means little more than what the dictionaries say it means: "the act of stealing goods on display in a store." But anyone who has ever been seriously tempted to shoplift, and especially anyone who has ever been caught in the act, will have a great sensitivity to that word. He will have strong feelings and memories associated with that common term, shoplifting, that even years after may give him the shivers.

Everyone knows the power that words have to hurt us or to make us happy. Semanticists call words that please, soothe, or compliment us "purr" words; they are intended to make us feel content like a well-fed cat purring its pleasure. On the other hand, as the term suggests, words which may cause pain by arousing unpleasant or harsh connotations and associations are termed "snarl" words.

Newspaper columnists with a flair for satire provide almost daily examples of the cutting power of snarl words to lay bare what the writer considers sham and pretense. Like Art Buchwald and Russell Baker, the syndicated columnist Mike Royko often demonstrates this power of language to attack. The following article was written after former President Richard M. Nixon's first long-awaited television speech regarding the Watergate scandal. Since a second such address resulted in lowering even further the president's rating in the polls, and a third address even more, Royko's bitter voice can be taken as representative of the doubts and misgivings of many who saw and heard the first address.

POLITICIANS, NOT THE PEOPLE, NEED "DECENCY AND CIVILITY"[7]

by MIKE ROYKO

Chicago—I want to be among the first to congratulate President Nixon for his bold new effort to achieve burglary with honor.

If anybody can do it, he can. And he is off to a rousing start.

In his TV speech Monday night, he began as if he intended to tell us something new about the Watergate case.

But by the time he ended, we were all marching off together, arm in arm with the President, Republicans and Democrats alike, in a crusade to rid political campaigns of any more dirty tricks.

It lacked only Kate Smith and the Mormon Tabernacle Choir belting out a chorus of "God Bless America," and the whole country could have gone to bed with a lump in its throat and a prayer on its lips for the man who is going to lead us to just and lasting grand jury investigation.

But if anything new came out of the TV report, it could only be that Mr. Nixon added a wistful grin to his stock of on-camera expressions.

Oh, he appeared to have said a few things.

For instance, he accepted the resignations of "Bob" (Haldeman) and "John" (Ehrlichman) and Atty. Gen. Kleindienst.

But when he finished saying what fine fellows they are, their resignations sounded like acts of heroism for which they ought to get medals in a ceremony on the White House lawn.

[7] *Chicago Daily News*, May 3, 1973, by permission of Mike Royko.

If you listened closely, you might have heard him accept "responsibility" for the entire mess. At least for a moment or two he accepted it.

Lowering his voice, as if trying to sing bass in a quartet, he disdainfully said it would be "cowardly" to blame somebody else.

Then he promptly blamed somebody else, by making a "pledge" that the "guilty" would be brought to justice.

The buck stopped at his desk just long enough for him to pick it up, pose manfully with it, then pass it as far downfield as he could.

Bringing the guilty to justice is no big deal at this point. People were being convicted when Mr. Nixon was still insisting it was a nickel-dime burglary case. And the way they are squealing on each other, more convictions will probably follow.

But Mr. Nixon didn't talk about the kind of "responsibility" that makes the Watergate scandal something to be nervous about: The fact that this crew of lock-pickers made it to positions of vast power in our White House.

In trying to calm our nerves, Mr. Nixon assured us that the "great majority" of people in politics are "honest."

If that is so, then how was he able to so completely defy the law of averages by hiring so many bums?

You would think that somewhere in American politics, he could have found people who thought breaking and entering, bugging, lying, double-dealing and hush-moneying were pastimes to be avoided.

The least he could have found was one man—just one would have done the job—who was honest enough to tell him what that other bunch of transom-climbers was up to.

But there he sat, telling us that he didn't know what was going on any more than we did. They fooled him, just as they tried to fool the rest of us. He seemed to be telling us—we are all in this together, folks.

The big difference is—he hired them.

But he didn't talk about that. So much for "responsibility." Now you see it, now you don't.

So let us move on to the next trick.

Having told us nothing about Watergate, he switched to matters of great global importance, ticking off awesome chores that await his attention.

Chancellor Brandt is coming to the White House; U.S. and Soviet negotiators and another round of talks; peace in Southeast Asia; inflation, and a better way of life for all Americans.

These larger duties should be claiming his attention, he said, not something as distracting as Watergate.

"I shall now turn my full attention . . . to the larger duties of this office. I owe it to this great office . . . and I owe it to you."

Just thinking about the weight of these "larger duties" would be enough to make ordinary TV viewers sink down past the springs of the sofa.

But hold on. Who was helping Mr. Nixon grapple with these "larger duties"? That's right. Some of those very same people who are now trotting off to a grand jury.

Mr. Nixon began sliding out of his TV "report" by asking us to join him in ridding politics of foul tricks, an easy enough request to comply with, as most people never bug phones or break into offices, anyway.

He shared with us the dreams he has for this nation: Peace, jobs, opportunity, a land where we can dream our dreams and have them, too.

And to use his very words—"decency and civility."

I guess we can never have enough "decency and civility." But I suggest that he save speeches about "decency and civility" for the people he hires. They are the ones who need them.

Like all journalists, Mike Royko in writing this article was working under the pressure of meeting a deadline, just as most students usually end up completing composition assignments in the same kind of frenzied rush. Neither literary effort will ever probably come to be rated as "great literature," but a professional like Royko has, as this piece shows, writing skills found in fine literary works. He can grasp and classify factual details, and then, whether right or wrong in his judgments, he also has the courage to speak out. It is evident he is not afraid to let his emotions come into play so as to stir up his imagination, which, in turn whets the tension and excitement enabling him to get started in the first place.

Being a good newsman, he looked for and found the kind of opening statement needed to grab the attention of his hurried readers: "I want to be among the first to congratulate President Nixon for his bold new effort to achieve burglary with honor." The literary device of making this opening a shocking stinger is called *verbal irony*—saying one thing but meaning another. The reader accustomed to Nixon's phrases expects to read "peace with honor" but finds "burglary with honor." This unexpected twist sets the pattern for almost all of the rest of the paragraphs and shows that ironic humor requires more than just word-switching: it takes an intellect trained to be consistent and alert for contradictions.

Royko's language throughout bristles with snarl words in expressions like "just and lasting grand jury investigation," "the entire mess," "nickel-dime burglary case," "crew of lock-pickers," "hiring so many bums," and "bunch of transom-climbers." He employs such harsh terms to point out what he considers the ugly facts which were glossed over or dismissed by the president.

The language or ironic humor works because writers with a sense of the comic have discovered that shocked laughter arises out of basic psychological needs. It is said, for example, that people laugh at painful situations in order to avoid crying over them. And they feel like crying when they are suddenly confronted by an unexpected and painful *reversal of situation.* We can all sadly identify with the victim of the mugging who when told, "Give me your money or your life," replied, "Take my life. I'm saving my money for my old age." Jonathan Swift's matter-of-fact tones make us smile in horror, when he proposes that the starving Irish babies of his times be sold as table meat to the wealthy who have already "eaten up" the impoverished parents. It is ironically, indeed, "A Modest Proposal."

Ironic humor makes the point that life is full of *incongruities,* that things are not often what they seem or should be. Hard work, cooperation, and scrupulous honesty are often unexpectedly not appreciated. Highly advertised and expensive products, like automobiles, frequently do not give the purchaser the pleasure and service envisioned when signing the 36-month payment contract. In short, anything that surprises or shocks because it is unexpected and out of place can be considered incongruous, and like the other daily columnists, Royko has a good eye for these irregularities.

Exaggeration also contributes to the ridiculousness of a situation as presented by an ironist. All humorous cartoons and caricatures are based upon such distortions, as are jokes such as this one: "He was so self-conscious about being tight with his money that when he heard a bird going 'chirp, chirp' he thought it was saying, 'cheap, cheap.'"

In the following article, "Wrenched Black Tongues," you will find how black students have reacted to the purr and snarl words they have found in books of "word-finders" like Roget's *Thesaurus* which reflect racial attitudes and prejudices. The ironic humor of parts of the article becomes truly "black"!

WRENCHED BLACK TONGUES: DEMOCRATIZING ENGLISH[8]

by LOUIE CREW

In "The English Language Is My Enemy," playwright Ossie Davis reported that fifty percent of the synonyms for Blackness listed in Roget's *Thesaurus of the English Language* are "distinctly unfavorable." One-

[8] *College Composition and Communication* 25 (February 1974): 42–45.

third of the remaining words are "related directly to race." As Mr. Davis observes:

> If you consider the fact that thinking itself is subvocal speech (in other words, one must use words in order to think at all), you will appreciate the enormous trap of racial prejudgment that works on any child who is born into the English language.*

Lest one think that Mr. Davis's own responses to Roget are biased, I found that forty Black students at Claflin College in South Carolina similarly rated a significant number of Roget's terms for Blackness (40% instead of Davis's 50%) as "distinctly unfavorable." Perhaps the slight (10%) decrease in negative weight is an index to the effectiveness over the last six years of the slogan "Black is Beautiful." In any event, the language itself, *at least as Roget selects it*, has not accommodated the identity needs of Black people; it remains an enemy.

A biased language is a curious anomaly from a strictly linguistic point of view. A biased language would clearly be an inferior language: yet linguistics does not recognize superiority or inferiority as properties of a language or of a dialect. Linguist R. H. Robins observes that the linguist "has no concern with preferring one dialect over another, nor with prescribing how people should use their language. Description, not prescription, is his work, and it is work enough."† According to linguistics, each living language is adequate to the cultural needs and experiences of its speakers: when the language threatens to become inadequate, the speakers change it. One can no more say that Eskimo is inferior to English because Eskimo does not, as English, have specialized words for atomic particles than one can say that English is inferior to Eskimo because English does not, as Eskimo, have specialized terms for the many grades of snow. English and Eskimo are both adequate to the needs of their speakers; both are able to accommodate new terms for atomic or niveous reality as the people's experience requires them. According to linguistics, the moment that English (or any other living language) threatens to become an enemy of its speakers, those speakers change it.

My studies of the language of Black students demonstrate support of the linguists' view of English. What Mr. Davis and my students are reacting to in Roget's list is not English per se, but *English as white folks use it*. Meanwhile, no language is the exclusive province of any one group of its speakers. All speakers of a language do indeed mold it to their needs; and the language habits of Black users of English demonstrate this molding in most creative ways. Language change is one of the most personal ways of measuring the cultural revolution taking place in America today.

* "The English Language Is My Enemy" in *Language, Communication, and Rhetoric in Black America*, ed. Arthur L. Smith (New York: Harper & Row, 1972), p. 51. A reprint from *American Teacher* (April 1967).
† *General Linguistics* (Bloomington: Indiana Univ. Press, 1964), p. 58.

The battle for a just response to Black language is one of the most significant skirmishes against white cultural imperialism. Miss Fidditch, the legendary white English teacher, must learn to talk and to understand Black English if she is not to continue tongue-tying her millions of Black charges.

To demonstrate that Roget's list does not reflect the biases and aspirations realized in the English of Black users of the language, I asked my forty Claflin students to participate in a two-part exercise. In the first part, each student anonymously composed ten sentences saying "White is ugly" without using the words *white* or *ugly*. In the second part, the same students composed ten more sentences saying "Black is beautiful" without using the words *black* or *beautiful*. This assignment provoked no consternation at all: the class was spirited, electric; sharing of responses with neighbors was frequently spontaneous. While clichés abounded, more interesting were the ways the students discovered to state the familiar ideas in fresh, original ways. Clearly the students were engaging in a language art well known to them, and their responses are, for the most part, vividly articulate. They speak as ones having authority. Here follows an important Black addendum to Roget's lists, including terms for Blackness and Whiteness employed by the students. Like Roget's lists (which included *nigger, darky,* et al.) this list does not purge all terms carrying social usage restrictions. Following Roget's lists, it does not try to include all of the most scabrous terms used. Again, like Roget's list, this list does not specify the fine shades of meaning and is a list of "synonyms" only in a most liberal sense of the term.

A Black Addendum to Roget

BLACKNESS	WHITENESS	
	NOUNS	
Soul Brothers	Whitey	Crackers
Africans	Bleachy	Southern pale trash
Africanism	Pinky	Buchra
Brother/Sister	Ghost	Honky
Dude	Superghost	Mister Charlie
Night	Pig	Peckerwood
Cat	Maggot	Hunk of funk
Eagle	Cancer	Redneck
Ram	Butcher	Rabbit-ass
Midnight (even "a midnight")	Cream-of-dung	Abominable snowman
Brown sugar	Buzzard	Pale face
Mystery	Hookworm	Snowy-faced monkies
	Dried Butt Meat	Chucks
	Pimpleface	Rice-patties
	(Skinned) Rabbit	

ADJECTIVES

Together	Puke-faced	Red
Natural	Bald-faced	Colorless
"Bad"	Frosted-faced	Pale-faced
Tanned	Pink	Raw
Radiant	Intestinal	Dead
Blended	Transparent	Salmon-faced
Shaded	Non-Black	Vanilla
Chocolate	Bland	Yellow
Naturally camouflaged	Flour-faced	
Tar		
Dark brown		
Brown		
Smooth		
Kinky		
Mystical		
Mysterious		
Delving		

Not surprisingly, English as these Black students use it has more negative terms for Whiteness even than it has positive terms for Blackness. Generally, all speakers of any language are more resourceful with hostility than with affirmation. So too, white Roget proved to be in his lists reflecting the anti-Black biases of English as spoken by whites.

Many of the students' best skills are not reflected clearly by merely isolating terms in the thesaurus fashion. Of particular interest are the imaginative ways in which the students frequently reversed the connotative fields of established words in Roget's white lexicon. For example, *ivory* in Roget's list would seem safely enough positive, suggestive of expensive artifacts stolen from aboriginal cultures and esteemed on the coffee tables and in the jewelry boxes of Europe and North America; yet observe its metamorphosis in one student's collocation "ivory-faced honky." Similarly "blue-eyed" is at worst innocuous if not positive until a Black metaphorically collocates "blue-eyed hookworms." Even traditional white standards of *snow* as "pure" and *soot* as "ugly, dirty" are wrenched in the Black language of another student: "The snow that fell into the soot surely made it murky as hell." Similarly witness the vicious diminutive wielded by another student: "that snowflake bastard." Very truly what you see is what you get: pollutants come in many colors, the white mentality to the contrary notwithstanding. One student almost phrenetically reveals the ambivalence-potential of biased words in his revision of the positive field for the white word *milk:* "As I came in my pants one day it reminded me of the milky people." The very color of the people who are white comes into a much closer scrutiny than whites themselves customarily employ, as is evidenced by the frequent emphasis upon the conspicuous blood colors in white complexion, in the terms *pink, red, raw, salmon-faced, pinky, pig, butcher, dried butt meat, redneck,* etc. (Frequently paintings by Black artists of white people demonstrate this greater sensitivity to the red pigments in white skin.)

The students were equally resourceful in wrenching Roget's words for Blackness out of the negative connotations they convey in the white lexicon. For example, one said, "I'm the sort of person that thinks of the charcoals as a pretty cool people." Another "redeemed" *nigger* with familiar vaunting: "The nigger is known for anything goes when it comes to sex." Another emphasized: "The raven is a very dignified-looking bird." In an almost Jungian or Gestalt fashion the students welcomed the opportunity to probe the positive side of what white society has tried to identify as negative, black, and threatening.

While some mindless approval and name-calling was encouraged by the brief exercise, often students accomplished both the affirmation and the negation with verbal inventiveness, as in the following samples, all of which were particularly popular with the students themselves:

BLACK IS BEAUTIFUL: SAMPLE SENTENCES

1. The darker the berry, the sweeter the juice.
2. He's an oil well.
3. Night is one-half of God's world too.
4. There is nothing like a cup of hot chocolate to keep a soul sister warm in the winter time.
5. She's deep, dark, delicious.
6. Joe Frazier's bony shoulders are stronger than Hercules'.
7. All those little kinky curls swirl on her head like those of a genuine goddess.
8. How blended are the pigments of the dark.

WHITE IS UGLY: SAMPLE SENTENCES

1. I thought I saw a walking ghost, but I cracked a joke and it turned pink.
2. Her legs were so pale I could count her veins.
3. I'll boil that rice honky till he puffs up.
4. Put the overcovering of your skin back on.
5. Her head looks like a pile of shit with curls of silk running from it.
6. You can let the hem out of those pants now because the flood has ceased.
7. I slapped his dirty face and he turned red.
8. Who the fuck is a snow fairy?

Here and also in the less inventive sentences are the positive values of allowing students to use their own language to affirm life from their own vantage, their own experience, to purge the alien that threatens to enslave their minds. The last group may be viewed as a way of exorcising the devil White Linguistic Tyranny. Not surprising are the numerous references to Black prowess. Over fifty percent of the students, unprompted, presented at least one sentence specifically affirming Black masculinity and femininity, and a similar majority wrote sentences denigrating white sexual identifications. Heavy emphasis in both lists was given to affirming exclusively Black biological experience (especially praises of hair and complexion) and to negating equivalents in the white experience as viewed from the outside. At times the students' fascination with the alien biology of whiteness is almost morbid. Frequently the white alien is seen as illusory, unreal, perhaps so perceived because he is not true to the Black personal experience (see nos. 1 and 4).

Blacks are not condemned to speak "a broken tongue," but rather are privileged to wield a tongue that breaks, ripping through the biases of English as whites use it to affirm a Black experience that is very much alive and linguistically resourceful. Meaning does not reside in words themselves; communities of people give meaning to words.

Six years ago Ossie Davis recommended that we democratize English. That process is occurring. It yet remains to be seen whether white America is listening. He that hath an ear to hear, let him hear. Blacks do not speak English as whites do, and they do not need a new language; they need only to get in touch with their natural imaginative linguistic resources.

FORT VALLEY STATE COLLEGE
FORT VALLEY, GEORGIA

Although seldom intentionally ironic, want-ads for jobs in classified newspaper columns often contain unconscious ironies of language. For example, how many unemployed people desperate for jobs would not find a classified advertisement like the following one highly appealing? Look at what every sentence in it does to arouse interest and high hopes.

This want-ad begins with a brief but very reassuring statement: "Consider: Good salesmen are trained . . . not born!" It states as an undisputed fact that anyone can be shown how to make it big as a salesman. Then to arouse visions of sure wealth comes the promise of "exceedingly large income your very first year." The qualifications demanded in the list under the heading of "You need to be" are general enough to encourage almost any high school graduate to think he has such a stock of marketable virtues. Next, he is promised more specific goodies under the heading "You Will . . ." and his imagination may

Help Wanted

SALES

CONSIDER

Good Salesmen Are Trained. . .Not Born!

And neither are doctors, lawyers, dentists or engineers.

You can be an outstanding salesman and earn exceedingly large income your very first year.

You Need To Be:

x Age 18 or over

x Ambitious, positive minded

x Energetic

x Competitive

x Have a high school education or better

You Will:

x Attend two weeks of school. Expenses paid.

x Have a $700 month Guarantee per month to start

REPRESENT AN INTERNATIONAL LEADER IN ITS FIELD.

If You Qualify, We Guarantee To:

x Teach and train you in our successful sales methods.

x You will advance into management as fast as your ability warrants.

Fringe benefits include unusual pension plan and savings plan.

Call NOW! for YOUR Personal Interview.

JOE HUMBLER

Mon-Tues-Wed, 9 am to 6 pm

235-8434

already be flashing him images of being an important representative of "an international leader in its field."

But now comes the catch! It appears in the form of a conditional statement starting with that formidable word "If"—"If you qualify." That "if" may topple all dream-castles the reader has erected while rushing through the earlier promises, but the most self-confident and desperate job seekers will hurry on to the final heady promises of affluence and success. They will be the ones who will do what the advertisement was set up and designed to produce: "Call now! for your personal interview." Only those who have experienced disappointment from answering previous such "Call now!" requests can really know what only too often lies behind such glittering promises.

In the Mike Royko article we have seen how a skilled journalist can make language a powerful offensive weapon, but in other hands and in other situations it can be an equally effective means of *defense*. Here, as an example, is the *voice* of a farmer's wife defending her husband and all owners of family-sized farms who are being harshly criticized for the high prices of meat in the supermarkets. The marginal comments accompanying her article point out some of her defensive tactics.

THE FARMER'S WIFE[9]
by Mrs. Albert Reifschneider

Opening with an expression of pride in her farmer husband, she backs up her pride with details of his achievements. She admits she is angry and wonders why injustice is being done them. She is speaking to the editor.

My husband is a farmer, and proud to be one. He's a young farmer—I call 36 "young" because in our area there are very few young farmers. He's a good husband, an excellent father of three children and has been named an Outstanding Young Farmer. He is also a cattleman. Never before have I felt so much anger for my fellow man, or for the President of this great country. The reason is the new ceiling on the price of beef, pork and lamb. Can you tell me what's the matter with this country?

Note the sharp request—"Tell me"—and the use of repetition: "long, hard hours—and I mean hard hours—" for emphasis; the details of stock-raising set forth to contrast with her next remarks on the soft city life of the "Great American Housewife."

Tell me, why should my husband work long, hard hours—and I mean hard hours—for people who don't give a damn? Take today, for instance: he's been up since early morning trying to feed cattle in blizzard conditions with 14 inches of snow and the wind blowing. New baby calves, some a few hours old, are sick and dying—and for what? The Great American Housewife, who likes to do a lot of griping about the cost of meat. Well, you sure don't hear about her boycotting any of the other things she's paying a big price for. So why beef over beef?

[9] From "My Turn," *Newsweek*, April 30, 1973. Copyright Newsweek, Inc., 1973, reprinted by permission.

Here she really allows herself to get sarcastic and let show her dislike of city housewives who will spend money on luxuries and yet complain about the price of meat. The last sentence picks up from the previous paragraph's "So why beef over beef?" and sums up the comparisons she makes, indicating she is knowledgeable of current jargon: "priorities."

A switch in point of view. She now speaks directly to all readers: "I agree with all of you." The "all of you" — all readers — become housewife-consumers with: "cosmetics . . . a pair of nylons for yourself." Again they are taken to task for mistakenly putting all the blame on the price of meat. Another question as an ending for a paragraph. Is this an effective device?

She is still continuing the direct attack but is now also pointing out all the work involved in raising cattle. She ends with a blunt accusation of selfishness.

She admits identification with the housewives she is scolding: "I know: I was a 'city' girl once myself." She raises questions aimed to shame those unthinking complainers and then gives answers detailing farmer hardships.

It's okay for the city housewife to go to the beauty shop every week and pay high prices to make herself look beautiful; or to take home a carton or two of cigarettes a week. She better not forget just a little booze for the party that she's having; she just has to have that cute little dress at that "nice little shop" down the street. Sure, you might hear her complain a little but, after all, all those things are absolutely necessary. But when it comes to the important things, like feeding her family a decent meal, she does plenty of griping. Somebody sure has their priorities confused.

I agree with all of you that prices are too high. But whose fault is that? It's yours and it's mine. You go to the grocery store with a practically empty purse, because you've already overspent on things that you thought you just had to have. You buy convenience foods that aren't necessary but that are nice to have. You pick up cosmetics, cigarettes, beer, maybe a pair of sneakers for the kids, a pair of nylons for yourself, a magazine or two. And by the time you get around to the meat counter, all you can see is that high price of beef, pork or lamb. You've forgotten that the cake mix is up 4 cents, or that tuna fish is 6 cents higher this week. So you're angry. But why does your anger have to focus just on the price of meat?

How many of you realize what it takes the cattleman to raise just one steer in order to put a roast, a steak or hamburger on your table? Have you ever thought about it? I'll bet not. Because as a housewife you have become too involved with just yourself. You've become so self-centered that you don't even realize that there is another side to the story.

To you, a cow is a cow! I know: I was a "city" girl once myself. How many of you know what a cow is? Do you know what a heifer is? Or what a steer is? Surely, you know what a bull is! A cow is pregnant nine months. And during this time the cattleman watches her and takes good care of her. He sees that his herd of cattle is fed, watered, has protein and salt blocks. He has to spray his cattle in order to kill fleas and in the summer he also sprays for flies. He has to brand, dehorn and castrate his bull calves in order to have steers so that he can fatten them and sell them to the packing houses. A heifer is a young cow that has not yet borne a calf. She's usually around fifteen months old when she is bred for the first time. And many a heifer having a calf gets into serious trouble when she is in labor, so she needs the cattleman to help her. Or else that heifer would die.

PULLING A CALF

Now she asks a question that leads into the brutal details of her husband's work.

Have you ever seen a farmer pull a calf? It's no pleasant sight. The farmer sometimes isn't so pleasant to look at afterward, either—with blood all over his arm because he had to reach into the heifer's uterus and turn the calf around so that it could be born. Sometimes it takes several men to do this job. And sometimes several hours. Oftentimes the cattleman has to load a heifer or a cow into the trailer and take it to the veterinarian to have a Caesarean. The vet usually charges $75 for this operation.

She continues to detail the labors, hazards, and hardships, especially those of winter.

During the summer, cattle herds are often transported hundreds of miles to new pasture, maybe because there's a drought in the area and there's no grass for the cattle to eat. In the winter, there's always the chance of a blizzard or, later, a freak spring blizzard such as southeast Colorado, Kansas and Oklahoma have recently experienced. So now we watch our husbands and the cattle suffering because of a snowstorm. And you sit there in your nice warm houses and say beef is too high!

She is not so angry and indignant, however, that she has lost sight of her original intentions in writing a defensive but yet, hopefully, a persuasive article.

I get so angry with the city people and their attitude toward the American farmer. I have heard several people observe in the last few months that they "don't need the farmer." Is this the attitude of the whole country? Is this the attitude of the President? I've always thought agriculture was the backbone of a nation. Well, I wish somebody would inform Mr. Nixon just what this means. What has he done for us? He's certainly not doing the farmers of this country any favors.

More questions voicing the central problems of the national economy as she sees them, showing she is well informed and why she thinks it illogical to complain only about meat prices. The final question is put to "America," not just the housewife, reenlarging her audience.

Now an abrupt switch to the defensive. By admitting the conveniences and appearances even of luxury to be found on her farm, she tries to disarm her critics.

I don't see a ceiling on the price of tractors, combines or other machinery that we need in order to do a good job of farming. Do you realize that a good tractor costs almost as much as some of your homes do? Do you see a ceiling on the price of lumber to build your new homes with? Do you see a ceiling on your wages? Do you see a ceiling on your new car? Well then, why, America, is there a ceiling just on beef, pork and lamb?

Sure, my husband and a lot of other farmers have nice machinery—air-conditioned cabs with radios and nice comfortable seats on their tractors. But why not? There are lots of days when my husband spends anywhere from ten to sixteen hours on a tractor, so why shouldn't he have the best? Businessmen in the cities have air conditioning in their offices, plush seats to sit on. But they don't have the expense of that equipment as the farmer does. Our city friends look at our nice homes, the new tractor in the yard, maybe a new car in the driveway and think we got it by sitting around doing nothing and drawing a big government check.

WAKE UP, AMERICA

She concludes by again addressing all of "America," not just the magazine editors and the housewives. She appeals to patriotism and the bonds of mutual need uniting city dwellers and farmers. She ends with still another question. Again, is this an effective device?

America, you've never been so misinformed about something in all your lives. Our husbands work hard for what we've got—and don't you ever forget it! Now for the first time in years the American farmer is making a little profit on beef, pork or lamb and Mr. Nixon puts a ceiling on them! Wake up, America, to your fellow man. Be proud to associate with your American farmer, as we are proud to associate with you. Don't you know we need you, and you need us?

Even more so than writing instructors, the editors of a national weekly—like *Newsweek*, which welcomed Mrs. Reifschneider's article—look for the arrival of interesting and publishable material, usually letters, from writers other than their staff. (Instructors might ardently hope a few such items may emerge from the stacks of "weekly theme assignments," but their jobs do not depend upon them.) No wonder, then, her voice of protest-mixed-with-pleading was accepted for publication. Aside from its colorful content, however, it also offers us a good example of the power of *informal* language: written "speech" which is personal and direct in tone and *point of view.*

Every word rings with sincerity and is something of a battle cry coming from one feeling herself under unfair attack. She "sounds" as if she were standing before the "city housewives" she is trying to set straight in their thinking on beef prices. To make her points, she is brutally frank in telling of such hardships of a farmer's life as "pulling a calf."

This article may not be professional writing in the sense that it has no claim—however remote—to being even on the fringe of "literature." But it well exemplifies the kind of writing that students might hope to equal when their own crucial personal situations call for such a response. It is a practicable model of effective communication—of person-to-person, informal but always "correct" language and statement.

Our language truly reflects the culture that has shaped us and given us our values and identity as well as the way we look at things and understand them. Everything in this chapter regarding dialect, voice, and word usage is meant to reflect this importance of language. Duke Redbird, an Ojibway Indian and poet from Canada, has pointed out in a recent article that the Indian's way of seeing and thinking is different from that of the white man and therefore makes the Indian easily misunderstood. He quotes from Carlos Castaneda's remarkable book, *A Separate Reality,* wherein a Yaqui Indian sorcerer tells Castaneda: "You must feel everything, otherwise the world loses its sense. . . . You think about yourself too much and that gives you a strange fatigue that makes you shut off the world around you and cling to your arguments. Therefore all you have is problems." It is this difference between seeing and looking that separates "the Indian's reality from that of the white man," and this "confusion inhibits communication." Redbird describes the differences between Indian language and English:

English as a language tends to have a built-in either/or quality about it. People who speak English tend to think in either/or terms. Up or down, black or white, good or bad. It's a device of language that is used constantly in the white community. The tendency in the Indian community is to view all things together as existing in an either/or dimension; not as separate conditions but rather as both conditions existing at one and the same time. Whites will often find it difficult to get Indians to take a firm either/or position on anything for this reason. The standard Indian answer to most questions of an either/or nature is "maybe," including invitations to dinner. The Indian is acutely aware of the changing and fluctuating nature of the universe so is therefore more comfortable flowing with these fluctuations than trying to fight them and suffer the attendant tension when the universe does not coincide with our schedules.

I find that I have difficulty many times trying to decide just where "right" leaves off and "left" begins when driving around with my Indian friends. It never bothers me, when inquiring which way to turn, to be told by an Indian to "go that way" accompanied by a gesture of the head or arm. However, when I have done the same thing to a white companion I find him becoming annoyed and demanding a "right" or "left" answer.[10]

Redbird's "voice" is that of the wise counselor who is sure of himself because he has had ample experience with white commissioners who misinterpret Indian ways and speech. American Indians have similar problems and for the same reasons, as the following analysis points out. Note the sympathetic—but restrained—voice of the author, William Hanlon, a young English teacher who recently spent 4 years teaching at the Pine Ridge Reservation.

GROWING UP INDIAN[11]

by WILLIAM HANLON

As average American city-dwellers, our notion of the American Indian has been formed, generally, through the vicarious experiences gathered from movies, the news media, and the growing number of books written by or about Indians.

In the good old days of the movies, we knew that, in the end, the Indians would be done in by the soldiers or the frontiersmen. The savages had, as everyone plainly knew, two mysterious strategical weaknesses: they would never attack at night, and the sound of a bugle would turn their warlike hearts to jelly. In our modern age of cinema, on the other hand, we can witness the Indians thumping the 7th Cavalry. We may even see the daily life of the native Americans portrayed as human, albeit different from that of our immigrant forebears.

Through the cooler medium of television, we have been exposed recently to other apparently conflicting views of the Indian. During the news, we see him capturing and ravaging government offices in Washing-

---

[10] Duke Redbird, "Declaration for Understanding," *Maclean's* 86 (May 1973): 26 and 28.

[11] William Hanlon, "Growing Up Indian," *New Catholic World* 216 (November 1973): 264–268. By permission of the publisher.

ton, or making a shambles of the small town of Wounded Knee. During a commercial, we see him shedding a tear at the litter being dumped by passing motorists.

Some of us have also read the books that recall the glories of Indian culture and religion or expose the white man's unconscionable handling of treaties and agreements.

Apart from these general sources of information, we may somehow know that Indians are stoic—just as Orientals are inscrutable—and that nobody can match their skill and daring as high-rise steelworkers. We may have been further instructed by bumper stickers which warn that "Custer Died for Your Sins" or theorize that "Indian Affairs Are Best."

In fact, much of what we have heard about the Indian and his situation is tainted with caricaturish exaggeration.

Four years experience on a Northern Plains reservation altered many of my preconceived notions about Indians and challenged my sometimes visionary solutions to their problems. I present here what I saw as the normal life on the reservation—especially, the normal life of Indian youth, with whom I was primarily involved and who, in fact, comprise about half the reservation's population. I should add that I am not an Indian and that my experience was on one reservation in the Dakotas.

Most younger children on the reservation lead unusually carefree and often happy lives. They do this against sometimes tremendous odds. A fair number of these children are deprived, for one reason or another, of one or both their parents. More than a few of them live, ordinarily with a generous supply of brothers and sisters, in one-room houses—some without electricity or water. And, as the U.S. Census Bureau has recently confirmed, they endure, more than any other ethnic group in our country, the multiple insults of poverty.

But there are some compensations. In the absence of a mother or father, there is often a kind grandparent and many aunts and uncles to see to the needs of the youngster. In lieu of a decent place to live, there are the unpolluted, rolling plains to roam. There always seems to be a horse to ride and friends to play with. The needs of children are usually simple and often, it seems, satisfactorily fulfilled on the reservation. This is not to say that there are not some tragedies of waste and neglect. But, generally, the life of the younger children seems pleasant enough.

With the dawning of adolescence, life on the reservation can become more difficult. The child's growing awareness can reveal that he is, somehow, different. He is a member of an ethnic group that attracts the curious and benign attention of many Europeans as well as Americans. Yet, for all the romance surrounding his people, their daily lives are far from idyllic.

Whether he be full blood or mixed blood, he is usually identifiable as Indian. If full blood, he is probably among the poorest of the reservation, but he has some link to the proud past through lineage and through his native tongue. If mixed blood, he probably has more money. But while often jealously claiming only Indian blood, he must do without the more direct links to the past that the full blood enjoys. In either case, he may now really for the first time recognize that the world at large considers him as different.

Psychologists like to talk about self-image and what happens to it during this period of life. Whether or not Indian teenagers, as a group, experience a breakdown of positive self-image at this stage is sometimes debated. At any rate, an Indian youth in these years of growing self-awareness is likely to face some situations that would not normally be thought to enhance self-image. Shopping in a neighboring white town, for instance, he may find that he is sometimes treated differently than a white person. He very likely will get into high school and find that he just can't read what the teachers are assigning. Eventually, too, he may find that some of his white teachers don't seem to expect him to accomplish very much. He may start thinking about what he is going to do with his life and find that his choices are severely limited by the opportunities.

It simply cannot be denied that there is prejudice against Indians in white towns that border reservations. It can, perhaps, be rationalized. For in any of these towns, established to fill the needs of hard-working white ranchers, you can usually see some drunken Indians loitering on the street corners. Of course, white people get drunk too—but usually not during the day and not so visibly. They do it in the more respectable surroundings of restaurant or community hall. Furthermore, some Indians have terrible work habits. People in these towns will tell you that they have hired Indians—to their regret. Indians, they say, rarely come to work on time, or on Mondays. And they always have a long, complicated excuse involving, say, the death of a grandmother in Montana. But the fact remains that they are not dependable and they are lazy. On top of that, some merchants will tell you that it is a mistake to extend credit to Indians. And these allegations are to some extent true—with regard to some Indians.

A glance back over the last hundred years or so of Indian history may help to explain the causes, if not eliminate the presence, of this apparent laziness and seeming irresponsibility. In the pre-reservation Indian culture, these problems simply didn't exist. A tribe or band naturally chose a place to live that was pleasant, defensible, and abundant in game. Chores such as hunting, scouting, and fighting were performed—and, from what we know, with consummate skill—for the survival or enrichment of the tribe. But not on a regular work-day basis. Later, the Indian was subdued, relieved of his chosen land, herded onto reservations, and made a ward of the government. The rest of the story is bleak. Everyone knows that as a guardian the government often assumed the role of the wicked, stingy uncle. And now, not too many years later, some Indians naturally have a difficult time fitting into what we consider a normal way of life and work.

At any rate, our young Indian has to cope with this situation. White people tend to have difficulty telling Indians apart, anyway, and so may think of him not as Tom or Lyle or Jim, but rather as an Indian. And as such he automatically assumes, in their minds, the listless characteristics mentioned above. In other words, he has to do more than the average American youth to prove his worth.

Prejudice is one outside pressure working on him. An even more constant pressure may be his daily school life. Many young Indians enter high school reading three, four, even five years below ninth grade level. Whose fault is that?

Partially, the schools'. A student in this fix has probably been the victim of "social promotions" through grade school. This policy is the school's admission that it doesn't know what to do to remedy the child's problem. The child's problem might have been something as easily corrected as poor eyesight and hearing or, in the case of a full blood, as baffling as a language barrier. Nearly all full bloods are bi-lingual and usually use their native language at home. Or it may be that his grade school's reading curriculum was not satisfactorily consistent. Teacher turnover at Indian schools is abnormally high. This naturally results, at times, in fragmented instruction. It should be remembered, however, that the current widespread interest in American Indians did not exist, say, ten years ago. Indian schools which now have a surfeit of teacher applications might then have been very hard-pressed indeed to fill their faculty rosters. We shouldn't be patronizing toward those who did a job that nobody else was interested in.

Or the fault may lie outside the school. Heavy absenteeism is a fact on the reservation. And while it can be argued that this, too, is really lack of student motivation on the school's part, it should also be said that the problems of transportation across the sprawling reservation or the lack of parental supervision may also be responsible. Wherever you place the blame, the young boy or girl is often educationally, as well as socially, handicapped.

Besides this possible reading difficulty, the young student may become more and more aware that some of his white teachers really don't expect much from him. And if it is true that the level of accomplishment tends to rise to the level of expectation, then our boy is in trouble again. Certainly, a realization of this sort would ruin any student-teacher relationship and contribute further to the student's possibly low image of himself.

In defense of the teacher it should be said that this attitude on his part is not usually intended. It may be that he came to the school with the noblest of intentions, worked very hard at his classes, and is simply frustrated by his inability to motivate his students. He may also have been unprepared for the type of instruction that he is compelled by the circumstances to give. Or, if he is a new teacher, the students' lack of cooperation may be their way of testing his reactions. After all, he is much more of an unknown to them than he would be to students in a white middle-class school. And these students may have reasons for not immediately accepting a strange white man as one who is concerned for their welfare. But if the teacher cannot cope with these problems and resorts to expecting little from his students, he has patently failed in his responsibility. Or more extremely, if he quits the students while outwardly proclaiming a victory he may really have reinforced the idea that they are hopeless.

Now even supposing that a student can manage his school work handily, sometime during high school he starts thinking about his future. Here again he faces a much more problematic situation than the average American youth. If he is capable of doing college work, his decision to go to college may be fraught with anxiety. He does not know how he will be treated off the reservation. He does not know how long he can do without the support of the extended family he is used to on the reservation. For better or worse he has probably learned to master the predictable routine of reservation life; he may be unsure about how he can handle himself off the reservation. He knows that students from white high schools are better academically prepared than he is for college work. And he knows, too, that statistically the odds against an Indian completing college are high.

Or he may start thinking about a job when he finishes high school. There are some opportunities on the reservation — working for the government, or in the one factory of the reservation, or at one of the church-related institutions — but they are limited and often do not even require a high school diploma. He really doesn't have much of an employment panorama on the reservation. On the other hand, if he lifts his sights beyond the reservation, he may be haunted by the knowledge of relatives or friends living in big-city Indian slums and decide that reservation life is, at least, better than that.

On top of all this, the teenager has to cope with the tough social atmosphere of the reservation. While other youths may be able to establish a kind of status through possessions or even academic achievement, a young person on the reservation will normally have to find his place in the pecking order through more physical means — toughness, daring, or drinking ability, for example. Heavy drinking is understandably an accepted facet of reservation life. It is the inevitable outgrowth of all the frustration, joblessness, and simple lack of other things to do. And at times the drinking erupts into violent beatings, stabbings, shootings, or vehicular homicide. Many deaths on the reservation, officially labeled as accidental, are believed by the residents to be quite otherwise. Tribal police are largely ineffective and FBI agents from off the reservation don't seem to get very far in their investigations of these accidents. The people of the reservation are widely interrelated through blood or marriage and, somehow, news travels very fast. In this situation, tribal police or potential informants often fear reprisals by a wrongdoer or his family against themselves or their families. A teenager has grown up accepting this social situation as normal.

Now to children or to older non-native residents, the rolling plains, though somewhat desolate, can hold a soothing enchantment. But to a native teenager, the thousands of square miles unspoiled by drive-in movies, record shops, McDonald's, or anything except livestock, can get to be boring. Emulating his elders, or possibly motivated by frustration at school or anger at his home situation, he can fall into this available pattern of social activity. He may get with a group, buy some beer, and drive around raising hell. Apart from other consequences, the combination of old cars, poor roads, and reckless driving frequently results in bad accidents. And an injury which could be easily treated in a city dotted with hospitals may be fatal on the vast expanse of the reservation.

Involved here, too, is the question of suicide among Indian teenagers. Hard statistics on suicide are always difficult to get. Although there are definite cases of overdose—usually among girls—there weren't, in my experience, as many forthright attempts at suicide as one would assume from popular articles on Indian youth. However, many people view activities such as the drinking, daredevil-driving syndrome as indicative of self-destructive behavior. These actions may indicate at least a willingness to get into situations that may result in injury or death. An injury could possibly bring individual attention and concern to a neglected youth. And death, he may reason, will release him from the troubles that almost certainly lie ahead.

These, then, are some of the daily pressures on an Indian youth. They often lead to his dropping out of school temporarily or for good. His parents or grandparents may be anxious that he stay in school. But often, either because it simply is their way or because they themselves are mystified by what goes on at school, they will not be firm. Unable to give much concrete advice, they will let him decide.

Sadly, dropping out is most frequent in the ninth and tenth grades. Some of these very young people will fall into the type of social behavior described above. Others will eventually get married, have large families, and often find themselves in the circle of poverty and welfare that too often is the norm on the reservation.

Those who make it through high school have accomplished quite a bit. But their future is still uncertain. I have already spoken of the difficulties concerning college. Some chose to enter the armed services. It must be admitted that this is one of the more attractive alternatives. It is a chance, at least, to get away from the reservation, to meet people who might not be prejudiced against Indians, and possibly to get some job training. Some choose to stay on the reservation, get what work is available, and try to make a better life for their children.

I have painted a fairly dim picture of normal life on the reservation for youth. For some life is better, for some worse, but for too many what I have described is their daily fare.

What about solutions? Everybody seems to have a solution to the Indian problem. And usually a person's confidence in the pragmatism of his solution varies inversely with his direct involvement in reservation life.

One obvious solution for the young is more Indian teachers in reservation schools. Obvious but not simple. Apart from instructors in the native language, culture, and crafts, there just isn't a great available pool of Indian teachers to draw from—for reasons which should be evident from this article. And one wonders whether it is advisable to hire too many Indian para-professionals if their position will enforce the students' notion that the Indian is second class.

Another possible solution, and clearly the most hopeful, is charismatic Indian leadership. Unfortunately, those Indians who do "make it," who could be models for Indian youth, often move off the reservation. They may become involved in Indian causes and enterprises—but at a distance. And perhaps they cannot be blamed for avoiding the unstable and feudish atmosphere of reservation life and politics. The local leadership, often plagued by charges of fraud, nepotism, and insobriety, is uninspiring. The militant leadership of the American Indian movement inspires a few but, in my experience, not many.

Money certainly must be able to cure some of these ills. It would seem so. But the loaves of bread designated for the reservation seem to be nibbled at in the bureaucracies of the BIA and the tribe and those who most need the nourishment get only crumbs. Private industry could perhaps accomplish more than the government. But the reservation is singularly lacking in natural resources. A private businessman may be reluctant to take on the difficulties of supply to a remote region or the uncertainties of getting local skilled personnel.

Finally, what about abolishing the reservation system, relocating people, and terminating the government's special relationship to Indian tribes. This involves gigantic moral and legal difficulties and to my knowledge has never been accepted by the Indian people as a viable alternative.

There must be other solutions. None yet tried has been very effective. Somehow, though, these young people must be given more to look forward to. In this land that was once theirs, they deserve to have the means of achieving a fulfilling life. Their mode of doing this may not be exactly ours for they are often very incisive detectors of the foibles and pitfalls in the "American way of life."

Their manner of achieving fulfillment must be their own. For too long Indians have been told what is good for them. And having subsisted on the fruits of what, in the past, was planted in their behalf, they may understandably be chary of our techniques. If we are to help in developing a strong Indian leadership and a better way of life on the reservation, we can only listen to their needs, understand what they wish, and where our abilities match their needs and their desire for our help, generously supply what we can.

I have tried in this article to present some of the problems of these young people without placing blame for their situation too heavily on any one group. I believe it is futile to wallow in collective guilt or excoriate the traditional whipping boys. Only wisdom, generosity, and patience will be productive.

Right off, William Hanlon shows a familiarity with popular misconceptions about Indians which reassures the reader that he knows what he is talking about, and when he says, "In fact, much of what we have heard about the Indian and his situation is tainted with caricaturish exaggeration," we are ready to agree with him. His plain, direct statement of his qualifications to explain what "growing up Indian" means to millions of people also strikes us as being reassuring. You may at first have thought he was refusing to look at the harsh side of Indian childhood, for he begins by going against another caricature: the one which portrays all Indian children as dull and on the verge of starvation. He finds positive features in their daily life although he admits they suffer "the multiple insults of poverty."

The facts Hanlon cites, explaining why as adolescents Indians do poorly in schools and despair of college, show that the author has read as well as observed a great deal. You will note he avoids drama, being content to speak in matter-of-fact tones, and is almost painfully "school teacherish" in his closing paragraph—"I have tried in this article to present some of the problems of these young people. . . ." His last two sentences well explain the restraint and objectivity which characterize the analysis: "I believe it is futile to wallow in collective guilt or excoriate the traditional whipping boys. Only wisdom, generosity, and patience will be productive." It is a worthy attitude. Agreed?

So far we have seen how two of the main creative sources energizing a literary work function: the writer's attitude toward himself and his attitude toward his subject matter. These two chief concerns of rhetoric involve also a third primary attitude making up the basic stance of a writer: *his attitude toward his readers.*

It is revealing to note that Duke Redbird's article appeared in *Maclean's*, one of the most respected and widely read Canadian magazines. What is more, the issue in which it appeared was devoted largely to the subject of Indian-white relations and history. Had either Redbird or William Hanlon aimed his article at some "underground" publication, he would very likely have written in a different tone and voice and from a different point of view. Note that Hanlon's article appeared in the *New Catholic World*, a periodical with a long publishing history which recently has been concerning itself especially with the intellectual and social problems of college-age readers.

So once more we see how close are the ties between the kind of language one naturally speaks and one's concepts of what life is all about. It appears that *we are*, in many respects, the language in which we speak and think. And that general language also has many "dialects," which are distinctive ways of thinking and feeling, as well as seeing and communicating. Which of these ways should be, in white man's logic, called *standard* or *nonstandard* remains an unsettled argument, but it is hoped that this book can serve as something of a "middle ground."

FOCUS POINT

1. Many words have two kinds of meaning: denotation and connotation.

2. As the study of "human interaction through communication," general semantics is concerned with the connotative meanings of words and symbols.

3. "Snarl" words are effective in writing that attacks, especially in irony and satire.

4. "Purr" words are confidence building and reassuring.

5. Informal language approximating good, direct speech is a powerful medium of expression.

TOPICS FOR DISCUSSION AND WRITING

1. What particular words and phrases rich in connotation do you know that can deeply affect the thoughts, feelings, and even the behavior of people? Write about your own experience — or a situation you may have witnessed — involving such words. Try to describe such a situation, the circumstances leading up to it, the exact language used, and the feelings and behavior resulting from it. Here are some suggestions to jog your memory — in and of themselves the words have "unloaded" meanings (a chicken is just a chicken, and a boy is a boy, after all), but each can be used in a "loaded" way as well:

The Expression	*The Situation*
"Fake!"	Someone is trying to be someone or something he or she is not.
"Chicken!"	Someone wants you to do something you have good reasons not to do.

"A wreck!"

"Boy!"

"Driver's license, please."

"Probation."

A bad car accident has just happened.

You are being insulted.

You have been stopped by a patrol car.

You have been given another chance.

2. Below are some of the slogans found in current advertisements intended to persuade the buying public to choose a particular brand of a general product or service. Looking through current issues of magazines, report on changes in these slogans and what events, if any, explain the changes in connotative language and appeals.

You've come a long way, baby. — [Virginia Slims]

Put some more flavor in your life. — [Lark]

Warning: The Surgeon General has determined that cigarette smoking is dangerous to your health.

Smile and say Cheeseburger. You deserve a break today. — [MacDonald's]

Carry the big fresh flavor. — [Wrigley's]

Join the Navy to get ahead. Be a success in the New Navy.

Westinghouse helps make it happen.

Making better cars to see the USA — [General Motors]

Anywhere, anytime, all the time — [Greyhound]

If you're without it, you're not with it — [Old Grand-Dad]

Travel light. — [Kodak]

Goodbye, Nick. — [Gillette Techmatic]

At $200 a ton, some solid waste shouldn't be wasted. Pass it on. — [Alcoa Aluminum]

Escape to a world where there's still room for man-size adventure. — [Western Writers of America Book Club]

3. Among the several letters appearing in a subsequent "Letter" column of *Newsweek* as a response to Mrs. Reifschneider's defense of meat prices are the two following. Be prepared to discuss them and their effectiveness of language as replies to her article. Then write your own letter of reply.

Your LETTERS column (unlike other magazines') has intelligent, pertinent responses. But one of the rejects slipped through and ended up under your column MY TURN. Mrs. Albert Reifschneider is an A-1 snob.

Most women can't afford the beauty parlor every week. The last time I saw the inside of one was six months ago, and it wasn't too fancy because I had to shop around for the cheapest. Who can afford cigarettes, or needs the extra lung pollution in the city? Why have parties when you live in a cramped apartment and can only afford chips and dip? Booze? Oh, yes, once in a while we can afford the small cans of beer.

I'd love to have that "cute little dress," but what I've got is what I had before marriage, except what I've sewn. My convenience foods include home-made bread and macaroni and cheese—when it's on sale. Cosmetics means the bare necessities, my daughter Lyn wears hand-me-down shoes, and when *my* nylons snag, I get a tan or wear pants! (By the way, how much did those earrings cost that Mrs. Reifschneider is wearing in that picture? I have two pairs.)

My husband works in a factory, packing metal all day. It's like a tin can, and he comes home sweating in the summer, working so we can afford groceries, which includes five meat dishes a week (if we're lucky).

I'm disappointed; that column should have been forwarded to Ann Landers.

SHIRLEY SCHELL
MONTEBELLO, CALIF.

Mrs. Reifschneider knows of what she speaks, and says it beautifully. Too many housewives busy themselves boycotting the meat market and getting their pictures in the papers or on TV, instead of staying home to prepare well-balanced meals at low cost with home-made soups, a variety of beans, fish, and gourmet dishes made with organ meats. After a hard day on the picket line or organizing committees to fight meat prices (nothing else), they only have time to pop a steak in the broiler just before dinner!

MS. GERMAINE LIPSCOMB
TEMPE, ARIZ.[12]

4. Many things going on today deserve satirical treatment because they are wrong and harmful, or at least sadly inappropriate. Show from your "common sense" point of view how incongruous and ridiculous some views or practices really are in fields such as the following:

Public transportation	Energy conservation
Television commercials	Law and order
Organic foods	Local politics
Professional sports	Parking
Children's TV programs	Latest fad
Student loans	Sex education

[12] From *Newsweek*, May 21, 1973, pp. 6–7. Copyright Newsweek, Inc., 1973. By permission.

5. Write a letter to the editor of a local newspaper wherein you are critical of the paper's stand on some important matter affecting your college or university. Remember to be brief, but make your point by backing it with the needed information.

WORD CHOICE

It is gradually becoming accepted that in general the "best" language is that which is most appropriate to the situation, the subject matter, and the audience you are addressing. Such consideration will include awareness of features such as the geographical area in which you live and the speech and culture patterns shaping it. All parts of the United States, for example, have regional dialects which are perfectly acceptable in those regions but which may sound strange to outsiders, such as these southern dialect expressions:

This here man's going.
That there girl's mine.
It's a powerful big fish.
That was powerful good.
I got a right smart of work.
I live a little piece up the road.
If she cries, pay her no mind.[13]

From the South, too, come words of African origin such as "goober" for peanut, "cooter" for turtle, "yam" for sweet potato, and "okra" for vegetable. Colorful Black English expressions also abound there and among them are these:

ham fat—a mediocre person
hams—human legs
handcuffs—engagement or wedding ring
roost—where one lives
rooster—a man
funky—truly felt blues mood in jazz
cop out—to make excuses
cool it—go slow, take it easy
alley—corridor in a hospital
clown—a foolish person

[13] From Louis Herman, *American Dialects* (New York, Theater Arts Books), p. 190.

pillow pigeons—bedbugs
ripped—unhappy
skate—to escape paying debts[14]

In personal letters or informal speech, such regional expressions and slang may be most appropriate; they are direct and colorful for those who "speak the language," but they may not be suitable for a wider audience who would not share the same connotations for those terms.

Grammatical usage is also important for communication and ready acceptance of messages. In everyday ("colloquial") speech many expressions readily suggest themselves but may be considered as not conforming to the kind of grammatical usage generally expected of educated people. Here are some of the faulty usages most commonly heard:

It *don't* look like rain. (doesn't)
Between you and *I*, I don't think he is as rich as he pretends. (me)
She wishes everyone would mind *their* own business. (his)
Both of us *was* interested in the job. (were)
Him and *her* are going steady. (he, she)
He felt *badly* on hearing the news. (bad)
Helen and *myself* are going to town. (I)
At the end of the day he was more tired than *me*. (I)

Just to reassure you that Americans are not the only ones who lapse into such usages almost as a matter of course, here is a brief list of some commonly heard in Canadian English:

It's *real* hot. (really)
She *dove* off the board. (dived)
The bear *clumb* a tree. (climbed)
My brother was sick *at* the stomach. (to, in)
He wants *to go out*. (He wants out.)
It was *laying* on the floor. (lying)
She's going to *bath* the baby. (bathe)
It's *behind the house, in back of the house.* (back of the house)
I'm *wore* out. (worn)
He *snuck* by. (sneaked)[15]

---

[14] From Clarence Major, *Dictionary of Afro-American Slang* (New York: International Publishers Co., Inc., 1970), p. 164.

[15] From H. Scargill and H. Warkeutzne, "The Survey of Canadian English: A Report," *The English Quarterly* 5 (Fall 1972): 72.

Every profession and trade also has its special vocabulary. Space exploration and "moon shots," for instance, have given us terms such as these: drogue parachute, flotation collar, fuel cells, meteor bumper, Apollo suit, backpack, moon car, fly-by, and splash down. And down on the earth, railroad workers also have a special vocabulary:

> dingbat—any bumbling, incompetent in authority
> doper—one who packs and lubricates car journal boxes
> drag—a long, slow freight train
> elephant tracker—a railroad detective
> flyer—an express train
> grease monkey—one who lubricates locomotives

In food production, even the Italian roll stuffed with a variety of Italian cheeses, meat, lettuce, tomato, onion, and garnishes has had numerous names given to it:

> submarine sandwich
> hoagie
> grinder
> rocket
> bomber
> Cuban sandwich
> hero
> poor boy
> torpedo
> zeppelin
> muscalatta[16]

So specialized are these vocabularies that they leave the reader who is unacquainted with them badly lost. As a result, the reader dismisses them as *jargon*, the term for the kind of language used by those writers and speakers who seem to delight in the overuse of technical terms, roundabout expressions featuring multisyllabic words, and worn-out phrases. Jargon consists of abstract, general terms instead of concrete specific ones that can be readily grasped. Thus, jargon generally is dull and pretentious writing lacking clarity and directness, as can be seen in this passage appearing in a current periodical addressed to university faculty members:

[16] From Edwin Jones and Howard Robboy, "The Submarine Sandwich," *American Speech* XLII (December 1967): 282–283.

In the internal labor market for an enterprise or an administrative unit such as a factory, a government agency, the managerial employees of a business, or a university faculty, the pricing and allocation of labor services, in general, is governed by a set of administrative rules and procedures for promotion from within and only indirectly by external economic variables. Continuity of employment for an individual is somewhat protected. The internal labor market is connected to the external labor market at those positions that constitute ports of entry and exit. In contrast, in enterprises where no internal labor market has developed (for example, the market for migratory agricultural labor), the pricing of jobs and allocation of labor fluctuate more directly with economic variables.

What is being said here that could not be more clearly stated in direct, simple terms? Behind all this abstract verbiage one detects these simple ideas:

In factories, government agencies, big business concerns, and universities, employees receive salaries and positions according to the rules established by their particular institution. They are not directly affected by changes in economic conditions and generally enjoy job security and can move within the system. But untrained, unskilled laborers outside such systems — for example, migratory workers — lack all such security and are ready victims of changes in economic conditions.

What is your reaction on reading this excerpt from a theme written by a very bright student?

Today in this our modern world we have to stand up to be counted, whatever our race, creed, or color. In the give and take of daily life in these troublesome times when things are in the saddle and no quarter is given, when everyone has to put his shoulder to the wheel and yet keep his eyes raised to the stars, we must all work with a will and hand to prove our mettle. Bloody but unbowed, or only tired but happy, every mother's son of us can thank his lucky stars to be living in the land of the free and the home of the brave. Citizens tried and tested all, raise your voices while our proud ship of state writes our destiny upon the marble tables of time immemorial!

Which of the following terms best describes this passage: eloquent, impressive, or hackneyed? Since the piece represents a deliberate attempt by the student to string together a series of trite, worn-out phrases — *clichés* — the term must be "hackneyed." As put together here, they are stock phrases so empty of meaning and out of place as to be ridiculous.

Clichés are trite expressions used without care for exactness or freshness of meaning. Many are tired figures of speech—similes and metaphors that once may have been colorful and expressive, such as these:

a blot on her character	as hungry as a bear
a reputation clouded over	meek as a rabbit
eaten by remorse	brave as a lion
the flower of the family	pretty as a picture
into the golden sunset	head over heels in love
the primrose path of dalliance	drowned in a sea of troubles
dangerous seas of passion	poor as a churchmouse
hidden depths of meaning	quiet as a mouse
land of dreams	dead as a doornail
a safe harbor	salt of the earth
any port in a storm	

Deadly to any style also are a host of ready-made phrases which have become badly shopworn, as have these:

tried and true	safe and sound
sadder but wiser	better safe than sorry
from rags to riches	without further ado
from start to finish	No way!
poor but happy	gone but not forgotten
poor but honest	long time no see

Excessive use of such ready-made expressions turns off the reader because it plainly tells him: "Read this crap if you want to punish yourself. You can see I don't have anything important enough to say to find the right words for it."

But not all familiar combinations of words are to be avoided in writing. To rule out as tired language one broad category of set phrases would be to deprive writers and speakers of one of our greatest language resources: idioms.

An *idiom* is a speech form that cannot be translated into any other language for the reason that it is peculiar to itself within the usage of a given language; it is an expression unique to a particular language. Confused? These examples should help clarify what idioms are and why they are important:

Shoulder
to cry on someone's shoulder
to put one's shoulder to the wheel
to rub shoulders with
to shoulder arms
to give a cold shoulder to
shoulder-to-shoulder
straight from the shoulder

Lay
to lay about one (to deliver blows on all sides)
to lay a course (to make plans)
to lay aside (to save)
to lay away (to save, set aside for future use)
to lay before (to present for consideration)
to lay down (to sacrifice one's life, to give up)
to lay for (to wait to attack)
to lay in (to store up)
to lay into (to attack with words)
to lay it on (to flatter)
to lay off (to put aside, to discharge, to cease)
to lay open (to open up)
to lay out (to spread before)

As dictionary makers admit, it is often difficult to know when a phrase which was once labeled "slang" makes the grade as idiom and thereby gives strength and vitality to the living language, as do these:

a square meal	a cop, fuzz
a dog's life	cop a plea
the hit parade	a dump, a dive
a hot dog	take a dive
a narc	behind the eight ball
a pick up	a cliff hanger
a raspberry	top banana
bump off	make a hit

It hardly needs saying that our language is rich enough to communicate all tones of feeling and shades of meaning if one will take the trouble to study its vast resources. Now another means of being precise and expressive is to use, as Swift said, "the right word in the right place," and to manage that, one must know something about synonyms.

A *synonym* is a word having a meaning similar to that of another word in the language.

Some of the usual sources of synonyms are dictionaries or a thesaurus, which is an index of general ideas and the words expressive of them. But helpful as such lists of words having the same general meaning may be to an author, he must know the fine shades of distinction in meaning each has if he is to use the term properly. Take, for example, these synonyms for the word "polite": civil, courteous, chivalrous, gallant, and genteel. All share the common meaning of "consideration for others" and "good manners," yet each is distinctive in meaning and should not be indiscriminately put into a "slot" which can be better filled by one of the other synonyms.

Civil suggests behavior merely refraining from being rude; *polite* suggests observance of proper etiquette; *courteous* implies a more sincere consideration of others, an inherent thoughtfulness; *chivalrous* suggests a disinterested devotion to the weak, especially to women (will this word fall into disrepute now that Women's Lib is here?); *gallant* denotes a dashing display of courtesy—again especially to women; and *genteel* suggests fine sensibilities and refined behavior—a pejorative term these days (one having a bad meaning), because it now suggests being too sensitive, too refined in manners and bearing.

Now consider the richness of meaning found in synonyms for the word "rude," which is the antonym of polite: rude, ill-mannered, impolite, discourteous, uncivil, uncouth. *Rude* implies a deliberate lack of consideration and connotes insolence or impudence; *ill-mannered* suggests ignorance of the amenities of social behavior in a person who may be well meaning but uninformed; *impolite* denotes the failure to observe social rules; *discourteous* suggests lack of dignified consideration for others; *uncivil* pertains to behavior showing disregard of the most elementary of good manners; and *uncouth* suggests behavior that is awkward, clumsy, or ungraceful.

To develop an interest in synonyms as a means of reminding oneself how many shades of meaning a general idea can have, a philosopher has made a "game" of collecting synonyms. Here is one of his examples as strung together in one sentence: "This conception, like others in the theory of meaning, is too vague, uncertain, unsettled, indefinite, visionary, undetermined, unsure, casual, doubtful, dubious, indeterminate, undefined, confused, obscure, enigmatic, problematic, questionable, unreliable, provisional, dim, muddy, nebulous, indistinct, loose, ambiguous, and mysterious to be the subject of careful logical scrutiny."[17]

[17] Quoted from memory by Alan Ross Anderson, "An Intensional Interpretation of Truth-Values," *Mind* 81 (April 1972): 348.

Being "word hungry" will help you to develop your capacity for self-expression. As you may have already found, discovery sparks discovery when you learn new words. So acquire the "dictionary habit" of looking up words new to you, but do not consider any dictionary as a judge and master of meanings. Dictionaries serve only to record changing word usages and meanings as these occur in current writing and speech; some of their material will be out of date by the time it is published.

To give what has been said in this chapter regarding your language perhaps a more direct bearing upon the future of many of you, we are including the following article, which appeared in a most prestigious business periodical.

DO YOUR WORDS OF WISDOM COME THROUGH CLEARLY?[18]

by JANE G. BENSAHEL

Children play a game that is really a caricature of what happens all too often in adult life. The game is called "Chinese whispers." To play it, a group of youngsters sit in a circle. One whispers something in the ear of the child next to him. Then that child, similarly, passes it on to the next, and so on, around the circle. When the message comes full circle back to the first child, everyone laughs at the incredible distortion the original message suffered in transmission. Everyone laughs, because it's a game.

But in adult life, getting the message through clearly is not a game. Yet distortions and misunderstandings occur—and they are not funny at all.

For the executive, particularly, effective communication is a critical skill. But it's a highly complex one to learn. There are an almost infinite number of variables that can affect accuracy of communication—the qualities, mood and feelings of both the sender and the recipient, as well as external influences competing for time and attention. But the most basic determinant of the quality of communication is the communicator himself. The more you develop your communication skills, the greater will be the probability of getting your message across.

To develop the skill of saying what you mean, and ensuring that your listener hears what you mean, here is a six-point checklist. Each of the six points is one of the personal attributes that social scientists have found to be the keys that allow a communicator to get his message across accurately.

---

[18] Reprinted by special permission from the November 1973 issue of *International Management.* Copyright © by McGraw-Hill International Publications Company Limited. All rights reserved.

Relate to others. This does not simply mean being affable, or having people like you. Rather, it involves the degree to which you're able to put yourself in the other man's place, to sense his point of view, to recognize and react appropriately to his feelings.

For example, suppose you have to criticize a report someone wrote for you. Do you just bluntly tell him what's wrong with it? Or do you allow for the time and effort he put into it? Do you realize that he may be proud of it? In either case, the point you want to make is how the report is to be changed. But if you say, "George, without additional figures to back up your points in the second section, this report is useless," chances are he will be hearing—and resenting—a lot more than just the need to get the figures.

Ironically, by keeping your message short, you're polluting your real point with a lot of messages you hadn't intended. He may hear that the report is useless, or even that *he* is.

Instead, you could say something like, "I'm looking forward to using this report at the next board meeting, George. But I think it would make the point even more effectively if you could give me some additional figures to back up the second section." Here, you are relating your message to his need for recognition and for knowing the ultimate importance of his effort. You are helping ensure his hearing what you really mean.

Choose the proper time and place. This is closely linked to how you relate to others. It means choosing the time when the other person will be most receptive to what you have to say. Generally speaking, anything of a personal nature such as a raise, a promotion, or even a demotion or firing is best left to the end of the day. This allows the receiver time to digest the message privately, outside the demands of the job. Also, giving assignments ought to come as close as possible to the beginning of his planning period, often the start of a week or a month. Thought-provoking meetings are usually best held just before lunch, so people can mull them through together, if they wish, during the daily break.

These general rules are useful for communicating major or unusual messages. But for more routine messages, your best timing involves some knowledge of the person you want to talk to, and of his work patterns.

For example, if you know your assistant takes a while to get started in the morning, then you know it's best to chat with him later in the day.

Or if you know that your boss has been working late this week on a big project, you might want to hold off some more routine requests until next week.

Or if you know that two of your subordinates have been at odds lately you may prefer to wait until things have cooled down a bit before getting them together to talk about something that involves both of their departments.

You may, of course, deliberately choose to give your assistant important assignments first thing in the morning. Or you may bring your feuding department heads together, no matter what. If so, your message will have additional implications to them. And that's all right, so long as the choice was deliberate. For part of the message you send is the time you send it. And, as long as you account for this, you'll be more likely to get across the message you mean.

Relate the speed of delivery to the content of the message. The more complex the message, the more slowly it ought to be transmitted in order to be received accurately and fully assimilated. Conversely, the simpler the message, the faster you should deliver it, so as not to wander from the point.

In either writing or talking a critical factor is the number of words you use to present your message. The more words you use, the longer you'll take to make your point—and vice versa. And this is something you can easily control.

For example, suppose you're presenting a person with a totally new plan you want him to implement. You would not give it to him during a chance meeting in the corridor. And you wouldn't simply say, "Here is an outline of the proposal, I would like results next Thursday." Rather, you would go into background details, explain the advantages of the plan fully, and give the impression of having as much time as necessary to explain further, to answer questions, perhaps even for him to try to explain it back to you. You should also supplement a complex oral explanation with a summary in writing so the recipient can go over it again later. For if you do not take ample time to deliver a complex message you cannot be assured that it has been fully understood.

Conversely, don't use such a laboured approach to ask your secretary to order certain supplies more frequently. She might get so lost in all the verbiage that she will not understand exactly which supplies you mean.

The medium is part of the message. For any given message, there are almost an infinite number of ways to send it. And the way in which you communicate often says as much as the actual message itself. So your means of communication, if well chosen, can enhance the strength of your point. Or, if ill chosen, the way you say it can even contradict your intended meaning.

Just think, when someone else is telling you something, what a difference is made by the words he chooses; whether he delivers them in person or by telephone, or in writing.

First, let's think about face-to-face communication. Let's suppose you have the duty of informing a manager that he is to be transferred to head a branch office. And suppose you start out by saying, "You've been doing a great job, John. In fact, you've been so good that this has really caused some problems in the executive group—we didn't quite know what to do with you." And then you tell him about the transfer. What impression would your opening words have made if you had been relaxed and smiling as you spoke them? And what impression would you have given, with the same words, with a tense, formal posture and a slight frown?

Words alone don't make the message, even face-to-face. And whether you choose to ask a man to your office, go to his, telephone, send a memo, even call a meeting sends some sort of message about what you have to say before you utter your first word.

Every executive has a "usual" means of communication with the people he works with. Suppose you usually call a colleague on the phone, but today you have a slight sore throat and decide to send a memo instead. Unless you tell him about your throat, chances are he will attach a great deal more significance to what you say than he would if you called him, and perhaps much more than you intend.

Or suppose you tend to call a lot of meetings to exchange ideas. Then, one day, you decide to go around and chat with your key people individually. They might well feel under greater pressure this way. Maybe this is the effect you want. But, if it's not, think through the implications of any switch from what people have come to expect from you.

Don't try to disguise your own feeling about the message you are delivering. Whatever it is, chances are it will show through, no matter how you try to hide it. You may be trying to convey straight facts, for instance. But if you have strong positive or negative feelings about these facts, your words will probably not sound as neutral as you intended. Or perhaps you're trying to build enthusiasm in someone else about something you yourself are actually less than enthusiastic about. Your chances of succeeding are poor.

Everyone has some feelings about whatever he says. Trying to mask them only produces an unclear message, because one's listener then gets conflicting signals. So, if you really want your words to get through, it's best to be candid at the start.

For instance, if your advertising agency has suggested that a different package could sell your produce better, you may not be too keen on the idea. Yet you may feel it's worth trying. You'll be more effective in your talk with your packaging manager if you say exactly that than if you try to pretend you believe a new package will solve all your company's problems.

Try to de-personalize the message. It's not possible to be completely neutral to another person. And it's instinctive to tailor your message to what you think of him. But most of us don't realize how transparent our feelings are, and how they can interfere with sounding the way we intend. It's hard to discipline someone one likes, hard to praise someone one dislikes. And it's so easy to praise a favourite or bark at an antagonist that often the words take on too much importance. The only thing you can do is to admit openly to yourself how you feel before you start. Then try to temper your words, your tone, your gestures to minimize the effects upon the message of your feelings toward the person.

These six steps should help you avoid the common pitfall of unconsciously sending out signals that garble the real intent of your message. This is the best method of ensuring that your listener will hear what you intended him to.

FOCUS POINT

1. Clichés and jargon dull a writing style.

2. Idioms make for strong, direct expression.

3. Study of synonyms makes for exact expression.

4. The "best" language is that which is most appropriate.

EXERCISES

1. Which of each of these pairs of expressions is the grammatical one?
   a. (i) He *set* at the table all evening. (ii) He *sat* at the table all evening.
   b. (i) She *knew* better than that. (ii) She *knowed* better than that.
   c. (i) *Them was* the days! (ii) *Those were* the days!
   d. (i) She has to choose between you and *he.* (ii) She has to choose between you and *him.*
   e. (i) *Bill and Henry, they* walked home. (ii) *Bill and Henry walked* home.
   f. (i) She *doesn't* trust him. (ii) She *don't* trust him.
   g. (i) Joe left his books *lying* in the rain. (ii) Joe left his books *laying* in the rain.
   h. (i) The sun has *arose.* (ii) The sun has *risen.*
   i. (i) *Neither* Ted *or* his mother *were* at home. (ii) *Neither* Ted *nor* his mother *was* at home.
   j. (i) He *climbed* the tall tree. (ii) He *clumb* the tall tree.

2. All of us in growing up have at one time or the other been greatly influenced by some word or expression that has deeply affected us. Write of your experience with such a command, warning, promise, or hope and what effects the expression may have had on you, or on someone you know.

3. Carefully read the article "Do Your Words of Wisdom Come Through Clearly" for the appropriateness of its language. Do you find clichés or stock phrases in it? If so, list them. Does it avoid the use of jargon? If not, give examples. Were there any expressions in it that struck you as being particularly apt and colorful? How would you describe the voice of the author?

4. Bring in a Xerox copy of writing that you consider so full of jargon as to be almost unintelligible. As was done with such a passage on p. 56 of this chapter, try to reduce it to simple, clear statements.

5. How effective do you find the following letter from the Canadian Government Travel Bureau sent in reply to a request for tourist information? Comment on its language, word choice, voice, and general suitability to its purpose. Is it rich in connotation? Which expressions do you find particularly inviting? Which, if any, arouse no response?

> Dear Sir,
>   Summer visitors to Canada West can't be blamed if they are sometimes confused about what to do and see first in this great holiday land. Don't worry. We have more suggestions than you will be able to use in summers and summers of vacations.°
>   Start at Vancouver, a jewel in a mountain-ringed setting but with the bustle and variety of an important international seaport. A great place to shop! Take the nighttime lift to the top of Grouse Mountain, dine with the glittering city spread out below. Victoria offers serenity, formal gardens, cricket . . . a piece of Olde England transplanted.
>   See the fjord-indented coastline from a sleek ferry . . . 20 beautiful hours to Prince Rupert. Or take the Trans Canada Highway that whisks you to vacation highlights; Banff, Jasper, Calgary's big Stampede (the Queen will be there July 25th in honour of the Royal Canadian Mounted Police Centennial), Edmonton's Klondike Days, pan Barkerville's gold.
>   Canada West is bursting with summer delights for fishermen, golfers, hikers, riders, boatmen and naturalists. Whatever your interests, you will find them in fascinating Canada West. Come and see!
>
> CORDIALLY YOURS,
DAN WALLACE,
DIRECTOR
>
> ° P.S. Return the enclosed card today for all the information you need for a great Canadian summer vacation. Suggested tours are expertly planned. D.W.

6. Bring in a list of 20 words with their definitions which are new to you and which you found in a recent issue of a periodical like *Harper's, Atlantic Monthly, The Nation, The New Republic, Commonweal, Commentary,* or *Esquire.*

3

Sentences: Word Patterns for Effectiveness

Right now you are reading a *sentence*. It is not so elaborate as some of the others you have read to get to this page, but it is a representative, run-of-the-mill kind of sentence often found in our American English language. In fact, by definition, that is all any language is: "the collection of sentences that a fluent person would be able to produce or comprehend had he the time, energy, and motivation."[1] Now if you have any curiosity about how many different kinds of sentences you possibly could speak or write, you should be interested in the study of grammar.

Do not shy away from definitions; they pin things down so that they can be examined. When looked at in the light of those possible sentences yet to come rolling out from the tip of your pen or the keys of your typewriter, the study of grammar makes sense. Grammar studies the "rules," or natural speech ways by which all the possible sentences in a language are generated and expressed. It shows us how our language enables us to use a great many basic word patterns or arrangements.

When you know these rules, these sentence forms, you can experiment with them in your own writing. You will also find them most helpful in your reading of difficult literary styles.

The particular "grammar" you will find at work in our analysis of sentence structures is a combination of traditional and transformational-

[1] Terence Langendoen, *The Study of Syntax* (New York: Holt, Rinehart and Winston, Inc., 1969), p. 1.

generative grammars. We promise to remain as nontechnical as possible, but we must have names in common for the word patterns that make sentences expressive.

KINDS OF SENTENCE MESSAGES

You may never have thought about it, but all your life you have been talking sentences having a wide range of meanings, as this family exchange illustrates:

1. "Joey, what are you doing in there?"
2. "I'm just looking out the window, Mama."
3. "Well, you'd better put those toys away like I told you."
4. "I will, Mama. Can I have my candy bar then?"
5. "Good heavens, boy! All that candy is going to give you more cavities."
6. "I'll wash my teeth right after it, Mama. I promise!"
7. "You had a Mars bar this morning already."
8. "But Ellen ate most of it. She's a grabber, you know, and she's a lot bigger'n me."

This homely dialogue also illustrates what sentences *do* in enabling us to communicate our thoughts and feelings. Looking closely at these eight statements, we find each one performs a specific function:

> Number 1 asks a question.
> Number 2 makes a statement of reply.
> Number 3 expresses a command.
> Number 4 makes a promise and then a request.
> Number 5 is an exclamation and then gives a warning.
> Number 6 makes a persuasive promise.
> Number 7 is an argument.
> Number 8 is a counterargument and identifies.

These are only a few basic services we daily call upon sentences to do for us; in addition we express our greatest hopes and visions as well as our worst fears and dreads in sentence forms. In fact, one way of looking at any effective piece of writing, whatever its length, is to see it as nothing more than an expanded sentence: a single basic "message" requiring many other supportive statements to make the desired point. How many autobiographies, for example, have had as their germinal start some such realizations as this one: "Say, I've really had an extraordinary life, haven't I?" Similarly, many short stories and novels have grown out of this half-phrased question: "What would happen if—?"

All those who have been brought up to speak some dialect of English share the same fundamental ways of speaking in recognizable sentence forms or structures, and with the aid of education—with or without much grammar—we have also learned to adapt those spoken messages into written sentences. Even if we do not make sense out of them, we would regard statements like the following as "sentences" written by English-speaking persons:

> *Kazoom shookled the berjum out of the lazote. With its snoopledee this qualpie escriggled and moolied the remper, helfing the snagerletzer to slipher sneep.*

Nonsensical and meaningless as the words themselves are, they are arranged in the kinds of word order we readily recognize as patterns we ourselves use daily, as these word substitutions show:

> *Mike shook the catsup out of the bottle. With its nose the rat jiggled and pushed the lever, causing the door to pop open.*

ORAL VERSUS WRITTEN SENTENCES

To further examine the relationship between the forms and patterns of everyday speech and written sentences, study the following passage from Eudora Welty's novel, *Losing Battles*. It is one of the many colorful conversational exchanges among members of a rural Mississippi family as they reminisce about a cyclone they had experienced as children.

"I wasn't but five years old that morning—and it all went dark, dark in the house, and I ran and got the door open. I says, 'Something's *coming!*' I heard it! 'Get out, Lexie! Run!' It was the *wind* I heard. The air was too thick to see through. Too thick to breathe any of. Too strong to stand up in. And I went down on my hands and knees and I shut my eyes and crawled," said Auntie Fay. She was telling it with her eyes shut. "Blind crawled."

"Where was you going?" asked Aunt Cleo. "Did you think it would do you any good?"

"I was crossing the road to go to school but I didn't know it," said Auntie Fay.

"You went off and left me," said Miss Lexie.

"You was kept home from school with the chicken pox. I *called* you."

"The rest of us children was already right where we belonged; inside Banner School with Miss Julia Mortimer telling us it was the best place to be," said Miss Beulah with her straight-lipped smile. "She taught right ahead. We could perfectly well hear all outdoors fixing to come apart. I reckon most of Banner was trying to get loose and go flying. All of a sudden, the schoolhouse roof took off and went right up to the sky. The cyclone was on top of Banner School like a drove of cattle. There was our stove, waltzing around with our lunch pails, and the map flapping its wings and flying away, and our coats was galloping over our heads with Miss Julia's cape trying to catch 'em. And the wind shrieking like a bunch of rivals at us children! But Miss Julia makes herself heard all the same. 'Hold on! Hold onto each other! All hold onto me! We're in the best place right here!' Didn't she?" she cried to the others.

"I thought I saw her throw herself down on the dictionary once, when it tried to get away," said Aunt Birdie. "But I didn't believe my eyes."

"Where was *you?*" Aunt Cleo pointed at Auntie Fay. "You started this."

"I was out on the schoolhouse step, hollering 'Let me in!' " she said. "And it seemed to me like they was trying a good deal harder to keep me out. Till Miss Julia herself got the door open and grabbed for me. And the wind was trying its best to scoop me and her and all of 'em behind her out of the schoolhouse, but she didn't let it. She had me by the foot and pulled me in flat. She pulled against the wind and dragged me good, till I was a hundred percent inside that schoolhouse."

"Finally we got the door shut again, and Miss Julia got on her knees and leaned against it, and we all copied her, and we held the schoolhouse up," said Aunt Birdie. "Every single one of us plastered with leaves!"

"And that chair—that's when this house was delivered that school chair, the one you're holding down this minute, Judge Moody. It blew here," said Miss Beulah, pointing at him. "And the tree caught it—Billy Vaughn's Switch did. If it hadn't, it might have come right in the house through that window into the company room. That chair's the only sample of the cyclone this house got. I reckon Grandpa was pretty strongly praying."

"What did it do to the store?" asked Aunt Cleo. "Stovall's store?"

"It was Papa's store then. Well, sir, the roof took off and it was just like you'd shaken a feather bolster and seen it come open at the seam," said Mr. Renfro. "I was watching the whole thing get away from Papa. Everything that'd been inside that store got outside. Blew away. And the majority of our house went right along to keep it company."

"What happened to the bridge?" asked Mrs. Moody.

Auntie Fay rattled her little tongue.

"No it didn't. It didn't even wiggle. I was paying it some mind, I was under it," said Mr. Renfro to his sister. "I was going a little tardy to school that morning, and when I heard the thing coming, the bridge is what I dove under. And it wasn't in the path, that bridge. No, the storm come up the river and it veered. The bridge stood still right where it was put, and a minute away, the rest of the world went right up in the air."

"It picked the Methodist Church up all in one piece and carried it through the air and set it down right next to the Baptist Church! Thank the Lord nobody was worshipping in either one," said Aunt Beck.

"I never heard of such a thing," said Mrs. Moody.

"Now you have. And those Methodists had to tear their own church down stick by stick so they could carry it back and put it together again on the side of the road where it belonged," said Miss Beulah. "A good many Baptists helped 'em."

"I'll tell you something as contrary as people are. Cyclones," said Mr. Renfro.

"It's a wonder we all wasn't carried off, killed with the horses and cows, and skinned alive like the chickens," said Uncle Curtis.[2]

Caught up in the art with which Eudora Welty narrates this account of the storm as the characters recall it, we may overlook the basic sentence patterns in which her people speak. And they are talking in sentences, although the author is a literary artist skilled in creating the effect of everyday talk. But however unskilled a student-writer may be— and the one quoted below has much to learn!—he will "talk-write" in distinguishable sentences:

Language is not to be made fun of. Although many people do, grammar or language was made for us to comonatate with each other. Here some modern language. Like hey man don't blow your cool or hey big mommy lets split to my pad. Or babie lets cut out these cats are to far out and still whose that big cat with big mommy, you know that crazy chick with the beautiful drumsticks. These is just some of our gram like man so I'm cuting scene so long you big cats and chicks.

THE SENTENCE AS SUBJECT AND PREDICATE

What is the most basic of all sentence-word patterns in our language? Let us hope you still remember enough language study to say, "The subject and the predicate!" Now if you have been blessed in having had somewhere in your 12 years of schooling a teacher who

[2] From *Losing Battles* by Eudora Welty. Copyright © 1970 by Eudora Welty. Reprinted by permission of Random House, Inc.

thought our civilization would go into a sharp decline if her students could not distinguish *subject* from *predicate*, you may still recall having learned sentence statements like this one: "The subject of a sentence is the thing or person talked about, and the predicate is what is said about it or him." Also now you may be ready to add, "Every sentence has to have a subject and a predicate, stated or understood, in order to be a complete sentence." Likewise, a *complete sentence* is one that deserves a capital letter in the beginning and a period, a question mark, or an exclamation point at the end.

Now one of the advantages of studying a foreign language like Spanish, French, or German is that you soon discover the need to learn the *eight basic parts of speech* in English: nouns, pronouns, verbs, adjectives, adverbs, prepositions, conjunctions, and interjections.

Of these eight classes of words, the two commonly found serving as the subject are the noun and the pronoun; the predicate is usually the verb with its modifiers. Every sentence will make a statement if it has these two basic parts, as we see by looking at some of the short Welty sentences.

Example:

SUBJECT	PREDICATE
Auntie Fay (noun)	*rattled* her little tongue. (verb)
You (pronoun)	*started* this. (verb)

Any noun may be given adjectives to describe it, identify it, or make its meaning richer. Had Eudora Welty wished us to have a picture of what Auntie Fay looked like in the above sentence, she could have added adjectives, such as "[The never-quiet, sharp-eyed] Auntie Fay rattled her little tongue." Similarly, any verb can be given adverbs to heighten the action of the verb or otherwise modify it, as in this example: "Auntie Fay [again loudly] rattled her little tongue."

Everyone in this Welty family can rattle off one sentence after the other. Look at this sample of Aunt Birdie's string of subjects and predicates:

    S V   conj. S   V

"Finally we got the door shut again, and Miss Julia got on her knees and

V   conj. S   V   conj. S V

leaned against it, and we all copied her, and we held the schoolhouse

S   V

up. . . . Every single one of us [was] plastered with leaves!"

In one flow of speech, Aunt Birdie has tied four sets of subject-predicate statements together by means of the coordinate conjunction "and." Her fifth sentence is an exclamation, which because it has a verb form— *plastered*—but not a finite verb, is called an *absolute phrase*.

But when as a student of grammar you begin to look closely at all the sentences that Aunt Birdie and the rest fire off in that exciting exchange of memories, you will find that all those sentences fall, as they must, under one of four basic word patterns fundamental to our English language, no matter what the dialect.

Here are those four basic grammatical structures, or word patterns, out of which a skilled writer can make almost countless variations and combinations to "invent" sentences.

1. *Subject and finite verb*

    Examples:

        S   V

    "You was kept home from school with the chicken pox."

         S   V

    "The cyclone was on top of Banner School like a drove of cattle."

    (A "finite verb" is a verb that indicates time, tense, person, and number.)

2. *Subject, finite verb, and direct object*

    Examples:

         S   V   O

    "You started this."

         S V O   V   O

    "She had me by the foot and pulled me in flat."

         S V   O

    "I called you."

    (The "direct object" is the word receiving the action from the verb;

it is also called "object complement" because it completes the predicate.)

3. *Subject, finite verb, and subject complement*

Examples:

S   V   SC

"The air was too thick to see through."

S   V   SC

"That chair's the only sample of the cyclone. . . ."

(The "subject complement" relates to the subject in that while completing the predicate it explains, describes, or identifies the subject.)

4. *Subject, finite verb, indirect object, and object complement*

Example:

S   V   IO   OC

"He gave her the repair bill."

As you can see, all four of these basic sentence patterns share the one common feature essential to any sentence: each has a subject and a finite verb. The subject is always a noun, a pronoun, or some grammatical unit—a noun phrase or a noun clause—serving as a noun. Always the noun and the verb may be modified, the former by adjectives and the latter by adverbs.

GRAMMATICAL TYPES OF SENTENCES

Let us assume that you know that each of the four sentence patterns mentioned above also can be called an *independent clause*—call it "base," "main," or "kernel" clause if you like—and that every sentence, to be complete, requires at least one such clause. Just as there are independent clauses, so there are also *dependent* or *subordinate* clauses. If they serve as adjective modifiers, these dependent clauses begin with what is called a *relative pronoun* (that, which, what, who, whoever). If the dependent, or subordinate clause serves as an adverb modifier, it will begin with a *subordinate connective* (if, since, although, till, until, while, when, where, after, because, etc.). A third use of the dependent clause is that the clause can act as a noun; it can be the subject of a verb (*That he was tired* was evident), a verb complement (I believed *what he said*), or the object of a preposition (He planned to give his money to *whoever needed it most*).

Everyone who knows this much of our grammar is probably also familiar with the kinds of sentence combinations these independent and dependent clauses can produce. Here they are as exemplified by sentences appearing in the Eudora Welty selection:

Simple sentence   (one independent clause)

> S   V
>
> "The air was too thick to see through."

> S   V
>
> "It was Papa's store then."

Compound sentence   (two or more independent clauses)

> S   V   S V
>
> "No, the storm come up the river and it veered."

> S   V
>
> "And the wind was trying its best to scoop me and her and all of 'em
>
>   S   V
>
> behind her out of the schoolhouse, but she didn't let it."

(The clauses are joined by the *coordinate conjunction* "but.")

Complex sentence   (one independent clause and one or more dependent clauses)

> S   V   V   S V
>
> "She pulled against the wind and dragged me good, till I was a hundred percent inside that schoolhouse."

> S V   S V
>
> "I thought I saw her throw herself down on the dictionary once, when
>
> S V
>
> it tried to get away."

Compound complex sentence   (two or more independent clauses and
one or more dependent clauses)

  S V   S V

"I was going a little tardy to school that morning, and when I heard

                   S   V   S V

the thing coming, the bridge is what I dove under."

Illustrating these grammatical sentence structures with Eudora
Welty examples leads us to note the appropriateness of these sentences
to the speech rhythms of the members of the family. The word-pattern
combinations resemble those that people normally adopt when "telling"
of an interesting experience. As such they form an essential part of the
author's *style* — the tone, the word choices, and the design — chosen for
this incident as well as for the rest of *Losing Battles.*

How these same simple, compound, complex, and compound-
complex sentences function in the kind of academic language you read
and hear in college classes can be seen in the paragraphs that follow.
The main point in calling attention to the existence and nature of these
sentence types is to show how valuable dependent clauses are in adding
meaningful details to the basic simple sentence statement. You should
be able to distinguish between the subject-verb markings (S-V) of the
main clauses and the S-V of the dependent adjective, adverb, and even
the noun clauses.

                       S   V

1. The fourteenth century opened with a series of famines brought on

                    S   V

    when population growth outstripped the techniques of food produc-

                                  S   V

    tion. [Complex] The precarious balance was tipped by a series of

                                           S

    heavy rains and floods and by a chilling of the climate in what has

    V

    been called the Little Ice Age. [Complex] — [Barbara W. Tuchman]

                                S   V

2. Month after month the cost of living rises. [Simple] High food

      S   V   S   V

    prices merely dramatize the fact that all the items in our budget go

    up and up and up. [Complex] Even with raises for seniority and ex-

                                S   V

    cellence, your higher paycheck barely stretches over living costs,

       S   V

    and it certainly doesn't bring the average worker that steady im-

       S   V

    provement in real wages Americans have grown used to. [Compound

                                  S V

    complex] As for the less lucky, they are really hurting. [Simple]—

    [Paul A. Samuelson]

          S

3. The use of non-validated data, such as assumed biological decay and

    transfer constants and absorbed dosages based on simulated model

                     V

    studies, became the acceptable standards after a period of time.

                                  S V

    [Simple] But since validations studies are generally never under-

                        S   V   S

    taken after the standards are set, these first armchair estimates be-

    V   S V

    come gospel fact. [Complex] The radiation safety field is replete

with such non-validated assumptions. [Simple] — [Associated Press]
  S   V   S   V

4. Few of us experience the world immediately, and we mostly live

   by abstract metaphors, snugly contained by our "institutionalized

   individualism," pursuing the fantasies of power of our "instrumental

   activism," and forever relieved of serious political commitments by
                                    S   V

   an education which "focuses on the development of an educated

   citizenry" . . . although not in the political sense. [Compound com-

   plex] — [Sheldon S. Wolin]
          S   V

5. The culture of the powerful is very infectious for the sophisticated
                                                           S

   and strangely addictive. [Simple] To be any kind of "success" one

     V   V
   must be fluent in this culture. [Simple] Know the words of the users,
                                           S V

   the semantic rituals of power. [Simple] This is a way into whatever
   S V S   V   V

   it is you are not now, but wish, very desperately, to get into. [Com-
                   S

   plex] . . . Being told to "speak proper," meaning that you become
                                 V

   fluent with the jargon of power, is also a part of not "speaking

S   S   V

proper." [Simple] That is, the culture which desperately under-

S   V   V

stands that it does not "speak proper," or is not fluent with the terms

V   S

of social strength, also understands somewhere that its desire to

V

gain such fluency is done at a terrifying risk. [Complex]—[LeRoi

Jones]

PUNCTUATING AND ENRICHING SENTENCES

If you can spot an independent clause when you see one and will memorize the following schema, you will have little trouble punctuating sentences.

1. If the sentence has only one independent clause, the main punctuation required is the final one: period, question mark, exclamation point:

Independent clause.

Example: He sadly went back to work.

2. If the sentence is *complex,* place a comma at the end of the subordinate clause when it precedes the independent:

Subordinate clause, independent clause.

Example: After he had lost all his money gambling, he sadly went back to work.

3. If the sentence is *compound* (two or more independent clauses) and has no connecting conjunction, separate them by a semicolon:

Independent clause; independent clause.

Example: India long has had the capacity to build a nuclear device; last year it set one off.

4. If the sentence is compound and the independent clauses are con-
    nected by a coordinate conjunction, put a comma before the con-
    junction.

Independent clause, and *independent clause.*

but

or

nor

Example: Because of food shortages two-thirds of the world is always
on the brink of starvation, and only the great grain-producing countries can be looked to for help.

5. If the two independent clauses are linked by the adverbial con-
    nectives—however, moreover, therefore, nevertheless, thus, or
    then—place a semicolon before the connective.

Independent; therefore *independent.*

however

moreover

thus

then

nevertheless

Example: Populations continue to grow in the so-called under-
developed countries; therefore it appears that no food-supply program
now available will be able to keep up with the ever increasing number of hungry mouths. (Note: if you wish, you may put a comma after
the connective.)

FIVE KINDS OF PHRASES

Coming down the scale of grammatical units of the sentence, we
arrive at the next largest group of closely related words—the phrase.
Phrases may serve as adjective or adverbial modifiers and therefore add
richness of meaning to nouns and verbs. Unlike clauses, phrases lack a
verb and sometimes even a subject.

We begin with the *prepositional phrase,* one that is difficult to define
clearly but is easy to spot in a sentence. A prepositional phrase consists
of a preposition with its object. Here is a list of some prepositions we
make phrases with almost every time we speak:

in	into	under	after
on	out	beyond	above

by	for	before	below
of	with	beside	inside
to	through	between	outside

Examples: In the car, on the table, by special delivery, of the house, to the door, into the street, out the window, for her, with much trouble, through the glass, under the tree, before dinner, beside him.

The following are student sentence examples of prepositional phrases:

Ival Lavaas is a Norwegian-born psychologist who uses a cattle prod

   (1)   (2)

in his work with autistic children. I have found his ideas most interest-

   (3)   (4)   (5)   (6)

ing *in light of my own negative reaction to the nature of past experi-*

       (7)   (8)

ments done *in this area and the conclusions* drawn *from them.*

Verbal phrases consist of some form of a verb, its modifiers, and its complement; they are found functioning in clauses as adjectives, nouns, or adverbs. Like wild flowers, they give real pleasure when they can be identified with their proper names. It is not too difficult since there are only three species of verbal phrases: participle, gerund, and infinitive. Let us take them one at a time.

The *participle* is a verbal form used as an adjective: The *singing* bird, the man *singing* in the shower. As a phrase, it is often found as a "free" modifier: one providing detail that is important but is not grammatically essential to the sentence: the information is parenthetical.

Examples: (1)

     Accepting her new responsibilities, the nurse is now able

                       (2)

     to take the pressure off the physician, *freeing him* to con-

                       (3)

     centrate his efforts on patients most in need of them, *allow-*

                       (4)

     ing him to be utilized as a referral man *checking only two cases in a hundred* whereas before he saw all one hundred.

(1)

Herodotus was an inventor of history, *sharing more the*

(2)

role of the modern historical novelist than *being an accurate recorder* of events.

The *gerund* is a verbal ending in *ing* that is used as a noun but still partakes of the nature of a verb. With its modifiers and complements, it can be found serving as the subject of a clause, the object of a verb or a preposition (prep.), and even as a subjective complement—in short, in any "slot" usually filled by a noun.

Examples: (subject)

It would seem that *setting up an experimental situation*

(subject)

with a rat in a Skinner-box and *arbitrarily punishing the
rat for a certain behavior it had been previously condi-*

(object of prep.)

tioned to perform could not be paralleled *to spanking a*

(object of prep.)   (object of prep.)

child for stealing or *for holding little brother's head under
the water in the bathtub.*

Examples of participles and gerunds in the same sentence are:

(gerund)

Probably the simplest way *of increasing profits* is to in-

(participle)   (gerund)

crease prices, *thus having the effect of increasing dollar*

(gerund)

amounts of gross sales and *of making the annual report
look good.*

(gerund)

In telling a story as a photojournalist, I use my camera the

(participle)

way a writer uses a typewriter, *trying* to include every

(participle)

significant detail and *making all* as vivid as I can.

Infinitives consist of the preposition *to*, either expressed or implied, and a verb: *to read, to have read, to have been reading.*

Examples:

> The goal of all good photojournalists is *to help, to question,* or *to comment.*

>   (1)   (2)
>
> The unwary consumer has *to trust the repairman to fix whatever is wrong* and must take his word for whatever was or was not repaired or replaced.

And then there is the most famous Shakespearean soliloquy:

> *To be,* or not *to be:* that is the question,
> Whether 'tis nobler in the mind *to suffer*
> The slings and arrows of outrageous fortune,
> Or *to take arms* against a sea of troubles,
> And by opposing *to end them. To die, to sleep;*
> No more; and by a sleep *to say* we end
> The heartache, and the thousand natural shocks
> That flesh is heir to, 'tis a consummation
> Devoutly *to be wished. To die, to sleep.*
> *To sleep,* perchance *to dream:* ay, there's the rub. . . .

Absolute phrases differ from verbal phrases in that they are constructions that appear to be independent clauses, but instead of having a finite verb may have only a participial phrase.

Examples:

The game having ended, the crowds began the rush for the parking lots.

The car brakes no longer working and *the downhill grade sharply increasing,* he took the first side road open to him.

His friends having taken off without him, he decided that having such friends he needed no enemies.

COMBINING SENTENCES

In the past, your own writing style has led you, knowingly or unknowingly, to make ready use of the sentence forms and word patterns we have so far been examining. Without realizing it, you probably have been writing complex sentences, for example, or made participial phrases one of your favorite grammatical devices. However, now that you have some knowledge of grammar and syntax (word patterning), you may wish to set to work and deliberately put into practice what you have learned.

Suppose you have been told, or have observed yourself, that you habitually write too many "and, and" sentences such as this one:

> He always came home from work tired, and he couldn't get a can of beer out of the refrigerator fast enough, and then he would settle down in his recliner chair and enjoy his drink.

This sentence consists of a series of independent clauses strung together as in the speech of one careless of the relationships among the facts being stated, making them all of equal importance. But there is a cause-and-effect relationship in those facts, and by subordinating the facts of lesser importance and leaving just one independent clause to express the main idea, we can form a more sophisticated sentence.

    (adverb clause)   (adverb clause)

When he came home from work tired, as he did every day, he could not

    (independent clause)   (adverb)

get a can of beer out of the refrigerator fast enough so that he could settle down in his recliner chair and enjoy his drink.

Or take this series of independent clauses:

> He was a devout believer; he accepted the Bible as the literal truth; he had a quotation for every occasion.

Are these statements all of equal importance, or should only one of them be given independent-clause prominence because it expresses the main idea? In its present form, the sentence has its three "he" clauses *co-*

ordinate with one another as equals. But looked at more closely, the clauses reveal a cause-and-effect relationship which should properly be expressed by making one subordinate, reducing another to a compound verb, and leaving one as the main clause.

(adverb clause)   (independent clause)

Because he was a devout believer, he accepted the Bible as the literal truth and had a quotation for every occasion.

It is possible, if you know some grammar, to design interesting as well as clear and concise sentences, but it takes some practice. For example, how would you go about combining the following simple sentences into one sentence having appropriate coordination and subordination of ideas?

> College students used to have telephone booth jamming contests.
> They used to have goldfish-swallowing contests.
> They engaged in panty raids.
> "Streaking" was the big campus fad in 1974.
> It was also called "organic running."

These five statements might appear in a weak writer's composition as paragraph sentences, all coordinate and apparently of equal importance. But which of the five facts is the main one in this context? The fourth one, of course. Yet it enjoys no distinctive position or grammatical prominence. Now there are many ways in which this main idea could be given a suitable design, but here is one, which reduces all to a single sentence:

> Although college students used to have telephone booth jamming contests, goldfish-swallowing contests, and panty raids, in 1974 they made "streaking"—also called "organic running"—the big campus fad.

It is true that few persons would in everyday speech come out with such a carefully structured complex sentence; if they did, they would probably sound stilted, artificial, and pompous. In almost any kind of academic writing, however, such constructions are commonplace, a fact which illustrates again how different "talk" is from writing. This difference can be shown also in the care needed in writing to maintain a consistent *point of view* throughout a sentence.

If the subject of a sentence is the thing talked about, it is reasonable to keep its reference clear throughout the sentence statement. In the examples that follow note how the revisions in the second sentence in each pair keeps a desired point of view consistency to make them clear and concise.

1. a. When a boy enters the teen-age world, the childish games that once held his interest are left behind.
    b. When a boy enters the teen-age world, he leaves behind the childish games that once held his interest.
2. a. By meeting the real problem, that of a challenge, the teen-age vandalism will be reduced.
    b. By meeting the real problem, that of a challenge, adults can reduce teen-age vandalism.
3. a. The school has a very good student body and a good faculty, but they are always needing money.
    b. The school has a very good student body and a good faculty, but it is always short of money.
4. a. Walking down the street, the empties cluttering up the sidewalk tell you it's my neighborhood.
    b. When you walk down the street, you can tell it's my neighborhood by the empties cluttering up the sidewalk.

FOCUS POINT

1. Sentences make statements, ask questions, make demands, promise, request, express surprise, and otherwise communicate "messages."

2. Sentences have only four basic grammatical structures:
    a. Subject—verb and modifiers
    b. Subject—verb—direct object
    c. Subject—verb—subject complement
    d. Subject—verb—indirect object—direct object

3. As determined by their clauses, sentences may be simple, compound, complex, and compound-complex.

4. Phrases are classed as prepositional, participial, gerund, infinitive, and absolute.

5. All such information regarding grammar and sentence syntax is worth little if it is not used to gain insights into how you can go about making your own sentences more interesting, meaningful, and concise.

EXERCISES

1. Identify the italicized expression in each of the following sentences as one of the following: an independent clause, a relative clause, a subordinate clause, a prepositional phrase, a participial phrase, a gerund phrase, an infinitive phrase, or an absolute phrase.
   a. *With amazing swiftness* modern art has split up into a multitude of divergent directions. — [José Ortega y Gasset]
   b. Art today is, *in Dewey's brilliant phrase,* "the beauty-parlor of civilization." — [Abraham Kaplan]
   c. These pictures, *taken by the thousands by journeyman workers and Sunday hobbyists,* were unlike any pictures before them. — [John Szarkowski]
   d. *If experience is the best teacher,* many of us are quite disadvantaged. — [Tish Sommers]
   e. By the end of the 1960s there were indications *that black artists and intellectuals were picking up Black English and making it a symbol of black unity.* — [J. L. Dillard]
   f. *On what grounds, then, can we ascertain* whether religious statements have cognitive or empirical meaning? — [William T. Blackstone]
   g. In his dark study, *vines clutching the bulging screen,* Herzog played Handel and Purcell — jigs, bourrées, contredances, *his face puffed out, fingers fleet on the keys, the music hopping and tumbling,* absent-minded and sad. — [Saul Bellow]

2. Try to experiment with the various types of sentences by writing at least a six-sentence paragraph on a topic such as one of the following. In your rewrite, indicate in parentheses after each sentence what kind of sentence it is — simple, compound, complex, or compound-complex.

   How I would like to be when I am 35 years old
   A teacher I did not appreciate at the time
   What our country most needs in 1976
   A kind of movie there should be more of
   Some thoughts on new uses of computers
   A new religious phenomenon
   Adventures in traveling

3. Combine the following simple sentences into one longer sentence having appropriate coordination and subordination.
   a. His mother was hurrying to catch the bus.
      She was worrying she was late for an appointment.
      She fell hard on her right arm.
      It was still in a cast from a fall the week before.
   b. Vice-president Gerald Ford was found to be an honest man.
      He is a loyal Republican party advocate.
      He was booed by some students during a commencement address at the University of Michigan.
      He was once a Michigan football star.
      In some 1974 speeches he seemed uncertain of President Nixon's guilt or innocence. As President he now faces great problems at home and abroad.

SENTENCE RHETORIC

As children we pick up the knack of talking sentences with apparently little difficulty, and we do so because our "audience"—the one we're speaking to—is right in front of us and generally tuned into our ways of thinking. But when on reaching school age we suddenly are asked to write even the briefest thank you note for a present received from a relative or a friend, we freeze up and may even panic. If made to "write something nice to Aunt Clara," the result is usually a scrawled, most skimpy, and misspelled message. Why? Because writing is not natural, in that the one being addressed is not physically present.

To find the language and sentence forms he hopes will affect his "invisible" readers as he wishes, a writer must be keenly aware of the needs, tastes, and strengths of his possible reader-audience. He naturally fears to say the wrong thing. Every sentence can become a kind of battle arena if *how* you have to say something is just as important as *what* you have to say. We all can take consolation from the story of how one of the nation's most important and literate leaders agonized over the writing of a very brief letter.

Until one Saturday in October 1973, Elliot Richardson, a brilliant, Harvard-educated lawyer, appeared to be the most indispensable man in the Nixon administration. He had served as Secretary of Health, Education, and Welfare, then as Secretary of Defense, and finally as Attorney-General for the United States. In that last position he was given full authority by President Nixon to hire a Special Prosecutor of his own choice to head the investigation of the Watergate and other 1972 election scandals. With the approval of Senator Ervin's select committee, Richardson appointed Archibald Cox to be that Special Prosecutor.

On October 10 occurred the events that have become known as the "Saturday Night Massacre." In quick succession, Richardson was ordered by the White House to fire Cox; when he refused and resigned, his Deputy Attorney General, William Ruckelshaus, was ordered to dismiss Cox and on his refusal was fired, leaving the actual final act of dismissing Cox to the next in line in the office. With this background we can see that Elliot Richardson wanted his letter of resignation to make its points clearly and justly. The following is Aaron Latham's account of what pains were involved in writing that letter.

A more somber mood settled over the Richardson household that evening as Anne and Elliot Richardson discussed the day's events and what might happen the next day. Once again, the attorney general labored over his yellow pad. He was making notes for the letter which he would write the President the next morning. At the top of the first page, Richardson printed an unusual title, one suggested by his wife to connote going out in style:

The Mahogany Coffin.

SATURDAY

October 20—On his last day as attorney general, Elliot Richardson arrived at his office at 10 A.M. His first task was a painful one: writing.

The attorney general carefully composed a letter to the President based on "The Mahogany Coffin." Richard Darman, who was angry, had worked up a draft of a letter which he thought his boss should send to the President. Darman's draft began: "I am returning herewith your letter of October 19. . . ." Richardson read the draft but rejected it. He could no more begin a letter without a formal "thank-you" than he could come to the office without a necktie. Consequently, he opened his letter somewhat oddly:

"Dear Mr. President: Thank you for your letter of October 19, 1973, instructing me to direct Mr. Cox that he is to make no further attempts by judicial process to obtain tapes, notes, or memoranda of Presidential conversations." In spite of the "thanks," Richardson went on to say that he disagreed with that order. He suggested that the Stennis authentication model might be used if and when future tapes were subpoenaed. Richardson says of the letter, "I was trying to clarify my position even though it might be too late."[3]

[3] Aaron Latham, "Seven Days in October," *New York*, 29 April 1974, pp. 54–55.

Now our own writing and composing efforts may never need to be expended on such a momentous "message," but we can sympathize with Richardson's "Mahogany Coffin" plight as a belabored author of sentences which might be important even to the readers of history, a great invisible audience!

We now ask you to take another step in exploring this domain of sentence forms and relationships. Great orators and writers of the past in their experiments with language patterns that would gain for them the effects desired from their various audiences invented a number of sentence styles which skilled authors still rely upon today. They offer you additional options for times when you feel the need to be especially dramatic. They bear these names:

1. The short, pithy sentence
2. The loose sentence
3. The balanced sentence
4. The periodic sentence

Each of these sentence forms is characterized by its own kind of *syntax* — its ordering of words.

As its name denotes, the *short, pithy sentence* is brief but carries a punch, as do these:

She came, she saw, she conquered.

Nice girls marry for love. — [SAUL BELLOW]

It was all-dark. The river-sound enveloped us as it never could have in light. I sat down beside Lewis and motioned to Bobby. He crouched down as well. — [JAMES DICKEY, *Deliverance*]

The *loose sentence* strings out details, adding subordinate information as it goes:

There is a sort of rude familiarity which some people, by practising among their intimates, have introduced into their general conversation, and would have it pass for innocent freedom or humours, which is a dangerous experiment in our northern climate, where all the little decorum and politeness we have are purely forced by art, and are so ready to lapse into barbarity. — [JONATHAN SWIFT]

Of what the world would call essentials, Enderby had few to pack. It was the bath full of verse that was the trouble. Kneeling in front of it, as though

—and here he laughed sardonically—he worshipped his own work, he began to bundle it into the larger of his two suitcases, separating—with reasonable care—manuscripts from sandwich-crusts, cigarette-packets, and the cylinders of long-used toilet-rolls.—[ANTHONY BURGESS, *Enderby* (New York: W. W. Norton & Co., 1968), p. 95.]

The *balanced sentence* relies heavily upon the principle of *parallelism;* that is, of using similar grammatical structures (syntax) for similar ideas.

The best man is he who most tries to perfect himself, and the happiest man is he who most feels he is perfecting himself.—[SOCRATES]

Ask not what your country can do for you, but what you can do for your country.—[JOHN F. KENNEDY]

Through wisdom is an house builded, and by understanding it is established: And by knowledge shall the chambers be filled with all precious and pleasant riches.—[PROVERBS]

The *periodic sentence* also frequently relies upon parallelism to keep in order the coordinate details making up the bulk of the sentence. The periodic sentence is the most formal since it is oratorical in effect and requires deliberate construction and arrangement of phrases and clauses. It is "periodic" in that it holds off its main meaning until just before the close of the sentence. It aims to keep the reader or hearer in suspense until the final phrase climaxes with the approach of the period, as in these examples:

If over-cultivation of the private sensibility leads to narrowness, limitation, and finally to a self-indulgent turning away from the external world altogether, commitment can lead to undesirable limitations of a different kind—limitations in kinds of subject-matter and in methods of rendering experience.—[ANDREW HOOK]

When the rock group produces its first record, it is not concerned with style or structure, but, rather, with a sense of immediate impact, with what the *Bandstand* panelists call "the great beat."—[CHARLES BELZ]

On these dark, drear January mornings, which daylight saving time makes nightmarishly unreal, when I am driving campusward hunched over the steering wheel, peering through rain-bleared side windows for invisible pedestrians—especially children ready to explode off street corners—looking almost frantically to follow worn-dim yellow traffic lane markers, dreading at stoplight changes that every set of headlights racing up to glare into the rear-view mirror may mean a rear-end crash, and wondering with other parts of my hardly awake mind whether the Christensen sentence exercise I have planned for my Wr323 class will work and why I forgot to bring my checkbook along, I feel I am rushing toward some disaster, which, if not on this particular morning, will yet claim me.

This last periodic sentence represents something of a stunt; it was written during one class period while each student worked out his own sentence in response to these directions written on the chalkboard: "Out of the following raw data, write a detail-rich sentence: coming to the campus on dark January mornings, special dangers now with heavy traffic, urgency to park and to make it to class in time, concerns about classwork, and special problems for today (personal)."

Here are several of those student sentences; note the variety of structures they exhibit.

Waking in the January darkness, he dressed, ate, stoked up the car, and left, plunging toward the blackened city with its freeways of headlighted obstacles between him and the school for which, no matter how early he rose or long he studied, he always seemed late, unprepared, or so bored he would fall asleep during the first two classes.

Riding a bus on these cold, dark and often wet January mornings to PSU is enough to make you wish your alarm hadn't sounded as you hustle through your morning routines of rising to a frigid floor and finding your slippers out of reach under the bed, to wait five minutes for your chilly wash water to become at least lukewarm and then attempting to juggle the makings of a peanut butter and jelly sandwich as you drink your morning constitutional of orange juice and consume that last bit of toast behind the slam of the front door; flying down the street and remembering you forgot your lunch, you turn the corner just in time to catch a glimpse of the seven-thirty bus you have missed by thirty-two seconds.

Long before the January sun has risen, I answer my alarm clock's beckon, dress, breakfast, slide onto the cold seat of my Volkswagen, and rumble off to pick up the other half of the car pool with whom I will hazard the perils of the daily thirty-mile trek up I-5, our noses toward the metropolis, our tongues relatively silent at this hour, and our minds on the day's activities and responsibilities awaiting us at school and, alas, the warm air slowly seeping out from between the covers of our beds back home.

These four sentences—all deliberately made long and detailed—display the complicated coordination-subordination sentence-element patterns found in various writing styles. As the following passage indicates, the periodic sentence derives from a Roman school of rhetoric, the "Ciceronian":

> The various traditional styles named *Attic, Isocratic, Ciceronian,* and *baroque* are recognizable by their various kinds of syntax, as the following sentences will illustrate. The Attic employs mostly simple sentences. As the Isocratic sentence runs to greater length, so it involves greater complexity; where the Attic would move forward clearly and directly, the Isocratic uses parallel clauses to balance and oppose the parts. Less artificial, and more likely to reveal its full meaning only after a series of details and interpolations, is the Ciceronian or *periodic sentence.* As for the baroque sentence, though it is pithy in its parts and dramatic in its total effect, its construction lacks the perfect symmetry of parallelism, for it develops gradually and by additions or modifications as it unfolds. Most writers of prose today want to achieve variety in style rather than to follow any one of these models. In good modern writing a long periodic sentence, reaching a climax only at its conclusion, may be followed by a short simple one. Nevertheless, these syntactically consistent styles are able, if subtly managed, to communicate the distinct individual quality of a work.[4]

Look closely at the sentences describing each of these four styles, and you will discover that each sentence exemplifies the style it defines!

But however elaborate or plain a sentence style may be, it cannot be an effective one, as has been pointed out earlier, unless it rings with a voice that means what it says. As the following account by a composition instructor makes clear, a piece of writing may be "correct" but dull and lifeless because it lacks the originality or vital tone that comes only from a writer who accepts challenges and does his best to rise to meet them.

> First, here is a run-of-the-mill essay by a student currently enrolled in the remedial English course at Berkeley:

> The University has established breadth requirements to broaden

---

[4] Marlies K. Danziger and W. Stacy Johnson. *An Introduction to Literary Criticism* (Lexington, Mass.: D.C. Heath & Company, 1961), pp. 45–46.

the student's educational scope. Certain courses must be completed at the end of a four year period in order for the student to obtain a degree. The abolition of the breadth requirements would promote a free educational atmosphere in which the student determines his own academic schedule. A student should not be compelled to enroll in Physics 10 if the subject does not appeal to his mental curiosity. An individual cannot force enthusiasm under this circumstance, and the University has no right to expect it. A great deal of valuable time is spent in satisfying these numerous requirements, time which should be devoted to studies supportive of a major.

Education is meant to be stimulating and involving; material should grasp the reader's interest to the point where one must force himself to cease. Breadth requirements in the latter sense are not representative of education; they are viewed as obstacles which must be conquered. It is imperative that a student select his own courses. These breadth requirements are not beneficial to the student and must be abolished.

If we evaluate this essay according to the criteria for writing established in Walter Loban's *The Language of Elementary School Children* (National Council of Teachers of English, 1963, p. 25), we find that the essay would barely qualify as "good" if the student were of elementary school age:

1. Uses limited sentence patterns
2. Uses few, if any, relational words
3. Begins to organize but strays from basis of organization
4. Displays monotonous vocabulary
5. Uses reasonably correct spelling and punctuation
6. Interprets only the obvious, barely achieving interpretation
7. Fails to be specific; tends to generalities

But this student is eighteen years old; he has had twelve years of instruction in English and has done well enough in other subjects in school to gain entrance to the University—none of which would matter except that the poor quality of this student's writing is typical of what we see in student essays written as remedial English assignments. Errors aside, the tendency to write a series of flat assertions, the lack of precise thinking and of any personal element, the monotony of language and sentence structure all make the essay boring, stale, clichéd, and, beyond that, pallid, thin and anemic.[5]

[5] Sabina Thorne Johnson, "Some Tentative Strictures on Generative Rhetoric," *College English* 31 (November 1969): 157.

WHAT ABOUT SENTENCE LENGTHS?

Now only a Hemingway worshipper is going to write completely in the *Attic* style of short simple sentences. And surely no one is going to be so *Ciceronian* as to make the periodic sentence with its often interminable lengths his mainstay—at least not for modern readers. Nor do you find many examples of the carefully constructed balanced *Isocratic* sentence in writing today. That leaves only the open-ended loose or *baroque* sentence as the most typical sentence style, but like baseball pitchers who "mix up their pitches" to get strikes on their batters, good writers also "mix up" their styles.

Are you aware of what kind of sentences you typically turn out? How long are they on the average? Is there any "proper" length a sentence should have? When is a sentence "too long" or "too short"?

These are not nonsensical questions, for they return us once more to the fundamental matter of rhetorical *stance*. Sentence lengths, like paragraph and whole composition lengths, may be judged for effectiveness in reaching the reader. That means the tastes and attention spans of your specific reader-audience should determine this matter of length. Now one pragmatic way to establish some standards for yourself is to do some word counting among examples of current professional and good nonprofessional writing.

The following article appearing in "The Talk of the Town" section of *The New Yorker* should show, when analyzed, how the editors of that sophisticated periodical regard the capacities of their readers.

NOTES AND COMMENT[6]

The Big Lie is a strategy for concealing the truth by putting forward a story so audaciously false that it disarms ordinary skepticism, which is ready to cope only with petty distortions and deceptions. The White House, in its Watergate maneuverings, has apparently adopted another strategy; that of the Big Snarl. Instead of putting forward a single, easily grasped false story that routs all other stories, including the complex true story, from the field, one who resorts to this strategy puts forward—and then often retracts—numberless clashing, mutually cancelling stories, so that before long the integrity of all the facts and the logic of all the justifications are destroyed beyond reconstruction. Instead of hiding in sim-

[6] Reprinted by permission. © 1973 The New Yorker Magazine, Inc.

plicity, one takes refuge in hopeless complexity. Instead of advancing a phony story that pushes aside the truth, one assails the very idea of a single truth and effaces from the public mind the memory of what truth is. In this way, a public figure can in effect shred a bothersome issue while working to debase public standards to the level of his own conduct. In recent weeks, such deterioration has been spreading in our political life. It has shown up, for instance, in some new ideas about two basic elements of politics — confidence and candor.

Several weeks ago, at the time of the nuclear alert, Secretary of State Kissinger appealed to the press and the country to show confidence in the Administration. "It is up to you, ladies and gentlemen, to determine whether this is the moment to try to create a crisis of confidence in the field of foreign policy," he told an assembly of newsmen. He also said, "There has to be a minimum of confidence that the senior officials of the American government are not playing with the lives of the American people." The implication was that the public and the press were hurting the country by losing confidence in the President. And certainly it was true that a minimum of confidence must exist. But the Secretary had seemingly forgotten where confidence comes from. Having confidence in the government is not a duty of citizenship, like paying taxes. No such obligation could ever be met, because confidence is a state of mind and cannot be willed. A person looks at what his government is doing, and either he has confidence or he doesn't have it. If he doesn't have it, he can fake it but he can't manufacture it. In matters of public confidence, it is on the government that the obligation falls.

Candor is one quality that officials must have if they wish to win confidence. But it is a much simpler quality than anything the White House currently has in mind, to judge from the Operation Candor that has been under way recently. Candor is sometimes painful, but it is rarely laborious. No "operation" is required. A "counter-offensive" won't help. Perhaps what the White House now has in mind is not candor at all but something quite different: credibility. Credibility is the modern version of candor. Candor entails truthfulness, but credibility does not. Credibility is the public-relations version of truthfulness. It is the truth's "image." And, like any other image, it can be manipulated and faked. Probably none of us should be surprised when politicians offer us credibility instead of the truth; what is odd is that the audience sometimes seems to be satisfied. For example, one Republican governor was heard to remark admiringly after a meeting with the President, "He was very believable today — more believable than I've ever seen him before." It wasn't quite that the governor *believed* the President; it was only that the President had been *believable* — credible. Instead of asking "Is it true?" people were asking "Is it credible?" Observers were saying that the President had "helped himself" by his operation, although the observers did not believe him themselves. All over the country, Operation Candor was being reviewed like a new musical comedy. It seemed to be accepted that the

President's candor, like the confidence that the Secretary of State was urging the rest of us to display, was an act—something forced or faked, which could be judged, like the skill of an actor. In this vision of our political life, it would be not only the performers but the members of the audience who would be actors. The President would perform and we would applaud. He would pretend to tell the truth and we would pretend to believe.

Doing some tedious counting, we find this piece runs to some 750 words and has 40 sentences, making the average sentence length around 18.75 words. These sentence lengths vary considerably from paragraph to paragraph: the first paragraph averages 35.6 words per sentence; the second, 17.7 words; and the third, 15 words. The longest—one of 61 words—appears in the opening paragraph. This average sentence length of 18.75 words may seem very low for a periodical which is generally thought to appeal to "elite" readers capable, presumably, of pursuing a complex thought through its intricacies and ramifications. But aside from that exceptionally long sentence of 61 words, the lengths are appropriate to readers of far less intellectual acumen, who, according to prevailing editorial judgment should not be asked to grasp the import of sentences averaging more than 25 words, the proper average for such minds being, according to the same thinking, a range of between 17 and 25 words.

It may come as a surprise, therefore, to find that the periodical which boasts of the largest circulation in the country, *TV Guide,* has average sentence lengths much higher than those in this *New Yorker* article. In the issue of February 2–8, 1974, for example, a count reveals these figures for three articles: 28 words, 38.2 words, and 23.7 words—all in excess of *The New Yorker* 18.75 average. In *TV Guide,* the opening page editorial "As We See It" had a 28 words per sentence average, with 60 words in the average paragraph. An article on "People Who Mimic Crimes on TV" averaged 38.2 words per sentence with 92.5 words to the paragraph; and a piece on Dom DeLuise—"I Grew Up with Garbage"—ran 23.7 words per sentence with 79 for the paragraph average.

From these figures we can only tentatively conclude that the *TV Guide* pieces were not readable for their intended reader-audience, whereas *The New Yorker* article was highly readable for its readers. But the only importance of these comparisons is that they may alert you to consider always the capacities of your readers.

Anyone interested in the various ways that readability of a work can be measured will do well to read studies such as this one: George

R. Klare, *The Measurement of Readability* (Ames, Iowa: Iowa State University Press, 1969).

FOCUS POINT

1. Coordination, subordination, and parallelism help to give sentences richness of meaning by adding carefully arranged details.

2. Four rhetorical types of sentences grew historically out of oratorical styles: the simple sentence (Attic), the balanced sentence (Isocratic), the periodic sentence (Ciceronian), and the loose sentence (Baroque).

3. It takes a personal *voice* to give your writing character.

4. Sentence lengths merit consideration in writing aimed at a special reader-audience.

TOPICS FOR DISCUSSION AND WRITING

1. Bring to class a short paragraph of sentences found in journals dealing with different fields of study (such as one of the sciences, social sciences, or humanities). What can you say about the length and word choice of these various sentences from different areas of study?

2. In *Readers' Digest,* find an article which originally had appeared in another kind of publication—a scholarly journal or a special-interest sort of periodical. When you compare the *Readers' Digest* version with the original, what can you say about the choices of language and sentence-lengths? In what ways has the difference in audiences affected the writers' treatment of the same subject?

3. If necessary, use your imagination and write letters to two persons in widely varying "culture levels," but say more or less the same things in both letters. For example, write a letter to your congressman or senator complaining about the lack of financial aids available to you as a student. Then make the same complaint in a letter home to your family or to a close friend. Be sure your sentence types, lengths, and voice reflect your awareness of your audience.

4

The Paragraph as Point Maker

Effective as single-sentence statements can be in expressing a feeling or an opinion, the lone sentence standing by itself seldom can do all that is desired. It may very well convey the questionable wisdom of homely proverbs, the caustic wit of aphorisms, and the zany humor of "one-liner" jokes.

Proverbs

A stitch in time saves nine.
Early to bed and early to rise makes a man healthy, wealthy, and wise.
Birds of a feather flock together.
A fool and his money are soon parted.

Aphorisms

My neighbor: someone who needs me but by whom I am not enchanted.
Nothing is more beautiful than cheerfulness in an old face.
The dispensing of injustice is always in the right hands.
Soldiers who don't know what they are fighting for, know, nevertheless, what they are not fighting for.[1]

Jokes

Progress means having machines rather than people insult you.

[1] Selected from W. H. Auden, *A Commonplace Book* (New York: The Viking Press, Inc., 1970), pp. 150, 208, 383.

It used to be if a student flunked a course, he wondered what he had done wrong, but now he wants to know what's wrong with the prof.

An avant-garde novel is one wherein an anonymous author takes 300 pages to pretend to tell what happened to nobodies you wouldn't let in your house.

Maturity is being able to look cool while your campus-visiting parents choke up on finding a girl sitting on your dormitory bed.

Similarly, writers of advertising slogans, bumper stickers, tee-shirts, and greeting cards cash in on the ability to turn out attention-getting statements. Even ministers hope to lure passersby into their churches by posting on sidewalk bulletin boards messages such as this one: "Conscience is what bothers you when you're alone in the dark."

But powerful as such lone sentences can be as stimuli to thought and action, they generally raise questions in the minds of thinking persons, who with good reason are skeptical about broad, sweeping statements. Being critical, they want details and explanations supportive of the judgments made, or implied, by such slogans. They especially distrust *stereotypes*—oversimplified, formulaic statements expressing viewpoints on subjects which are highly complex. Understandably, they disapprove of "Archie Bunkerisms" regarding race, color, national origin, or religion. They object to all blanket assertions and sweeping judgments that lump together people or actions as "types."

It takes more than a sentence to convince and persuade such thoughtful persons to accept as "truth" any unsupported judgment. They know that the botanist examining a wild flower, or a fire inspector looking for traces of arson in the charred ruins of a building sees a world of complexities and relationships invisible to untrained eyes. So does the department store executive studying the flow of store-patron traffic, or the professional football quarterback diagnosing the strengths and weaknesses of an opposing line. And only a dull-witted newcomer to a neighborhood will accept a simple judgment about it as the "whole truth"; for like everything else, a well-established neighborhood has a highly diverse character all its own which you need to know well if you are to survive in it.

The fact that nothing really is simple explains why compositions require use of the *paragraph*. In reading, you readily identify the familiar indented line and preceding white space as an indication that something "new" is being introduced, just as in listening to a speech, you can tell, if you are attentive, when the speaker is taking up another and different aspect of his topic.

You may also already know a great deal about paragraph writing. You probably have been writing them—or trying to, at least!—for years. If you have ever taken a typing course, you have even learned just how many spaces are regularly allotted for the indention on the left margin. And in many English classes you must have often heard truisms such as these:

A paragraph develops one complete idea.

A paragraph usually has a topic sentence, stated or understood, which tells the reader what idea is being dealt with.

It should have *unity*—that is, it should develop only one main idea.

It should also have *coherence*—that is, it should present the sentence ideas in some order and tie them to one another with transition devices.

Topic-sentence ideas can be developed by giving examples, definitions, comparison, and contrast, etc.

Now the trouble with such prescriptive lists is that they give the struggling young writer the wrong impression. They lead him to think that all he needs to become an effective writer is to learn the "rules" of paragraphing; he can then automatically write good paragraphs with ease. Facing a comp assignment, however, he may, despite having read the "formulas," be in the position of this young correspondent:

Dear Ann Landers: I've read your booklets on dating and nowhere does it tell how to kiss a girl. I am especially interested in the first kiss because I have not had it yet, but I'm expecting to try May 1. In case you haven't guessed, I am a guy and I do not to wish to get my face slapped.

For starters, should I kiss the girl on the cheek or would that be chicken? If I aim for her lips, how can I be sure I'll hit dead center and not get her chin or her nose? What should I do with my eyes? Open or shut? I practiced with a volleyball, kept my eyes open and got crosseyed. If I close my eyes, how can I see what's going on?

I realize this sounds dopey, but really, Miss Ann, I need some answers —Springfield, Mo.

Dear Mo: A lot depends on the chick. If she is eager and puckers up, that means no cheek. Nature's radar will lead you to her lips. If, however, you get slightly off target, you can quickly alter your course. About your eyes: Closed or open? Keep 'em closed. Nothing you see can possibly be as interesting as what you are doing.[2]

---

[2] Ann Landers, Publishers-Hall Syndicate, The Oregon Journal.

It is apparent that the source of the trouble the young man was having is that for him "kiss" was still an abstract term, a *concept* or vague notion in his mind but, nevertheless, an exciting one. Now the term "paragraph" may not be so exciting nor our own advice regarding it so amusing, but until—for you—paragraph becomes more than just a concept, all talk about it will fail to sink in. You need to experience what the term stands for, just as for them to have real meaning, other abstractions like "justice," "corruption," "sportsmanship," "integrity," freedom," and "delinquency" must be learned through observation or experience.

Reluctance and fear to examine for yourself what terms like the sentence, the paragraph, the essay, or the composition *mean* will cripple your efforts as a student-writer. Such unwillingness to square abstractions with what you know in real life results generally in writing that is trite, hackneyed, and lifeless. This accounts for the *jargon* or "gobbledegook" found in bureaucratic writing, as this observer notes in describing the painful psychological state this fear of facing up to abstract terms produces:

> The result of all this is that a wet hand of fear rests on the heart of every nonprofessional writer who merely has a lot of important knowledge to communicate. He writes every sentence with a self-conscious horror of doing something wrong. It is always compatible to him if he can fit himself into some system such as that of a business or government office which provides him a *model.* It is thus that gobbledegook comes into being.[3]

This same kind of personal insecurity with its resultant wandering off into the woods of obscurity has produced also much jargon in the field of English and especially that of Composition, as this article appearing in a professional journal attests.

PROPOSAL FOR A NEW LEXICON[4]

by SALLY ALEXANDER LUTTRELL

In order to have our dictaphones, our four secretaries to every instructor, our carpeted and panelled offices, our phones upon phones, and our conference money, we must be more relevant.

---

[3] Donald J. Lloyd, "Our Mania for Correctness," in *Essays on Language and Usage*, eds. Leonard F. Dean and Kenneth G. Wilson (New York: Oxford University Press, 1963), p. 309.

[4] *College English* 35 (October 1973): 52.

Herewith is a vocabulary list drawn from successful grants, privileged departments, and verbal young project directors. Use of the words on this list will dazzle the layman, captivate the dean, and open the pocketbook of the corporation research sponsor.

Professor	Human Resources Analyst
Grades	Integrated Software Projections
Student	Monitored Systems Contingency
Fellows	Parallel Resources Task Force
Tests	Information Organization, Consolidation, and Retention Techniques
Teaching Assistant	Audio Verbal Technician
Department Chairman	Functional Managements Director
Secretary	Contingency Operations Assistant
Department of English	Center for Information Resources and Directed Operations Flexibility
Classes	Systemized Monitored Time Phases
Papers	Recorded Data Function
Conference, panels, etc.	Synchronized Investigations Data Exchange
Failing Grade	Optimization Potential Procedure
Faculty Meetings	Systems Personnel Mobility Program
Tenure	Responsive Transitional Contingency
Faculty Committees	Systems Analysts for Procedural Resolutions
Journal Articles	Output Effort

A few further words to the renovation technician analyzing the archaic functions titles for possible output: One does not merely study, one "analyzes the data." Work in progress is "data being examined and analyzed for possible revision procedures"; anything that one hears, sees, reads, is "input," while any new teaching procedure should be referred to as "experimental manipulation of response modes." Photographs in the texts are "ideographic forms," and audiovisuals are "dynamic pictorials." A completed paper has been "brought to its appropriate terminal point"; classroom lectures should be referred to as "simulational developmental techniques." Any classification of students is a "potential behavioral taxonomy regarding simulation content characteristics." Moreover, research efforts are "empirical investigations" and department organization charts are properly described as "manpower utilization models." One does not contract, deal, or negotiate, but "plays the game."

We sincerely hope that our empirical data brought to its appropriate terminal point has encountered all possible contingency manifestations within the apprehended output recipients.

To avoid all such inanity and gibberish in your own writing, you will want to *experience* paragraphing, and you can do this in two ways: by examining for content, technique, and form paragraphs appearing in current reputable magazines and books, and by deliberately trying to follow their example in writing ones of your own and daring to experiment in them. But before plunging into these means, it may be helpful to look at some of the other psychological aspects.

First of all, writing a paragraph is always a challenge. (You can believe this one is for us!) Challenge—that is another much abused word. We like this meaning a renowned psychologist gives it: "To be challenged—by a person, by God, by a possibility that has been imagined, a problem or a crisis—means that an individual *cannot* ignore the situation at hand and devote his attention elsewhere. Challenges, almost by definition, are attention-grabbing."[5]

Learning to write paragraphs suggests recognizing how much you need to rely upon your memory, your imagination, and even your "hunches" as well as your best sense of logic. Second, the paragraph, like the sentence, is a unit of power in an article or essay if phrased in language that the writer feels, or knows from experience, should create the kind of effect he wants. As an intelligent person, he adopts means to a desired end, and the more he knows about writing skills, the more choices of means he has at hand with which to work.

Writing a paragraph, then, is something of an adventure. It involves exploring and welcoming strange and puzzling thoughts and memories, reevaluating old experiences, and seeking new combinations of ideas. There is nothing mechanical about the process; and if at times you work with some ease and speed, it probably means you have settled on a style—a mood, a tone, an approach—that works, at least for the time being!

Now let us try to give the term "paragraph" some more concrete meaning by taking a close look at a specimen of persuasive composition in the form of a letter consisting of six paragraphs.

[5] Sidney M. Jourard, "Toward a Psychology of Transcendent Behavior," in *Explorations in Human Potentialities,* ed. Herbert A. Otto (Springfield, Ill.: Charles C. Thomas, Publisher, 1966), pp. 369–370.

April, 1973

Dear Friend:

As a Senator, but more important, as an American, I am concerned about insuring justice for all our citizens. Without justice and equal opportunity for all, a democratic society cannot survive unscarred.

There are 12 million Spanish speaking citizens in the United States. Too many still face the barriers of discrimination in our schools, our businesses and our courts. The result is a high unemployment rate, substandard housing and a low level of educational attainment. It is of the utmost importance that these injustices be corrected.

During the past five years, the Mexican American Legal Defense and Educational Fund has worked steadfastly to bring about positive change in our society through both legal and educational channels. The MALDEF litigation department has challenged in the courtroom the most blatant forms of social and economic discrimination, with considerable success. But equally as important, MALDEF has established an Educational Grant Program which has financially assisted 275 qualified Chicano law students over the past three years.

Significant progress has been made through MALDEF's efforts. Jobs and the opportunity for advancement have increased for Mexican American employees; education for Chicano children has improved in quality; housing and business opportunities have been expanded -- but there is much, much more to be done.

And this is MALDEF's purpose -- to use the law to open doors for Mexican Americans where they have been shut by the forces of discrimination. To do this MALDEF needs our help, all of us. By sending your contribution now, either for litigation purposes or student scholarships, you will add your encouragement to mine; that Spanish surname Americans may find freedom from all forms of discrimination and inequality.

Thank you.

Sincerely,

Ted Kennedy

Edward M. Kennedy

P.S. Contributions made to MALDEF are tax deductible.

Readers friendly to Senator Kennedy will probably agree that this letter makes some impressive points, the main one being, of course, a plea for contributions to the worthy cause symbolized by the acronym MALDEF. But readers hostile to what they regard as his presidential ambitions may brand the letter as nothing more than an attempt to win the Mexican-American vote. What for one group will be a sincere and moving plea on behalf of an ill-treated people will thus be dismissed by others as "propaganda," blatant favor-currying, and grandstand posturing as a "liberal." But for now, let us move from considering the rhetorical impact on possible audiences to an analysis of the individual paragraphs.

In the Kennedy letter, every paragraph has its special contribution to make as part of a quite effective whole. The first one, consisting of two sentence statements, places the writer in the role of a zealous and patriotic legislator "concerned about insuring justice for all our citizens." The second sentence voices a lofty principle with which few would disagree: "Without justice and equal opportunity for all, a democratic society cannot survive unscarred." Note, however, the implication that even "without justice and equal opportunity" the democratic society would survive although "scarred."

The second paragraph at once gets down to the statement of specific facts of "injustices" suffered by many of the "12 million Spanish speaking citizens in the United States." The use of "barriers of discrimination" operates as a reversal of the first paragraph's "equal opportunity for all." Then we are given two sets of cause-to-effect lists: the barriers "in our schools, our businesses and our courts" are the causes for these effects: "a high unemployment rate, substandard housing and a low level of educational attainment."

How these injustices are being remedied makes up the content of the third paragraph, which briefly sums up the 5-year history of the organization known as MALDEF. That progress is being made, thanks to MALDEF effort, is pointed out in the fourth paragraph. It ends with the warning: "but there is much, much more to be done."

In sales letters devoted to arousing the reader to take some definite action—*Order now, mail the coupon today, hurry to be one of the lucky ones, if you order today we will* etc.—the paragraph that specifically calls upon the reader to make a definite response is called "the hook." It urges the reader to do what the letter was designed to impel him to do. In this particular letter, "the hook" is to send in "your contribution now," and thereby join the charismatic Kennedy fellowship as well as help a worthy cause promoting "freedom from all forms of discrimination and inequality" for "Spanish surname Americans."

The brief but confident "Thank you" paragraph followed by the intimate "Ted Kennedy" signature suggests it would somehow be disloyal not to respond as requested. And the postscript reminder—"Contributions made to MALDEF are tax deductible" is a pocketbook assurance to the self-interest of those who like to have their cake and eat it too.

HOW LONG SHOULD A PARAGRAPH BE?

We shall return to the matter of length again to rest the fears of word-counters. Our heading above is misleading; it implies there exists somewhere certain prescribed rules determining how many sentences, how many words a paragraph should have as its maximum and its minimum. The question, however, makes a good starting point from which to plunge into closely-related matters.

It is true some instructors in hopes of making their students "think in depth" may require paragraphs to average at least 100 words. (Being instructors ourselves, we must confess having also gone that route, but soon found that just as "you can't legislate morality," you cannot compel students to "think in depth" if they do not want to do so.)

The fact is, the paragraph is only a literary device, an agreed upon convention for marking off divisions in an essay or narrative to indicate that it makes a distinct contribution to the whole. As such it is a natural and practicable device growing out of the rhythmic process of writing and speaking as the natural way of following up on and expanding a judgment, an observation, or an expression of emotion. Any verbal judgment or flat statement of opinion we make—say, about sports, music, films, classes, or jobs—generally requires us to hurry on to explain or justify why we feel or believe as we do. In conversing, we go on explaining or defending until we feel the need is satisfied—unless we are chatterboxes! In doing so we get caught up in a kind of rhythmic utterance that is sustained by the excitement rising from that need to explain, to justify, or to attack. One thing suggests another as additional thoughts come one after the other in the heat of the exchange.

What Noam Chomsky, a very creative linguistics scholar, has said of sentence lengths applies also to paragraphs: "Because of the creativity of language the set of the sentences of a language is in fact an *infinite set*. In the more limited and more precise mathematical sense, this means that no matter how long a sentence—for instance, of English—one may utter or write, the language has devices that enable one to create a still longer sentence."[6] The only sensible limit to set to such lengths should be determined by consideration of the interests of the readers. For example, in the leisurely days of the nineteenth century—leisurely at least for the well-to-do upper classes—essayists like William

[6] Quoted by John Viertel, "Generative Grammars," *CCC* 15 (May 1964): 66–67.

Hazlitt often trusted their readers' capacity to absorb long single sentences like this penetrating analysis of the psychology of laughter:

> If everything that went wrong, if every vanity or weakness in another gave us a sensible pang, it would be hard indeed, but as long as the disagreeableness of the consequences of a sudden disaster is kept out of sight by the immediate oddity of the circumstances, and the absurdity or unaccountableness of a foolish action is the most striking thing in it, the ludicrous prevails over the pathetic, and we receive pleasure instead of pain from the farce of life which is played before us, and which discomposes our gravity as often as it fails to move our anger or our pity!—
> [WILLIAM HAZLITT, "On Wit and Humor," from *Lectures on the Comic Writers* (1819)]

Analyze the syntax of this 103-word sentence and you will find it is a compound-complex one having three independent clauses, four subordinate adverbial clauses, and two adjective clauses. As the three independent clauses indicate, this one long sentence could have been written as a three-sentence paragraph, had Hazlitt so desired, and it might have appeared like this:

> If everything that went wrong, if every vanity or weakness in another gave us a sensible pang, it would be hard indeed. But as long as the disagreeableness of the consequences of a sudden disaster is kept out of sight by the immediate oddity of the circumstances, and the absurdity or unaccountableness of a foolish action is the most striking thing in it, the ludicrous prevails over the pathetic. [It is thus] we receive pleasure from the farce of life which is played before us, and which discomposes our gravity as often as it fails to move our anger or our pity!

However it be written, this statement explaining what makes us smile or laugh at the foolish actions of others deserves careful study, word by word, comma by semicolon.

So the length of any paragraph—the number of words in sentences it takes to support or illustrate the key idea—depends upon how many details you, as the writer, decide are enough to satisfy the readers you have in mind. One way to test your copy is to let it lie for at least a few hours and then come back to read it aloud, pretending you are a critical or even hostile reader ready to challenge your point of view on the topic. If you find your work cannot withstand probes such as the following from your imaginary reader, sit down and rewrite it:

"How's that again?" — Is your basic meaning clear?

"What's *that* word mean?" — Does any term need defining?

"Not *again!*" — Are you repeating the same idea needlessly?

"Whoops! How did you jump to *that*?" — Do the sentences "flow" from one to another in good order?

"Get to cases!" — Should you include a specific example to pin down the point you are trying to make?

"Why are you telling *me* this?" — Who are your readers and under what circumstances will they probably be reading what you write?

This last question is of special importance to journalists and reporters writing for readers who hurriedly scan the news while on the run or while distracted by household affairs at home. To meet such conditions, reporters employ brief paragraphs of the kind found in this account of a congressional inquiry into the "economic status of women."

Washington, D.C. — For seven days of occasionally bitter debate recently — and for the first time in U.S. history — a Congressional committee took a free-swinging look at the economic status of women in America.

And what the Joint Economic Committee came up with was a pattern of discrimination against women in almost every aspect of their lives: In job availability, pay scales, and promotions; in credit and insurance plans; in Social Security and private pension programs; in federal income tax structures; in the armed forces; in public assistance programs; in inheritance and estate laws; and in the policies of educational institutions, to name a few.

The conference learned, according to its chairman, Rep. Martha Griffiths (D-Mich.), that the biggest single discriminator against women is the federal government, which overtly discriminates against women, while it fails to enforce its own anti-discrimination laws on behalf of others.

The root of the trouble, as Mrs. Griffiths and witnesses stated, is that society still regards working women as out on a lark, earning "just a tad of pin money" — and that they are cared for by men. But these are the facts given the committee by government and private sources:

Three-quarters of all the women who work for pay either have no husband, or a husband whose income is under $7,000 a year.

Women are now 40 per cent of the work force, and are its fastest growing segment.

Between 1960 and 1972 the number of households dependent on women increased 56 per cent.

Most women will work 25 or more years regardless of marriage and children.

Half the mothers of school age children now work.

Witnesses invited the committee to compare such statistics with these:

The average full-time working woman who is as well-educated as the average working man earns only three-fifths as much as he earns.

At least 20 per cent of the difference between men's and women's wages is due to sheer discrimination.

Women with five or more years of college education have a median income of only $14 more than male high school graduates.

Women's unemployment is 35 per cent above men's, and getting worse.

Mrs. Griffiths, whose hard-hitting questions rattled several government witnesses, didn't mince words. For example, she told one Labor Department official, "The real truth is that 40 per cent of the labor force is female, and they are being discriminated against. That is the reason why the welfare rolls have increased, almost exclusively. And the Department of Labor should forget about taking care of only men and see to it that they take care of all who work . . . and all of us are working."

While over three-fifths of all the adults in poverty are women, the Labor Department's manpower training programs train far more men than women.

The Labor Department's "skill-complexity" classifications list "foster mother" equally with "restroom attendant" and "parking lot attendant," and below that of "newspaper delivery boy." . . .[7]

Note the many short paragraphs. Of the 17 paragraphs, 16 consist of only one sentence. At a glance the reader is attracted, first of all, by the white space the indentions provide to break up the solid mass of print. Furthermore, the separate "slots" given each of these sentence statements lend them the valuable quality of *emphasis,* making them stand out to the eye and appear as important points.

Looking closely at what each of these paragraphs contributes as a "statement" of information, we find that the first one leads off with the main general statement of fact that the rest of the article expands upon and supports. This prime sentence also has the merits of providing answers to the key "Five W's" reporters are trained to supply the reader in opening paragraphs: Who? What? When? Where? Why?

The second paragraph sums up the areas explored by the now specifically named "Joint Economic Committee" and becomes a detailed list of apparently all of the kinds of economic "discrimination" to which American women are being subjected. Not until the third paragraph does the name of Congresswoman Martha Griffiths appear as the central

[7] Karen Peterson, *The Oregonian,* September 29, 1973, by permission of the Oregonian Publishing Company.

figure of this conference, and in the 10 very brief paragraphs that follow, the reporter names the specific "facts given the committee by government and private sources." The rest of the article goes on to give additional and more detailed testimony presented at the hearings.

How effective do you find this kind of paragraphing? Is it suited to its purposes? Does it reveal a clear purpose and some significant design?

If your answers are in the affirmative and you now have a more realistic concept of "economic discrimination" against women, you may conclude the paragraphing has done its work as intended by the reporter.

As a practicable approach to setting paragraph-length guidelines for yourself, why not examine specimens of paragraphs written by reputable writers today in current periodicals or books? It can probably be assumed that, like Marshall MacLuhan, they are keenly aware that "The medium is the message" and that television screen images are "cool" whereas print is "hot," meaning the printed page requires more complete attention than does watching television. Also the professional writer, unlike some academic scholars writing for an intellectual elite, must be concerned with effective communication. He, too, writes to be swiftly read and understood.

There are several methods of determining the average length of paragraphs in any piece of writing, but most are indebted in one way or the other to studies such as Rudolf Flesch's *The Art of Readable Writing.* Using his procedure, select random pages and count the total number of words on the page and then divide that total by the number of paragraphs. (The same method applies to determining the average sentence length.) We can apply his procedure to demonstrate what the proper sentence length is judged to be by a given periodical's editorial staff.

All questions of "proper length" thus can be settled by applying one criterion: *appropriateness.* If the "message" reflects the mood and apparent purposes of the author, the paragraphs making up that message are right. Paragraphing is basically a matter of personal style, of individual choice and decision as to the most effective means available at the time the writer composes the piece. After all, the thought or emotional unit of expression we call a "paragraph" is only a partial statement of what the whole essay, or article, attempts to say, and it is a response to tensions being experienced by the writer who is trying to say what must be said, and say it in the best manner possible.

How individual these responses can be is well exemplified in this moving personal statement of a woman who before her entry into history was herself a struggling journalist.

THE BRIGHT LIGHT OF HIS DAYS[8]
by JACQUELINE KENNEDY ONASSIS

What I think about the last decade is how much we missed him in it.

When he came to the Presidency it was a time when the world seemed new — when it was right to hope, and hopes could be realized.

He gave everyone around him a desire to excel — not in the harsh competitive sense, but in the ancient Greek sense that a life is not worth living unless all one's faculties are used along lines leading to excellence.

There is a passage in his favorite book, *Pilgrim's Way*, by John Buchan, that describes Jack so well, though it was written about the son of a British Prime Minister killed in World War I — that he had "great beauty of person; the gift of winning speech; a mind that mastered readily whatever it cared to master; poetry and the love of all beautiful things; a heart as tender as it was brave. One gift only was withheld from him — length of years."

Then the glass shattered. All he had put together, as well as many people's dreams, lay in fragments.

One must not let oneself be numbed by sadness. He would not have wished that. I don't know how he would have coped with the problems that lay there like sleeping beasts, but I know how he would have approached them. . . .

For those who shared his days it is too painful to look back. But for the young it can be helpful.

That is why I care about his Library. It can't replace him, but it can help people who believe " 'tis not too late to seek a newer world." God grant us always young people who feel that way. That is my prayer.

If they care, then in his Library they can find ways of solving problems through government.

It will be a repository of ideas, of approaches, of accomplishments — of his time and of time since. The wisdom and experience of dedicated men will be there, to be drawn on and used, not merely studied.

One of his earliest themes was the importance of service. I remember his Senate campaign speeches when he would say over and over that the Greek word for idiot meant one who took no part in the affairs of his state.

The problems are so huge now. Man seems so tiny in this technological age. Resignation is tempting.

But then I think of Jack — the bright light of his days. He would be older now, and wiser, and he would still maintain his deep belief that problems can be solved by men.

And so they must be.

---

[8] From *McCall's*, November 1973, p. 81, by permission of Jacqueline Kennedy Onassis.

FROM SENTENCES TO PARAGRAPHS

Under special circumstances, almost any sentence statement will call for additional statements to explain, describe, define, or exemplify the idea it expresses. Certainly observations like these would call for more information:

She was a strange woman.

Human civilization is an outgrowth of language, and language is the product of advancing civilization. —[ALFRED NORTH WHITEHEAD]

The doer does, the observer sees, the witness and artist chronicles and converts. —[RICHARD STERN]

In *A Portrait of the Artist as a Young Man,* James Joyce shows Stephen Dedalus experiencing some beautiful moments of epiphany.

Economists have found three new reasons for this rapid inflation.

Such sentences serve as *signals* alerting the reader, or the listener, to the fact that more is to come to fulfill the promise implicit in the statement. The common term for them is *topic sentence.*

In the paragraph, the topic sentence bears the same relationship to other sentences as does the independent clause to the other parts of a sentence. Just as subordinate phrases and clauses are added to the main clause to make the sentence clear and rich in meaning, so additional sentences make the topic into a properly expressive paragraph.

We have already seen (p. 108) that a single sentence may itself convey a wealth of detail suitable for a whole paragraph, as does this one:

Having had to go without her usual breakfast of a big glass of orange juice, two poached eggs, three slices of crisp bacon, and hash-brown potatoes plus toast, marmalade, and coffee, Lonnie, suffering acute hunger pains, ate a tremendous lunch, dreamily downing a bowl of creamed tomato soup, two MacDonald quarter-pounders, two sacks of fries, and a chocolate milkshake—all topped off with a banana split—after which, she allowed, she could get along until dinner time unless, of course, somebody forced her to go somewhere for an afternoon snack.

In paragraph form, the same complex sentence might well have been written like this:

> Lonnie made up for having had to go without her usual big breakfast. Through force of circumstances, she had to pass up the big glass of orange juice, the two poached eggs, the three slices of crisp bacon, and the hash-brown potatoes as well as the toast, marmalade, and coffee that generally made up her morning meal. No wonder that by noon she was suffering acute hunger pains. At a MacDonald's she ordered and ate a hearty lunch, dreamily downing a bowl of creamed tomato soup, two quarter-pounders, two sacks of fries, a chocolate milkshake. Then still not satisfied, she topped all that off with a banana split. Afterward, she allowed, she now could get along until dinner unless, of course, somebody forced her to go somewhere for an afternoon snack.

This six-sentence paragraph begins with the topic sentence, one from which the others generate. The remaining five sentences closely relate to the opening one and clearly follow from it in a cause-to-effect sequence.

While pointing out how similar the function of a multisentence paragraph is to that of a highly expressive sentence, we should also note just how these six sentences are smoothly bridged one to the other by means of *transitional devices* as well as thought-sequence order that taken together give a paragraph the desired quality of coherence. Transitions are words or phrases which help the reader make the move from one sentence idea to the next by giving suitable connective links. Sentence two, for example, opens with the phrase "through force of circumstances" which explains why Lonnie was deprived of her usual breakfast. Sentence three begins with an expression drawing a logical inference from sentence two: "no wonder that by noon. . . ." By starting sentence four with "At a MacDonald's," the reader is prepared for what Lonnie orders, just as in the opening of sentence five the phrase "Then still not satisfied" serves to add a surprising revelation. In sentence six, the opening adverb, "Afterward," leads the reader to the climactic conclusion suggesting what a big eater like Lonnie might do when she had to go without her usual breakfast.

As the following layout shows, this paragraph also is one thoroughly developed by the cause-to-effect method:

Lonnie made up for having had to go without her . . . breakfast.

Through force of circumstances, she had to pass up. . . .

No wonder by noon she was suffering acute hunger pains.

At a MacDonald's she ordered and ate a hearty lunch. . . .

Then still not satisfied, she topped. . . .

Afterward, she allowed she now could get along. . . .

This sentence layout indicates the kind of thinking and arrangement that goes on in the mind when we try to be logical in explaining or defending a viewpoint. Three of the "effects" are *subordinate* to the topic idea "cause" and yet are *coordinate* with each other. In addition, the last one is followed by two other subordinate statements. Good writing thus is "tight" writing; sentence statements are either equal, main supports of the topic sentence idea, or else evidence supporting one or the other of those main supports.

How to tie in sentences that are coordinate or subordinate in meaning always presents a problem, but learning to think in terms of *transitions* helps considerably. It is true that once your thinking catches you up in a kind of rhythm, you will find sentence ideas growing one out of the other, but to knit them together so that the reader can readily see what your point is and how you are making it requires that you know how transitional words and phrases work. For every effect you want to make in going from one sentence to the next in your writing, you are actually making judgments, as the following categories indicate.

CONTRAST: but, yet, on the contrary, on the other hand, opposed to, however
ADDITION: also, again, in addition to, still another, included in, moreover
RESULT: therefore, consequently, in consequence of, thus, as a result
TIME: now, earlier, later, at the time, before, during, after, while, once, again, since
MANNER: like, as if, as though, as seen by, as viewed by, in this manner, as accustomed, unlike, apropos to
FACT: as proved, as shown, as learned, the fact that, indeed, as indicated by, as established, on the basis of the evidence

Yet another means of keeping your sentence ideas on track is to maintain, as much as is convenient, the same *point of view* throughout the paragraph. You will recall we saw earlier in discussing sentence coherence that keeping the same subject reference made for easy reading. The same applies to paragraph coherence, as the questions in the margin of this one are meant to point out.

1. Who in the opening topic sentence are the ones singled out and who serve as the point of view plural noun?

2. In sentence two, how do the pronouns "their" and "they" clue in the reader?

3. In sentence three, what does repetition of the pronoun "they" serve?

4. In sentence four, to what noun or nouns does the pronoun "their" refer?

5. And to what does the "they" in the final sentence refer?

Catholic priests and other clergy have been doing more than anyone else to help the victims of terror in Chile and they have emerged as the only group that has been openly challenging the regime. At increasing risk to their immunity, they have been pursuing every legal means available to secure information on people who are missing and to arrange the release of prisoners or publication of charges against them. They give moral and financial help to the thousands of Chilean children who have recently become orphans, to families in which the wage earners are dead or jailed, and to those who want to emigrate. Much of their time is spent trying to find lawyers to defend the poor, weak, and ignorant. (In fact, because so many lawyers have been persecuted or disbarred, they are also helping to find counsel for the well-to-do.)[9]

Now let us examine a paragraph of *exposition,* of explanation, for the way thought-statements related to one another emerge from the hard thinking of an author trying to work his way through a most difficult problem. Our example is a paragraph from a review of *Rabbit Boss,* a recent novel about the Washo Indians by Thomas Sanchez. The paragraph begins with a topic sentence partly stated in the language of the reviewer but largely a quotation from the novel.

Though not Indian, Sanchez did not conceive of himself as writing *Rabbit Boss* from a white man's point of view "any more than let's say Shakespeare conceived of himself writing from the point of view of an Elizabethan playwright when he was writing about Juliet, a Renaissance teenager. An artist is always a proteus. He can always change his shape or form, if he really indeed is an artist. That means, first of all, that he has to completely admit himself and submerge himself in the particular character that he's portraying. That's one of the reasons *Rabbit Boss* took more than seven years to write. It was very, very difficult, not only because of the poetry that was involved in speaking of the Washo Indians — the way they talked — but I had a great problem with the American consciousness. I

[9] Rose Styron, "The Amnesty Report" in "Terror in Chile," *The New York Review of Books,* 30 May 1974, p. 45.

knew that most Americans would not understand what *Rabbit Boss* was unless *Rabbit Boss* was an *experience* of perceiving through the consciousness, through the poetry inherent in the language what the Washo Indians were going through and what they were submitted to."[10]

Mr. Sanchez is trying to explain aspects of that mysterious process always at work when a writer creates fictional characters who are different from the author himself in temperament, outlook, and experience. Because he is not a Washo Indian, born and brought up in the culture and settings he is writing about, Sanchez feels he must defend himself against possible accusations that he is in no position to write about Washo people. He begins his defense by citing as an example Shakespeare creating a character like "Juliet, a Renaissance teenager." In the second sentence he names the quality that enables a writer to make real such imaginary men and women: "An artist is always a proteus." A "proteus" is defined in the next sentence: "He can always change his shape or form, if he really indeed is an artist." This statement, in turn, requires explanation, and it is immediately forthcoming: "That means, first of all, that he has to completely admit himself and submerge himself in the particular character that he's portraying."

After these first four introductory and preparatory sentences, Mr. Sanchez now can go on to relate the problems he has had to cope with in trying to portray the Washo experience and character in terms understandable to "the American consciousness." He starts with the simple sentence: "That's one of the reasons *Rabbit Boss* took more than seven years to write." And the concluding sentence describes the method he finally chose in order to give his readers the kind of empathy they had to experience if he were to communicate successfully the poetic quality of the Washo nature and experience.

In conversations with well-informed people who are also interesting talkers, paragraphs often grow out of topic sentences that call for a typical example of the point being made, as does the following informal one.

> On his work in the sixties with porpoises in the Virgin Islands and Hawaii, Gregory reports:
> "Porpoises are capable of learning to learn, we verified that. It's one of the few things we did get on them. The trainer was instructed not to reward the porpoise with a fish unless she—the porpoise was a female— did something, quote, '*new*.' The porpoise would come out of the holding

[10] Barbara Cady, "Sanchez Book Is Well Researched," *Los Angeles Free Press,* 21 September 1973, p. 20.

tank and would go through two-thirds of the fifteen-minute session doing what had been rewarded in the last session, and then would more or less accidentally do something, quote, 'new.' The trainer would reward that, and then the next session she'd spend two-thirds of the time doing *that*.

"Between the fourteenth and fifteenth session the porpoise got awfully excited in the holding tank, slapping around. She came on stage for the fifteenth session and did twelve new things one after another, some of which nobody'd ever seen at all in that species. She'd got the idea. . . . It's a nice case of the pressure of contradiction making her jump a level."[11]

In the first paragraph, the topic sentence is a compound one: "Porpoises are capable of learning to learn, we verified that." In the second, the topic sentence comes as a conclusion to the anecdote: "It's a nice case of the pressure of contradiction making her jump a level." Like many another anecdote or story, this one tells what happened in *chronological* order, relating what occurred first and then what followed in time.

Care for *coherence* to lead the reader from one paragraph to the next is often on display also in letters-to-the-editor columns of daily newspapers. Here is a spirited attack on an article by James Kilpatrick entitled "The Nixon War on Poverty Fat."

OTHER SIDE TO STORY

To the Editor: Re James Kilpatrick's article, "'Compassion that works' goal of Nixon war on poverty fat."

What is the point the writer intends to make? How does repetition of the word "side" clue in the reader?

I am writing this to inform Mr. Kilpatrick that there is indeed another side to his dismal tale of the Neighborhood Youth Corps program. There is a side that would reveal young people gaining meaningful experiences as aides in hospitals, aides to activity coordinators in centers for the retarded, as well as participants in exciting Youth Tutoring Youth projects.

What is the function of the opening phrase of this paragraph? Incidentally, is this long sentence too involved for newspaper readers?

In addition to these enriching activities, NYC funds, when administered properly, are providing opportunities for young people from welfare homes to be exposed to the world of work — to examples of people who hold down

[11] From Stewart Brand, "Both Sides of the Necessary Paradox: Meditations on Gregory Bateson and the Death of the Bread-and-Butterfly," *Harper's* 247 (November 1973): 34–35.

8 A.M.–5 P.M. jobs, who feel that it is their responsibility to be on time and to be present every day (even janitorial jobs can teach this, Mr. Kilpatrick), whereas at home these are oftentimes not the types of examples that are present.

To what do the words "this program" refer? How do they lead to the writer's own experience with the program? How does she establish her authority?

Admittedly, I am viewing the success or failure of this program on a much smaller scale, but possibly on a more real one. The Kilpatrick statistics can tell any story he wants them to. My comments stem from my work with some 50 young people who are participating in this program. My evaluation comes not from someone's statistical report, but from daily seeing faces light up, attitudes change, hearing comments like, "I feel important now," and seeing shy, self-conscious teen-agers blossom when given responsibility and praise for a job well done.

How does the NYC abbreviation serve as a connective?

NYC can give opportunities for positive work experiences and opportunities for success stories in the lives of people who may badly need them.

What is gained by the repetition again of the word "side"?

So you see, there is another side to the story, a side with a potential that can alter lives and ease burdens. And isn't that what it's all about?

(NAME WITHHELD)[12]

PARAGRAPH DEVELOPMENT THROUGH DETAILS

"I want to believe you! Give me some good reasons why I should!" So friendly readers will welcome the report or explanation of any troubled writer. Hostile readers will, on the other hand, pose the threat: "We're not listening to you if you can't prove what you have to say with hard facts and sound reason!" In either situation the reader has the right to expect sufficient detail to make acceptable what has been said.

Scanty explanation means scanty paragraphs. It is not enough to dash off a few general sentences which more or less repeat the same ideas. What is wanted is the following types of information:

[12] *The Oregonian,* May 16, 1973.

Example	Definition
Cause and effect	Description
Comparison and contrast	Analogy (metaphor)
Illustration	

Only when you have learned to approach and develop any subject matter through such avenues of inquiry can you hope to give it adequate detail.

The best way to familiarize yourself with these various means of expanding a topic and exploring its possibilities usually is the method of *example,* or *illustration.* The paragraphs which follow are models of these means of presenting details and deserve close study.

Development through specific detail in the form of examples

"How can you stand it?" This is the first thing the transient visitor to Florence, in summer, wants to know, and the last thing too—the eschatological question he leaves echoing in the air as he speeds on to Venice. He means the noise, the traffic, and the heat, and something else besides, something he hesitates to mention, in view of former raptures: the fact that Florence seems to him dull, drab, provincial. Those who know Florence a little often compare it to Boston. It is full of banks, loan agencies, and insurance companies, of shops selling place mats and doilies and tooled-leather desk sets. The Raphaels and Botticellis in the museums have been copied a thousand times; the architecture and sculpture are associated with the schoolroom. For the contemporary taste, there is too much Renaissance in Florence: too much "David" (copies of Michelangelo's gigantic white nude stand on the Piazza della Signoria and the Piazzale Michelangelo; the original is in the Academy), too much rusticated stone, too much glazed terracotta, too many Madonnas with Bambinos. In the lacklustre cafés of the dreary main piazza (which has a parking lot in the middle), stout women in sensible clothing sit drinking tea, and old gentlemen with canes are reading newspapers, sensible, stout, countrified flowers like zinnias and dahlias are being sold in the Mercato Nuovo, along with straw carryalls, pocketbooks, and marketing baskets. Along the Arno, near Ponte Vecchio, ugly new buildings show where the German bombs fell.[13]

Development through cause and effect

It cannot be denied that the *St. Jerome* is a good example of an attractive painter's work. But what was there about this picture that made it

[13] *Mary McCarthy, The Stones of Florence* (New York: Harcourt Brace Jovanovich, Inc., 1963), pp. 1–2.

worth a whole gallery of Rembrandts in 1780 and as costly as any picture in England at the end of the Napoleonic wars? There seems to have been a special glamour, today somewhat unintelligible, surrounding huge soup-brown religious pictures that had been raided from the altar of a church or pledged by esurient monks or nuns. Till the end of the nineteenth century, English taste favoured very large pictures, and payment by size was all to the advantage of the seventeenth-century Italians, among whom life-sized figures had been an occupational disease. Moreover the huge well-smoked altarpieces went particularly well with even smokier ancestors. The taste was responsible for the Murillo cult as late as the 1840's and 1850's, and the market was only killed by the demands of living art. In order to hang *Alpine Mastiffs*, 93 ins. × 75 ins., something else that was eight feet high had to go.[14]

Development by comparison — contrast

The leveling effect of the numerous influences I have discussed is appalling. The tense and perilous times in which we live demand an invigorating dialogue. Yet we seem largely incapable of conducting one because of the growing rightist tendencies in the nation that demand conformity — or else. We are inhibited when we should be unrestrained. We are hesitant when we should be bold. It is not enough to be anticommunist. We need the irrepressible urge to rejoin the human race. We need to contribute moral and political leadership — as well as technical and financial help — to rebuilding a new world order controlled by Law rather than by Force.[15]

Development by analogy (metaphor)

The historian, then, is an individual human being. Like other individuals, he is also a social phenomenon, both the product and the conscious or unconscious spokesman of the society to which he belongs; it is in this capacity that he approaches the facts of the historical past. We sometimes speak of the course of history as a "moving procession." The metaphor is fair enough, provided it does not tempt the historian to think of himself as an eagle surveying the scene from a lonely crag or as a V.I.P. at the saluting base. Nothing of the kind! The historian is just another dim figure trudging along in another part of the procession. And as the procession winds along, swerving now to the right and now to the left, and sometimes doubling back on itself, the relative positions of different parts of the procession are constantly changing, so that it may make perfectly good

[14] Gerald Reitlinger, *The Economics of Taste: The Rise and Fall of the Picture Market 1760–1960* (New York: Holt, Rinehart and Winston, Inc., 1961), pp. 7–8.
[15] William O. Douglas, *Points of Rebellion* (New York: Random House, Inc., 1969), pp. 31–32.

sense to say, for example, that we are nearer today to the Middle Ages than were our great-grandfathers a century ago, or that the age of Caesar is nearer to us than the age of Dante. New vistas, new angles of vision, constantly appear as the procession—and the historian with it—moves along. The historian is part of history. The point in the procession at which he finds himself determines his angle of vision over the past.[16]

Development by definition

Style exists on two levels. It is practiced and produced; something akin, creatively, to breathing. And it is talked about. One is art and the other is polemics. The connection can be tenuous.

Style—the product—is a reality, with or without polemical explanations. It is automatically and inevitably the result of all the confluent factors of a culture and a particular moment. It cannot be created artificially or imitated successfully. That is why the forger's hand is almost always revealed, through slips of style beyond his control.[17]

I asked Wambaugh what he meant by the "emotional danger" of police work.

"I'm talking about the kind of emotional violence done to Bumper Morgan by 20 years on the job—the trauma, the emotional battering that has left him unable to love, unable to commit himself to anything or anyone. This is the real danger of police work. It's what all my books are about, essentially. It's what engages me as a writer. Shootings bore me."[18]

Description by spatial arrangement

In Kamayama Park most of the trees were pines, and here the colors did not change with the seasons. It was a large, hilly park. The trees were all tall and they had no leaves until fairly high up. There was something disquieting about the sight of this park with all its countless, naked tree trunks crossing each other irregularly. A wide path led round the park; it was full of uneven slopes, and when one thought that it was going to rise, it would instead go down. Here and there I noticed tree stumps, shrubs, and little pines. Near where the great white rocks emerged from the ground in which they were half buried, the azaleas blossomed with a profusion of purple. Under the cloudy sky their color looked as if it harbored some

---

[16] Edward Hallet Carr, *What Is History?* (New York: Alfred A. Knopf, Inc., 1969), pp. 42–43.

[17] Ada Louise Huxtable, "In Love with Times Square," *The New York Review of Books,* 16 November 1973, p. 45.

[18] From an interview with Joseph Wambaugh by Bob MacKenzie, "Violence Is Not Beautiful," *TV Guide,* 10 November 1973, p. 14.

evil design. We climbed up a small hill and sat down to rest under an umbrella-shaped arbor. Below us on an incline was a swing, on which a young couple was seated. From where we were, we could see the entire park spread out to the east, and in the west we could look down through the trees onto the waters of the Hozu River. The constant creaking of the swing reached us in the arbor like the grinding of teeth.[19]

FOCUS POINT

1. Paragraphs are generally sentence-sequences supporting some basic statement.

2. The basic idea which a paragraph expands or describes in some detail may, or may not, appear as a topic sentence.

3. The length of any paragraph depends upon the writer's judgment of how much detail—in the form of examples, definition, comparison, contrast, or other means of driving home the point—is necessary for completeness and effectiveness.

4. Sentences following one another in some perceptible order give the paragraph-statement coherence, a desirable feature that helps keep the reader on track.

5. Rhetorical analysis is an important means of learning how skilled authors adapt the many devices and strategies of persuasive writing to their particular purposes.

PARAGRAPH WORKSHOP

1. Certain paragraphs in any piece of writing have special tasks to fulfill. Among these are paragraphs that are introductory and those that are final, operating as opening and closing statements. Analyze and identify the following for the desirable qualities they may demonstrate as introductions or conclusions.

   a. If we overlook the unloveliness of the term and accept for the sake of argument that it is wicked to be softheaded, what is the evidence for the prevalence of this quality among judges, Federal or other? (I say "for the sake of

[19] Yukio Mishima, *The Temple of the Golden Pavilion* (New York: Berkley Publishing Corp., 1971, original ed. 1959), pp. 138–139.

argument" because there has been a respectable tradition for some millennia that sympathy and a willingness to consider claims for leniency are not altogether incongruous traits for judges.) That there are degrees of hardness (punitiveness) and softness among the wide varieties of judges no one could doubt. But enough to be a major evil and a major cause of anything, let alone crime? That everyone should doubt—or, simply, reject. Two grounds for rejection (leaving aside that the accuser—thus far—should have the burden of proof) seem sufficient for now: (1) some concrete, if unscientific, observations of my own; (2) the statistics of American judicial punishment.[20]

b. I had a job interview several weeks ago. Friends warned me not to be too aggressive. During the interview, I tried to present myself as a competent candidate, able to "think like a man" and yet not to be a "masculine" female. After fielding several questions relevant to the job, I suddenly heard, "Miss Stern, are you in love?"[21]

c. Women should not be given an even break in education and careers, says a clichéd argument, because they will get married and quit anyway. But that's because they are given an arbitrary, unfair option which men aren't forced to accept—either career or marriage. Career opportunities and salary levels for women are so poor that a calculating female would figure marriage is a better bargain. Once married, she can stop fighting the stereotypes and start teaching them to her children.[22]

d. Thus, in the end, Hesse may have been more right about himself than he knew, in the reply which he was too exhausted to give to the young seeker after truth at Baden. In his writings, the "patterns of language stuff, of language yarn" contain the secret; they do possess that "immeasurable worth" greater than "the measurable worth of the content." It is, very simply, that the serene style (concealing ugly episodes, tensions and self-doubtings), the careful selection (and rejection) of detail, the measured, dignified treatment of his small range of themes is in fact *all*. There are no answers, no solutions: only the posing of a series of questions which similar self-doubters could understand, appreciate and derive consolation from because Hesse had asked them in ways which helped to make them valid. His widespread latter-day influence may not exactly have been invigorating; but it has, in its mild way, been positive and beneficent, a

[20] Marvin E. Frankel (United States District Judge), "An Opinion by One of Those 'Softheaded Judges,'" *New York Times Magazine*, 13 May 1973, p. 41.

[21] From Paula Stern, "The Womanly Image: Character Assassination through the Ages," *The Atlantic Monthly* 225 (March 1970): 87.

[22] Ibid., p. 90.

gentle, discerning, eminent minor writer's critique of a real world which has moved farther and farther from the ideal which he imagined himself to be defining.[23]

e. Calvin Coolidge once told us that "the business of America is business." The fashion has been to judge this notion quaint. But the late President is owed something better than condescension. He should be thanked for laying down an Orwellian stepping-stone to a perception of our true condition: Big Business is government.[24]

f. The concentration of economic power is well advanced. There is still time — probably not much — to halt the process and maybe even reverse it. If we fail to act swiftly, those who hold concentrated economic power will bring it increasingly to bear on our democratic institutions. They may come to dominate them. Such a manifestation of self-protection and aggression is their natural thrust. We may learn the hard way, and too late, that a free society and massive concentration of economic power cannot for long co-exist. This power can be diffused. Its growth can be stunted. These are feasible goals. We will make suggestions looking toward their achievement. If these suggestions should strike the reader as less than ideal we can only offer him the consolation of Alexander Hamilton. "I never expect to see a perfect work from imperfect man," he said.[25]

2. To prove to yourself the practicability of the various means of developing a paragraph through giving details, take your choice of one of the following means and write a paragraph of some length. You may wish to expand on one or the other of the suggested topic sentences given for each kind of development.
   a. Development by means of example
      i. From experience I would say owning a car can be a headache.
      ii. I have good reasons for not feeling safe on the streets at night.
      iii. Moving into a new neighborhood brings problems.
      iv. Riding a bicycle to campus may be quite adventurous.
      v. GI education benefits are not adequate.

[23] Alan Brownjohn, "German Protestant in Guru's Clothing," *Encounter* 41 (October 1973): 107–108.
[24] Norton Mintz and Jerry S. Cohen, "Prologue," *America, Inc.: Who Owns and Operates the United States* (New York: The Dial Press, 1971), p. 1.
[25] Ibid., p. 33.

b. Development by means of cause and effect
   i. Nostalgia for things of the past makes people do strange things.
   ii. Dress styles are affected by high prices of clothes.
   iii. Inflation makes owning your own house difficult.
   iv. Having frequently to change schools creates problems.
   v. Watergate scandals have affected many things.
c. Development by means of comparison and contrast
   i. Rock music is changing.
   ii. Everything is more expensive now.
   iii. Christmases aren't celebrated the way they used to be.
   iv. Public morality is more lax these days.
   v. Life on a farm has seen great changes.
d. Development by means of description
   i. It was not the cleanest apartment I have ever seen.
   ii. You run into one of them at every party.
   iii. We arrived just after the accident had happened.
   iv. The place gave me the strangest feeling.
   v. It was a typical family holiday dinner.
e. Development by means of definition
   i. Alcohol is really a drug.
   ii. You know what *inflation* means when you have to pay for things with your own hard-earned money.
   iii. Can any well-known athlete today be called an "amateur"?
   iv. You know what pollution is when you . . .
   v. Is marriage still regarded as a "sacrament"?

5

Thinking and Feeling for Writing

FIVE KINDS OF THINKING

By now, we are sure, it is safe to say you are more than aware that writing, like all the other arts, proceeds from the creative forces we associate with thought, emotion, and imagination. Unlike the other arts, we also well know, it communicates its message through language flowing in rhythmic statements in conformance to the rituals and symbols governing the written word. How our thoughts and our feelings help or hinder us in trying to find something significant to say and then trying to communicate it effectively requires some special attention.

To begin with, all of us know that any attempt to start writing something—be it a letter, analysis, report, examination answer—may stir up some ideas, but those often wild mental images will immediately start emotions churning. If we start with words—say of an assignment on "campus fads" and the term "streaking" pops up—the same kind of emotional reaction may occur. It works both ways: ideas and mental images produce feelings, and, in turn, feelings give rise to other ideas and words.

There appear to be at least four basic kinds of thinking or mental activity going on in our minds at almost any minute. Each usually is accompanied by certain emotional states which will vary greatly in intensity according to the temperament and situation of the individual. We can classify these five kinds of thinking as follows:

Purposeful thinking
Daydreaming
Indecisive thinking
Creative thinking
Meditation

Other classifications and terms may be proposed, and at times anyone may swiftly alternate from one to the other of these mental–emotional states. Only the highly self-disciplined can begin to regulate them with any great success. We want to take up these ways of thinking, one by one, to see how they help or hinder us in our writing attempts.

Purposeful thinking

All manner of mental responses to any problem, danger, threat, or crisis as well as to any unexpected but appealing challenge or opportunity are considered purposeful thinking. We are involved in purposeful, or decisive, thinking every time we find ourselves in a situation calling for mental responses such as the following:

Making a decision or accepting one made by someone else
Solving a problem, especially one involving our well-being, health, or social position
Considering the applicability or relevance of a judgment, opinion, or assumption
Sizing up a situation and appraising its possibilities
Safeguarding or defending something from attack
Engaging in any kind of planning
Weighing the choice of alternatives when confronted by a dilemma

By their very definition the terms "judgment" and "choice" imply that purposeful thinking involves psychological conflicts: "A judgment refers to any verbal reaction (or its equivalent) that is the direct product of the individual's processing his sensory inputs in combination with his memories of stored experiences."[1] "A *choice* is the behavior of a person who, when faced with a number of possible alternative courses of action, acts so as to carry out one of those courses."[2]

[1] P. C. Wason and P. N. Johnson-Laird, *Psychology of Reasoning* (Cambridge, Mass.: Harvard University Press, 1972), pp. 3–4.
[2] Sidney Segel, *Choice, Strategy, and Utility* (New York: McGraw-Hill Book Co., 1964), p. 1.

All forms of purposeful thinking, then, are accompanied by confusion-creating surges of emotion set off by the stress and pressures of the situations being encountered. Painful and disturbing feelings of perplexity, puzzlement, frustration, desperation, worry, and perhaps even despair go along with such thinking, just as do those of hope and confidence when one finds he has discovered a satisfactory response to the troublesome situation.

If we are appalled or overwhelmed by the problem confronting us, we may even experience the frightening sensations described in terms like "My mind just went blank. I couldn't think of anything. I was petrified!" The sort of endocrine gland action accompanying fear or anger causes the body to go into action through flight or fight, but is not conducive to moving the mind into action. Education, even self-conditioning as a form of education, helps us to control the flight-fight impulse (as in the actor's or speaker's stage-fright situation) and even to use that energy. But in and of itself, it is not conducive to intellectual activity, unless it can be recognized for what it is and be forced to give way to calmer consideration.

EXERCISES

1. In our daily lives all of us constantly must make decisions. Fortunately, most of them do not require much deliberate "purposeful thinking," but some do, and such decisions can be most perplexing and even painful. Try in writing to recall one such occasion and describe the various emotions and ideas you had to cope with and how you fared in trying to concentrate.

   Some situations involving "purposeful thinking":
   When I first had to decide—
       to try out for the team
       to come to this campus
       to become a major in—
       to work for a political candidate
       to approve (disapprove) of Woman's Lib
       to choose military service
       to own a car
       to get a job
       to go steady
       to take a stand on drugs
       to join a social group
       to work for or against—

2. Write a report in which you try to recreate step by step the various stages you went through in trying to find a suitable subject for a recent comp assignment. Discuss how you dealt with the difficulties, how you made the decisions you did, and with what results.

3. In worthwhile novels, biographies, films, and other works of art people are shown in dramatic situations having to do some serious thinking. Choose one such work and show how skilled the artist was in presenting such conflicts.

Daydreaming

Daydreaming may be a "natural" escape hatch from some anxieties. This type of mental-emotional activity includes all forms of fantasy in periods of relaxation wherein the mind is allowed one might say: "to wander and woolgather." In daydreams, you usually visualize yourself as a hero or a heroine overcoming with ease difficulties perplexing to others, especially the solving of problems of the kind being evaded by this lapsing into exotic fancies. In such rosy dreams all bad memories of earlier defeats disappear, all personal slights and shortcomings are remedied. It is an egocentric state of dreamy make-believe and escape.

Perhaps as much as 90 percent of a person's waking time may be given to this self-indulgent, wishful thinking. Pleasant as it may be, however, it ordinarily will not help you to meet the demands of a composition assignment, which generally calls for "purposeful" thinking and considerable self-discipline. Yet daydreaming does have "creative" aspects, as psychologists' studies of children's fantasies and daydreams show. In adults it may serve to relax the mind and at times even lead to sudden intuitions, but too much indulgence in rosey-hued escapism, especially if helped along by alcohol or drugs, may even increase feelings of defeatism as a result of such copping out.

Indecisive thinking

Often what begins as purposeful mental energy intended to lead to some practicable resolution ends up at cross-purposes, resulting in the very painful and distressing indecision and perplexity we have been discussing. Instead of reaching a solution to the problem, the attempt to meet one problem leads to additional problems aggravating the original situation. Only too frequently the situation that appeared as one to be met easily with some ready-made judgment or opinion turns, on closer study, into one raising a series of kaleidoscopic facts—puzzles never remaining in focus long enough to be dealt with one at a time. You tell yourself, "I can't make head or tail of it. What used to work no longer does."

Then myriads of excuses present themselves, and we find "good reasons"—rationalizations—to put off the writing task. Listening to a record, watching television, even staring out the window or making a telephone call—all become suddenly desirable alternatives to glaring down at a blank sheet of paper. Or we tell ourselves, "I've got plenty of time. I'll put it off until I get a better idea. Besides I work better under pressure."

So what starts as purposeful and decisive thinking often turns into vexing indecisiveness and then degenerates further into flights of escapist daydreams. This is a cycle that all writers must cope with as one of the psychological hazards of their craft. But even the least experienced student-writer caught in the toils of composition problems may find himself capable of the fourth kind of mental activity—creative thinking—and through it achieve a measure of success, sweet to effort-wearied nerves.

Creative thinking

We can be very grateful that creative thinking works, even if we do not understand how. It is most mysterious because it involves as yet unexplainable mental-emotional capacities and produces results at times that are truly amazing. It is distinguished by these features:

It provides new approaches and solutions to problems.
It envisions new possibilities and alternatives.
However surprising, its results when regarded closely appear to be a kind of logical outgrowth of familiar things.
It is spontaneous and intuitive, "accidental" rather than planned.

Scientists and poets alike rely upon the intuitions that emerge from this unexplainable process we call creative thinking. Intuitions are flashes of immediate understanding, "hunches," truths felt in the bones. They come of their own accord and cannot be forced. James B. Watson, the author of *The Double Helix*, has admitted that the idea leading to his discovery of DNA and the secret of genetic inheritance came to him while he was in a movie theater watching a film. C. P. Snow, scientist turned novelist, has pioneered in efforts to show that the "two cultures" of science and literature both depend upon intuitive processes for discoveries.

Poets often begin poems with a phrase or a line without having any clear idea of what will follow next. They rely upon the tensions of emotion mounting within them to propel into consciousness the words that memory and imagination working together will bring into awareness. It is a process of surprise, for as Robert Frost said, "No surprise for the poet, no surprise for the reader."

Meditation

This exciting process of discovery often grows out of periods of meditation, a state of mind in which you will deliberately concentrate your attention upon some proclaimed "truth" or even some disturbing experience of your own which you would like to understand. All of the great religions have made meditation an essential part of their processes of arriving at truth through achieving some kind of "higher consciousness." It requires self-discipline so as to discourage distractions and to keep the mind focused on the chosen subject.

Growing awareness of "hidden" facts is one of the features of successful meditation. In his autobiographical book, *In the Castle of My Skin*, George Lamming vividly details what his meditations upon childhood experiences have revealed to him regarding feelings and words.

We walked through the grape vine disentangling our feet from the leaves. We uprooted the patches of moss and fern that covered the narrow dirt swamps. And we didn't look back. It was hours since we had left home. We had talked and talked and talked. We had talked a lot of nonsense, perhaps. But anyone would forgive us. With the sea shimmering, and the sand and the wind in the trees, we received so many strange feelings. And in the village, in the cellar, at the school, in this corner or that corner of the house, something was always happening. We didn't notice it then, but when something bigger appeared like the sea and the sand, it brought with it a big, big feeling, and the big feeling pushed up all the little feelings we had received in other places. We weren't ashamed. Perhaps we would do better if we had good big words like the educated people. But we didn't. We had to say something was like something else, and whatever we said didn't convey all that we felt. We wouldn't dare tell anybody what we had talked about. People who were sure of what they were saying and who had the right words to use could do that. They could talk to others. And even if they didn't feel what they were saying, it didn't matter. They had the right words. Language was a kind of passport. You could go where you like if you had a clean record. You could say what you like if you knew how to say it. It didn't matter whether you felt everything you said. You had language, good, big words to make up for what you didn't feel. And if you were really educated, and you could command the language like a captain on a ship, if you could make the language do what you wanted it to do, say what you wanted it say, then you didn't have to feel at all. You could do away with feeling. That's why everybody wanted to be educated. You didn't have to feel. You learnt this and you learnt that, and you knew a Jack for a Jack and Ace for an Ace. You were all right. Nothing would ever go pop, pop, pop in your head. You had language to safeguard you. And if you were beginning to feel too strongly, you could kill the feeling, you could get it out of the way by fetching the words that couldn't understand what the feeling was all about. It was like a knife. If you wanted to slaughter the pig, you got your knife. The knife hadn't a clue what was going on in the pig's head, but when you wielded it, the job was done. It was so with language. When the feelings came up like so many little pigs that grunted and irritated with their grunts, you could slaughter them. You could slaughter your feelings as you slaughtered a pig. Language was all you needed. It was like a knife. It knifed your feelings clean and proper, and put an end to any pop, pop, pop in your head. Perhaps we would do better if we were educated. For the time being we weren't going to say a word to anybody. Not a word.[3]

It is this kind of awareness that makes life and the world around us real and meaningful. As the author says, things go "pop, pop, pop in your head" until you hear the words grown-ups use to account for them or to dismiss them. Most of the time, however, as Lamming points out, adults use language like "a knife" with which "You could slaughter your feelings as you slaughtered a pig."

European literature is especially rich in records of such great moments of highly charged meditation and the discoveries growing out of them. Take, for instance, this passage from the well-known novel, *Zorba the Greek,* by Nikos Kazantzakis, wherein the contemplative young aesthete makes a great discovery about himself.

We arrived at our hut. I had not the slightest desire to eat, and sat on a rock by the sea. Zorba lit the fire, ate, was about to come to sit beside me, but changed his mind and lay on his mattress and fell asleep.

[3] George Lamming, *In the Castle of my Skin* (New York: McGraw-Hill Book Company, Inc., 1953), pp. 127–128.

The sea was dead calm. Beneath the volley of shooting stars the earth also lay motionless and silent. No dog barked, no nightbird shrieked. It was a stealthy, dangerous, total silence, composed of thousands of cries so distant or from such depths within us that we could not hear them. I could only discern the pulsing of my blood in my temples and in the veins of my neck.

The song of the tiger! I thought, and shuddered.

In India, when night falls, a sad, monotonous song is sung in a low voice, a slow, wild song, like the distant yawn of a beast of prey—the song of the tiger. Man's heart flutters and seeks an outlet as he waits in tense expectation.

As I thought of this fearful song, the void in my breast was gradually filled. My ears came to life, the silence became a shout. It was as if the soul itself were composed out of this song and were escaping from the body to listen.

I stooped, filled my palm with sea water, moistened my brow and temples. I felt refreshed. In the depths of my being, cries were echoing, threateningly, confused, impatient—the tiger was within me and he was roaring.

All at once I heard the voice clearly. It was the voice of Buddha.

I started walking rapidly along the water's edge, as if I wished to escape. For some time now, when alone at night and silence reigned, I had been hearing his voice—at first sorrowful and plaintive, like a dirge; then, becoming angry, scolding and imperative. It kicked within my breast like a child when the time has come for it to leave the womb.

It must have been midnight. Black clouds had gathered in the sky, large drops of rain fell onto my hands. But I paid no heed. I was plunged into a burning atmosphere; I could feel a flame flickering from both my temples.

The time has come, I thought, with a shudder. The Buddhist wheel is bearing me away; the time has come for me to free myself from this miraculous burden.[4]

To determine what exactly Kazantzakis means by "The song of the Tiger" and "the voice of Buddha" it is necessary to read the whole novel and then to meditate further, but it is clear that the experience recounted has been a "creative" one for the narrator. But it is not necessary to journey to exotic islands like Crete to enjoy moments of creative awareness; this is evidenced by the following two attempts at poetry written by students in a staid classroom.

[4] Nikos Kazantzakis, *Zorba the Greek* (New York: Simon & Schuster, Inc., 1952), pp. 63–64, by permission of Simon & Schuster, Inc.

ON CLASSROOM DISCUSSIONS
BY RICHARD WALSH

Watching closely, listening hard.
Shifting positions,
Thinking of bad times, and other times, too,
In the back row always understanding
The futile efforts of a few
Impressing others with avant-garde intellectualism,
Shifting positions,
Losing sight now.

MY CHILDHOOD FLOWED IN TIME
BY BRIAN MCLAUGHLIN

My Childhood flowed in time
Like water down a hillside.
Rivulets of experience gathering together
In quiet harmony.
Some muddy and full of debris,
Others clear with the light of discovery.
So much of my childhood has seeped back into the hill.
The path of my life is marked by cracking mud,
And an occasional flower,
The product of my passing.

FOCUS POINT

1. Indecisive thinking accompanies confusion and bewilderment when one is torn by conflicting ideas and impulses.

2. Daydreaming is a natural escape into realms of pleasant fantasies free from all present difficulties and frustrations.

3. Creative thinking of the kinds found in both art and science is a most mysterious process involving intuitive understanding.

4. Meditation is a prominent feature of all such creative thought.

EXERCISES

1. As an exercise in developing "awareness" and making a "discovery," choose a place, a time, and other circumstances favorable for your close observation of one thing such as the following. Take notes on what your senses record—what you see, hear, smell, feel, and perhaps even taste as you "see" and meditate.

a flower	a gutter
a pebble	a stairway
a tree root	a classroom
a leaf	a sink
something edible	a car floor
a work of art	a bus seat
a religious object	a table

2. Relate a vivid childhood experience wherein you made a discovery of a "truth" important to you. Be sure to describe in detail the scene as you reconstruct it in your memory.

3. Bring in a poem of your own composition and along with it a brief statement of how you came to write it.

FORMS OF APPLIED REASONING

Problem solving

To begin with, let us regard writing on any topic or subject, whether an imposed or a self-assigned project, as a *problem* having certain steps necessary for its possible solution. Like all other forms of purposeful thinking, problem solving usually is accompanied by emotional reactions and stresses, but these, if properly regarded, can add zest to the game of finding right answers. And knowing just how to go about problem solving builds confidence. As it is taught in schools of business, psychology, law, and education, here are the steps helpful in arriving at the best judgment and solution possible. For the sake of clarity and brevity, they are stated as simply as possible.

1. What exactly is the problem I am facing?

a. Can I state it clearly and fully?
b. How important is it?
2. What kind of problem is it?
   a. Is it one of fact?
   b. Or is it one of change of policy?
3. What do I already know about it and its backgrounds?
   a. From firsthand experience?
   b. From having received reports on it?
4. What alternative solutions are offered?
   a. Which ones will not meet the demands of the situation?
   b. Which is the more preferable alternative?
5. Can I propose an even better alternative?
   a. Will it work under the conditions contemplated?
   b. Will it be more in harmony with basic principles?
6. Whatever my final solution, can I predict what its long-term results may be?
   a. Will these results be acceptable?

Consider the following newspaper editorial as an attempt to deal with a most serious problem. Do you find steps such as those listed above reflected in the article?

TERRORISM'S TOLL[5]

There is little value in decrying fruitlessly the carnage of the Arab terrorist fire-bombing of a Pan Am jet in Rome, the hijacking of a nearby Lufthansa jet and the execution of one hostage. Altogether, 32 innocent bystanders died, victims of criminals whose goals are still not completely understood. Two key questions must be asked about this tragedy: (1) What lessons can be learned from it? (2) How can the international community prevent a repetition?

As to the first, it has become obvious that attacks on airlines offices or hijackings of planes—usually in Europe—have become a favorite tactic of terrorism originating in the Middle East. Eight of the nine Arab terrorist international incidents this year were focused on airline offices or on large jet planes. Also, Israeli retaliation to one incident resulted in the forced diversion of a jetliner into Israel in August.

A second lesson appears to be that this form of terrorism feeds on success: Prisoners released and ransoms paid encourage further criminality.

[5] *The Oregonian*, December 19, 1973.

It also is evident that absence of extradition treaties between nations where hijackings originate and states where the terrorists finally surrender—with resultant failure to prosecute and imprison terrorists—amounts at best to a deplorable gap in the machinery of international relations and at worst to covert cooperation with international killers and kidnapers.

Although the initial techniques used by the terrorists Monday in Rome were almost the same as those employed by Black September guerrillas at Athens airport on Aug. 5 (three people killed, 60 wounded), it is apparent that security measures at Rome airport were inadequate for a similar confrontation. Security measures at all major international airports must be greatly tightened, for commercial jets are such long-range and ubiquitous mechanisms that terroristic forays can begin anywhere—even areas far more remote from the Middle East than European airports.

The action by Japan Air Lines in July in refusing to pay ransom for hostages, the action Tuesday of Lebanese officials in blocking runways in Beirut against an unwanted landing by the hijacked jet and refusal by other nations to give hijackers sanctuary are techniques which, if publicized in advance and subsequently adhered to, will discourage anyone but those bent on suicide missions. And it is clear that this latest group of terrorists, as ferocious as were their actions and as loud their avowals of willingness to perish, still hoped and counted on a way out of their dilemma. Such hopes must be denied.

Finally, attempts should be made through the United Nations to reach accord on international extradition procedures for terrorists when bilateral treaties do not exist between affected states.

If politically inspired criminal violence against innocent persons goes unpunished, it will inevitably be repeated. Thus, unless the hijacker-murderers, who have surrendered to Kuwaiti authorities, are severely handled, terrorism's toll can be expected to rise.

Applying our six-step "model," we can see how the author thought through this particular problem in trying to find a solution for it.

1. *What exactly is the problem I am facing?* By stating a most recent example of Arab terrorist airplane executions and hijacking, the opening paragraph pins down the very serious problem, which is clearly stated in terms of the two questions: "What lessons can be learned from it?" "How can the international community prevent a repetition?"

2 and 3. *What kind of problem is it? What do I already know about it?* There appears to be no doubt regarding the violence of such hijacking.

The problem also clearly is one of a "change of policy" because the article attacks the present policy of lack of agreement on what steps to take. The second, third, and fourth paragraphs are direct answers to the problem-questions and call for a new policy.

4. *What alternative solutions are offered?* The "lessons" cited also suggest the new measures that are needed: refusal to release prisoners, refusal to pay ransoms, and necessity to prosecute "international killers and kidnapers." Additional steps required are those of improving airport security precautions and taking actions such as those taken by Japan Air Lines and the Lebanese officials.

5. *Can I propose an even better alternative?* It is, of course, impossible for a reader to tell whether the insistence upon United Nations action on international extradition procedures in the paragraph beginning with "Finally" is a new alternative. It does serve, however, as a climactic point in solving the problem.

6. *Whatever my solution, can I predict what its long-term results may be?*

The concluding paragraph does have the tone of prophecy; it warns that if the steps proposed are not applied to the problem "terrorism can be expected to rise." The tone of the whole article is one of confidence that these steps will bring about satisfactory results.

Especially in the studies of law and history, problem solving centers upon the "issues" involved in the controversial aspects of the problem. One way of ferreting out these main points of contention is to decide with what kind of problem you are dealing. In the terrorist problem just examined, we have defined it as one calling for a "change of policy." To help you arrive at the main points to be considered in proposing or attacking any such change, study the following questions. They can be applied to any debatable proposal calling for dropping a present practice and adopting a new one.

For the "old" policy

1. Is the present policy in harmony with traditional values and standards?
2. Is the present policy working satisfactorily and fairly?
3. If not, can it be changed or corrected so as to continue to serve well?

For the "new" policy

4. Is the proposed new policy in harmony with traditional values and standards?
5. Will it work effectively in the realistic situations it must face?
6. Is there no other possible policy which may be better?

To make these "models" of thinking through a subject even more concrete, here is a student's attempt, somewhat edited, to apply the "model" of problem solving to a matter of overwhelming national concern.

The Problem: *Should the busing of school children be the way of bringing about racial integration?*

1. *What exactly is the problem I am facing?* Is the present policy and practice of United States courts to order school districts to bus black children and white children out of their neighborhood-school areas to other and more distant schools a practicable and beneficial policy?

2. *What kind of problem is it?* It obviously is a change of policy argument problem. The old practice and policy of expecting children to go to neighborhood schools has now been changed, but this new policy is still under attack. Many powerful voices, both black and white, continue to argue for reversal of such court rulings. I can see I have to run through the six questions given regarding "a change of policy" argument, and I need "facts."

3. *What do I already know about it and its backgrounds?* It grew out of the 1954 Supreme Court decision on the *Brown* v. *Topeka Board of Education* ruling that separate but equal schools were unconstitutional. But the issue of busing itself was not determined until April 20, 1971, when the Supreme Court announced its decision in the case of *Swanson* v. *Charlotte-Mecklenburg Board of Education.* Justice Warren E. Burger said in that unanimous decision, "that although the judiciary had neither the mandate nor the desire to set a fixed mathematical racial balance of white and black students in public schools, government-ordered busing was a proper constitutional remedy in districts where segregation was officially sanctioned and school authorities offered no other acceptable plan for desegregation."

This decision and others enforcing such busing have raised and continue to raise questions regarding this busing policy: questions and objections raised in the North as well as in the South and among blacks as well as among whites.

4. *What alternative solutions are offered?* For one, Senator Walter F. Mondale has urged that if school systems would look into their districting policies, there might not be need for unnecessary busing. He cites court decisions which attack old practices of deliberately fostering school segregation and assigning of teachers on a racial basis—practices found continuing segregation in countless communities in the North as well as in the South.[6] Also it is only just that if school systems in one part of the country like the South, are compelled to adopt busing programs to end former "separate but equal" practices, all other regional school systems should also be made to adopt the same prescribed busing programs.

In the 1972 presidential election campaigns, first Governor George Wallace made busing one of his main targets and called for an end to busing as a means of ending segregation. Then President Nixon, apparently in order to win the southern vote, also joined in condemning busing as the means of bringing about racial integration.

Anyone acquainted with the problems encountered in the busing programs—school boards, parents, teachers, and children (especially black children)—also know the hardships the program involves and the costs of maintaining fleets of buses—money many blacks themselves think could be better spent on improving neighborhood schools.

Militant blacks even insist that the best alternative would be to end busing of black children and to build and maintain neighborhood black schools that would be so excellent—especially if taught by qualified black teachers—that white children would want to go to these schools.

5. *Can I propose an even better alternative?* It still seems to me that busing of school children for the purpose of achieving racial balance and eventual desegregation is a very superficial program. The time when youngsters learn to play together and to like each other as children is not when they are sitting in the classrooms, but rather after school when they go into each other's homes, when they go to shows and parties together. Busing does not direct itself to this problem at all. And perhaps the attempts to place the major responsibility for social reform on one institution—education—must be doomed to failure, for one institution alone cannot foster the changes needed for such social reform.

[6] Nathan Glazer, "Is Busing Necessary?" *Current* 140 (May 1972): 20.

After all, schools are for learning and not for bringing about major social reforms in the terms now proposed.

6. *Whatever my final solution, can I predict what its long-term results will be?* As a black college student myself, I can only repeat what I have already said: Busing in itself can never do what its proponents hope; it cannot bring about racial integration. To be successful integration programs must be built upon the principles laid down by the Supreme Court of the United States in 1896: "If the races are to meet upon terms of social equality, it must be the result of natural affinities, a mutual appreciation of each other's merits, and a voluntary consent of individuals."

Far less important problems may also be headaches demanding solutions. Everyone who owns an automobile sooner or later runs into problems. In an amusing article, the editor of *Harper's* tells of his problems in owning a secondhand car in New York City and how he solved them. All of the issues and the painful decision-arriving process typical of our "model" appear in this brief account.

THE IMPOSSIBLE CHOICE[7]

by ROBERT SHNAYERSON

What is the problem?

Owning a car in New York City means you spend your life parking it. Each morning you have to shift the thing from one side of the street to the other (on pain of a $25 fine) so the sweepers can clean up after urban man's worst enemy, the dog. It's a frustrating, competitive, crazy, unrelenting process that I endured for six years after I moved here. Once, God granted me a miracle: a blown-down No Parking sign that no one else noticed. But after grabbing that space, I naturally couldn't use the car; weekends, I sat in it, imagining myself in the country. Eventually the cops dislodged me; an obscure ordinance says that everything on wheels here must be moved once every twenty-four hours.

[7] Copyright 1973 by Harper's Magazine. Reprinted from the April 1973 issue by special permission.

Plunging back into the space race, I found myself screaming at other parking crazies, even beautiful women. Near brawls were routine. I rarely used my once-beloved Thunderbird to *go* anywhere, not in this traffic. In six years, I put 4,000 miles on it, most of it parking. I used the thing mainly as a hideaway, a curbside gazebo. Others used it as a spare-parts depot; one year I replaced three stolen batteries, two aerials, and a generator. Junkies got all four hubcaps. From disuse, the car gradually rotted and rotted and rotted.

The end came one day when I was merely sitting in the grounded Bird, a fugitive from some familial chore. Three cracked tires blew in rapid-fire succession—pop pop pop. A passing couple gawked and guffawed. All the stored-up rage and frustration consumed me. I decided to get rid of the car instantly.

It wasn't easy. Civic conscience intruded. I couldn't blithely litter some block with yet another rusting heap (one of 50,000 cars abandoned here each year), so I resolved to heed the law and deliver my ton of junk steel, as rapidly as possible, to the Sanitation Department. Off I drove, on the rims, while helpful pedestrians shouted, "Hey, mister, you know you gotta flat? Hey, a *flat*." Three miles later I screeched up to Sanitation headquarters, only to be greeted with incredulity by the insouciant Sicilians who run that part of our civil service.

"Hey, Rocco, here's a guy wantsa *give* a car to the city!"

"I hate it. Just take it."

"Why, this car's only got 16,000 miles. Whyn't ya sell it?"

"I hate it. Just take it."

"How da we know ya even *own* it?"

Yep, I was some kina nut. In fact, that year I was apparently one of only nine New Yorkers who disposed of an unwanted car in this manner. It took almost two hours of negotiations, but finally the right piece of paper was found and signed, and the Bird-albatross became the city's problem. Shortly thereafter the Bird vanished into a mammoth compacting machine that,

What was the first alternative solution?

What was the second alternative?

What is the final solution?

thwack-thwack, mashed her into a steel brick, the size of weekend suitcase.

I've got a confession, though: last summer I caved in to wheelomania again and bought another faded beauty, a '66 Ford Galaxie convertible with only 40,000 miles. These days I'm parking well and truly, as Dr. Hem would say, but I'm getting crazier and crueler in the process — and a little worried. I can't decide whether it's more frustrating to keep it, or to try to get rid of it.

FOCUS POINT

1. Problem solving calls for systematic thinking.

2. Evidence and logic, therefore, are both essential.

3. Some trial-and-error activity also often is involved.

4. In dealing with problems requiring personal judgment, one needs to be especially alert for possibilities of error.

TOPICS FOR DISCUSSION AND WRITING

1. Write an account of a problem you — or someone you know — recently faced and how logically or illogically a solution was reached.

2. Bring to class a newspaper editorial dealing with a problem that interests you. Be prepared to discuss how systematically the problem is presented and "solved."

Deductive reasoning

Readers of Robert Shnayerson's misadventures with street parking in New York City will have little trouble arriving at the general judgment that being without parking garage space in that city makes car ownership there almost impossible. That conclusion underlies all of his attempts to solve his parking problems and well exemplifies what is commonly called *deductive reasoning.*

For centuries this was the only acceptable kind of reasoning prevailing in the Western world; it was first systematized by Aristotle and then in the Middle Ages made absolute by Thomas Aquinas, and finally "modernized" in the sixteenth century by Descartes. Despite all the attacks upon it, it still seems to represent for many people the only way the human mind operates.

Needless to say, our whole intellectual culture and the approaches to "thinking through a subject" or "solving a problem" are affected deeply by this method of arriving at "truth." Deductive reasoning is the kind of thinking wherein we logically apply some generalization or general principle to a particular situation or thing. Grant that man is a "rational animal," one capable of arriving at reasoned conclusions. According to the Aristotle-Aquinas-Descartes schools, man builds his store of knowledge upon the conclusions he has previously learned or accepted, and then when confronted by any situation identifiable as being covered by that general principle, he can *infer* (draw a conclusion) that the general rule applies.

For example, I know from experience and believe that whenever I am compelled to sit for a long time in an unheated room, I will very likely catch a cold. I am chilled now after having sat in an unheated library for several hours. I will not be surprised if I come down with some form of the common cold. This homely example illustrates how the principle of deductive reasoning works. But as logicians use it, this going from the general to the particular has special terms and rules so as to ensure the validity, or correctness, of arriving at the inevitable conclusion.

Because of space restrictions, our explanation here must be a most simple one, doing little more than outlining the procedures. To begin with, this process—applying a general principle to a particular instance and arriving at a valid conclusion—produces what is called a *syllogism*.

Example:

1. Government regulations are restrictive.
2. Rationing is a form of government regulation.
3. Therefore, rationing is restrictive.

Statements 1 and 2 are called the *major premise* and the *minor premise*, respectively. As can be seen, the *conclusion* is derived from those two premises.

Example:

Major premise—Fossil fuels in short supply are expensive.
Minor premise—Gasoline is a fossil fuel in short supply.
Conclusion—Gasoline is expensive.

Reliance upon deductive reasoning encourages the building up of a chain of syllogisms called "sorites," wherein the conclusion of one becomes something of a general principle for a succeeding one.

Example:
1. Fossil fuels not in short supply need not be rationed.
2. Coal is a fossil fuel in great supply.
3. Coal need not be rationed.

1. But all fuels producing sulphuric dioxide are harmful to the environment.
2. Coal when burned gives off sulphuric dioxide.
3. Coal as a fuel is harmful to the environment.

Usually instead of going through all of these steps in such a formal manner, we take short cuts by omitting one or the other of the premises and going directly to the conclusion. This shortened form of the syllogism is called an *enthymeme*.

Example: He wouldn't shoplift anything. He's an honest person.

1. No honest person will shoplift. (major premise)
2. He's an honest person. (minor premise)
3. He wouldn't shoplift anything. (conclusion)

I don't trust her. She likes to lie.

1. People who like to lie can't be trusted.
2. She likes to lie.
3. She can't be trusted.

Behind all deductive thinking, therefore, we find reasoning that relies upon some authority, whether it be the pronouncements of authority figures or merely popular views which are accepted without question as being "true." All dictatorial governments demand their fiats and decisions be regarded as general principles to be applied to all relevant situations. Likewise, all moral codes and ethical principles at work in a society serve as major premises guiding individuals to make conclusions acceptable to that society. Terms like "morality," "decency," "honesty," "sin," "offence," "honor," "right," "wrong," "legal," "illegal," and "guilt" are applied to acts involving acceptable or unacceptable attitudes and ideals.

General statements that are commonly accepted as true, and so are taken for granted, are called "assumptions." Writers building support for a thesis often rely upon assumptions. How such assumptions can oppose one another and give rise to serious problems in almost any classroom is the subject of the following article.

BLACK CULTURE IN THE CLASSROOM[8]
by GENEVA GAY and ROBERT D. ABRAHAMS

As the impact of Black nationalism and cultural awareness increases we can expect the sources of irritation and tension between Black students and white middle-class teachers to increase unless teachers begin to understand the implications of their students' behavior. White teachers are quite right that their Black students are "hostile," "resent the authority they represent," "quick to anger," and "have chips on their shoulders." The question here is why are these attitudes so prevalent, and how can teachers go about understanding them?

To begin with, teachers need to recognize the fact that these attitudes are prevalent among all kinds of Black students, those who are receiving good grades as well as those who are about to drop out of school. Admittedly, it can be said that all students, regardless of racial or ethnic identity, are questioning teacher authority, but if we dismiss the relationship between Black students and white teachers as merely that, we are belittling the point if not avoiding it altogether. There is an additional factor that must be considered which compounds the Black student's reactions to suggestions of authority and discipline from white teachers. This factor is the Black experience with racism. White teachers are symbols of the racism that these students have known throughout their entire lives. The student, therefore, reacts to the teacher not so much as a person but as a member of a group which is defined primarily by skin tone and other physical attributes—just as they are used to being reacted to.

Second, when the white teacher becomes very assertive as a disciplinarian, especially if these actions are regarded as arbitrary and autocratic, the Black student's reaction is that a white man is *still* trying to tell him what to do, and current events have done a lot to convince him that he no longer needs to be submissive and docile. Merely saying that, "I understand why he should feel this way," means nothing. Understanding the

---

[8] From Geneva Gay and Roger D. Abrahams, "Black Culture in the Classroom," in *Language and Cultural Diversity in American Education*, Roger D. Abrahams and Rudolph C. Troike, eds., © 1972. Reprinted by permission of Prentice-Hall, Inc., Englewood Cliffs, New Jersey.

complexities of life for a Black person in this country does not come that easy. It does not stop the teacher from becoming frustrated—even frightened—nor will it stop the student from being resentful. If we revamp our educational philosophies and activities toward changing the student's attitudes we will be wasting our time. That has been tried before and it was a miserable failure. Black students will continue to carry their own culture into the classroom, and they will continue to misunderstand their middle-class teacher as profoundly as she misunderstands them. It is the teacher who can be taught to expect and deal with cultural differences before she enters the classroom, and it is the teacher who should and will have to do the changing. These changes must begin with the teacher's acceptance of the fact that despite the desire, she may never be accepted as a person by her Black students. Resorting to traditional measures to remove the hostile students from class serves no purpose whatsoever; they only delay the inevitable confrontation between student and teacher and heighten hostilities.

A few years ago Black people in general and particularly students were interested in doing whatever they could to remain in the good graces of the white folks. If the student were to do anything to anger the teacher, he was told to apologize, to avoid an all-out confrontation. This is no longer the case. Black people are too sensitive about always having to be the ones to "give" in interracial relations to be receptive to this approach any longer. Now, when a white teacher tells her Black student that she does not like his attitude, he is likely to answer in word and/or action, "that's tough, I don't like yours either, but you've got to live with it." Especially bewildered are teachers who were accustomed to the previous reaction, now trying to cope with this new attitude.

A third reason why Black students resent white teachers is that they are convinced of their racism and prejudice. The students' perceptions are very important in determining the direction of their relationship with the teachers. Regardless of how often the teacher professes her liberalism and unbiased attitudes, if the student perceives her differently all her testimony proves to no avail. This conviction may result from a certain movement, the way the teacher places herself in the classroom, the recurrent use of a certain word or phrase, or other idiosyncrasies which connote to the student an air of superiority. These speculations are areas which must be explored more deeply if teachers are to come to understand why Black students act and react as they do.

To test an assumption or judgment of the kind appearing as the thesis of "Black Culture in the Classroom" is no easy task. It calls for determining the truth and reliability of a statement wide in scope and open to many situations. But one can raise basic questions such as these:

1. What are the qualifications and reputation of the "authority" advancing the thesis or general statement?
2. What reliable evidence is presented in support of its validity?
3. Is the principle really relevant to the situation being discussed?
4. Are there other general principles which may actually offer better alternative approaches?

Applying these criteria to "Black Culture in the Classroom," we find that the authors dealing with the problem of black student hostility in white teacher classrooms are reputable scholars widely recognized for their studies in cultural behavior. The "general law" or thesis stated in the opening sentence is relevant to the problems being examined: "As the impact of Black nationalism and cultural awareness increase, we can expect the sources of irritation and tension between Black students and white middle-class teachers to increase. . . ." No evidence is introduced to show that "Black nationalism and cultural awareness" will "increase" and have more "impact," but the assumption seems reasonable in light of recent trends. And looked at in the light of question 4, the thesis seems to be the most likely approach and explanation of the problems being discussed.

Basic to all deductive reasoning is the emphasis placed upon *concepts,* or general ideas from which judgments are made. Any notion we have of what constitutes "the real world," for example, is a concept; it may be a picture we have in the mind, a familiar term we give to the associations we have of a particular place or person, or anything else that guides us in everyday living. Probably most concepts operate as a strong feeling or as an image such as those suggested by these ways of looking at things:

It's a dog-eat-dog kind of life
Get the other fellow before he gets you
Do unto others as you would have them do unto you
No girl is good enough for my son
I want to marry a girl like dear old mom
Money talks
America the beautiful
A Howard Johnson restaurant
The Man
Rapping

One very popular form of expressing concepts is *graffiti* — messages found scrawled in public places. These written-in-secret observations are often witty statements of popular concepts. A report on graffiti by a senior at the University of Northern Iowa points out how concepts can find strange utterances.

GRAFFITI[9]

by VICKI GACH

A frequently overlooked form of communication, used particularly by college students, is the anonymous graffito. Each graffito expresses a thought, wish, or attitude. Through graffiti, students communicate attitudes and feelings they would hesitate to utter publicly. Unlike spoken communications, graffiti provide safety from direct rebuttal, are more permanent than the spoken word, and reach larger audiences over a period of time.

The word *graffiti* (singular: *graffito*) comes from the Italian verb *graffiare,* meaning "to scratch." Graffiti are a variation of an ancient art form, sgraffito, which is etching or scratching designs in glass and clay vases. In their present form, graffiti are statements and drawings penned, penciled, painted, crayoned, lipsticked, or scratched on desks and walls, particularly restroom walls. Stonehenge carvings, Lascaux cave drawings, pyramid hieroglyphics, and Pompeiian wall writings are among the past forms of graffiti.

Graffitists (writers of graffiti) recognize their art as a form of creative expression. Some graffiti are about graffiti.

> The major form of creativity in America today is graffiti.
> These desk-top poets, so full of wit, should have their names engraved in shit.
> They all write biggest so they may be heard, but I write little cause I am cripple.
> Will someone please write an intelligent question on this desk?
> On table graffiti, this one rates a C—dean of UNI.
> Quit reading this desk and get back to work.
> This desk should be a museum.
> This desk is in its 10th printing.
> This chair soon to come out in paperback edition.

Descriptive phrases and statements in most graffiti are good examples of creative writing.

> The comic idea in a nutshell—what's funny is worth laughing at.
> Comp. is for burnt-out comic book writers.

9 *College English* 35 (December 1973): 285–287.

Double negatives are no-no's.

Confusing remarks in other graffiti require the reader to rethink what he has just read.

> I know that you think you know what I said, but I'm not sure that you realize that what you heard was not what I meant.
> I feel more like I do now than I did when I first got here.

Semantically, many graffiti use word games and words with double meanings in a context that can be interpreted as meaning either.

> Smoke marijuana—say "hi!" with conviction.
> Elsie the Cow is on grass.
> The pigs have been asking about my joint bank account.

Take-offs on advertising slogans for common products and from movie themes require special interpretations.

> Love means saying I'm sorry every five minutes.
> LSD melts in your mind, not in your hand.
> Hashish—Breakfast of Champions.
> A day without sex is like a day without sunshine.

Literary allusions in graffiti, as well as references from other academic fields, make more sense when the reference is familiar.

> Holden Caulfield—patron saint of the confused, misunderstood and thoroughly fed up.
> Frodo gave his finger for you.

Platitudes and quotations are altered.

> Give me liberty or give me meth.
> Vasectomy means never having to say you're sorry.
> Remember, girls, the way to a man's heart is through his left ventricle.
> If at first you don't succeed, you're about average.

Word games in graffiti are witty in themselves, but differ from graffiti about words.

> I'd rather be a small ot than a bigot.
> Live spelled backwards is evil.
> Russian Rape—Ivan Toratitov.
> Russian fingers, Roman hands.
> Words are facts in action, acts are truths beyond facts.
> My words trickle down from a wound I have no intention to heal.
> If an idea cannot be expressed in language that a reasonably attentive 7th grader can understand, someone's jiving someone else.
> —I. A. Richards

Graffiti also contain many of the technical devices and figures of speech of poetry and literature.

> *Climax:* I came, I saw, I flunked.
> *Syllogism:* God is love. Love is blind. Ray Charles is God.
> *Alliteration:* Hemp, Hemp, Hooray! / Life is as tedious as a twice-told tale, Vexing the dull ear of a drowsy man.
> *Assonance:* No Moe Woe. / She offered her honor, he honored her offer. And all night long it was honor, offer, honor, offer. . . .
> *Simile:* Sex is like snowfalls—you're never sure how many inches you'll get.
> *Metaphor:* Life is a bowl of pits—somebody else got all of the cherries. / Truth is *tits* sometimes.
> *Allusion:* Frankenstein Lives.
> *Epigram:* Honesty is good for the soul.
> *Apostrophe:* Small people of the World!! Unite!
> *Euphemism:* Fighting for peace is like making love for virginity.
> *Eulogy:* In memory of those who died while waiting for this class to end.
> *Irony:* Barabas lives for your sins.
> *Hyperbole:* Males are usually basically ignorant.
> *Interrogation:* Is it going to be all right?

Spelling and punctuation errors occur less frequently on college campuses than in public places although sometimes deliberate misspelling is used to create an effect.

> Ar we al Fols to think we kan liv forever?
> If your stoned (I wish) and you cann read thiss ant you donn't thunk your seaing things than maybee your knot ass stoned has u think u r?

Although the graffiti I have collected at my college include certain local topical allusions, many graffiti subjects are universal. The following graffiti, which I found at the University of Northern Iowa (Cedar Falls, Iowa), are representative of graffiti found not only on campuses but outside of the academic community as well.

> God isn't dead—He just doesn't want to get involved.
> Reality is a crutch.
> > —Harvard Lamont Library
> God is dead, but don't worry, Mary's pregnant again.
> > —96th Street, Manhattan
> Christ is the Answer—What was your question?
> > —Alabama

Withdrawal is something Nixon's father should have done years ago.
Vietnam—love it or leave it.
Kill a Commie for Christ.

—Vietnam

Graffiti are much more than doodles or vandalism. They are the written thoughts, wishes, hopes, and dreams of individuals. From a historical
viewpoint, graffiti record contemporary events with ordinary people's
outlooks. These observations are in the vernacular of the people and reflect their lifestyles. As Robert Reisner, author of *Graffiti: Two Thousand
Years of Wall Writing,* has stated, graffiti were, are, and will continue to
be, "a sensitive barometer of change in popular preoccupations . . . a
twilight means of communication between the anonymous man and the
world."

On being original: inductive reasoning

"Make up your own mind! Think for yourself! And take a good look
at the world around you!" What such exhortations are calling for is
inductive reasoning, which includes all forms of arriving at generalizations or judgments through personal observation. At its best, inductive thinking is the kind of thoroughly tested conclusion or theory that a
scientist reaches after repeated observations of a phenomenon under
carefully controlled circumstances. At its worst, it is the kind of hasty
or "snap" judgment made by anyone smarting from some painful or
unpleasant experience which leads him or her to say things like, "Take
my word for it—they're all alike. You can't trust any of 'em."

History scholars and students of political science, like all social
scientists, rely upon the inductive process to arrive at hypotheses and
theories. It means examining the significance of what at first glance may
appear to be wholly unrelated actions and events but which may be
found to have a bearing upon one another. The process leads to the arriving at original conclusions the hard way—through careful, objective
evaluation of a wide range of details. Storied detectives like Sherlock
Holmes and the television characters like Columbo or Kojak well exemplify this piecing together of parts to make a significant whole.

But as the following account shows, it is not always easy even for a
most privileged young man to arrive at a necessary decision by "thinking for yourself," at least so Professor Blinderman says in his re-creation
of the thought processes of Henry Adams.

AN ERA TO MAKE YOUNG AMERICANS DESPAIR[10]
by ABRAHAM BLINDERMAN

> For I am certain, O men of Athens, that
> if I had engaged in politics, I would
> have perished long ago and done no good
> either to you or to myself.
>
> —Socrates, in his apology

When Gordon Strachan concluded his testimony before the Senate Watergate Committee, he advised young Americans to shun political careers in Washington, echoing the words of Henry Adams almost a century before in a letter to his friend, Sen. Cabot Lodge. "I suppose," wrote Adams, "every man who has looked on at the game has been struck by the remarkable way in which politics deteriorates the moral tone of everyone who mixes in them. The deterioration is far more marked than in any other occupation . . . except the turf, stock-jobbing, and gambling. . . . I have never known a young man go into politics who was not the worse for it. They all try to be honest and then are tripped up by the dishonest (i.e. practical politicians) and degrade their own natures."

Why should a man as eminently qualified for political greatness as Adams regard statesmanship so cynically? The great-grandson of John Adams, the grandson of John Quincy Adams, the son of Charles Francis Adams, a graduate of Harvard, and secretary to his father, U.S. minister to England during the Civil War, Adams at 30 seemed destined to emulate his renowned ancestors in some branch of public service. He was one of post-Civil War Washington's many young men "greedy for work, eager for reform" who needed a leader to direct their goals. Had not a war-weary people given Grant an overwhelming mandate to impose order in the land?

But Adams was soon suspicious of Grant's intentions and dismayed by Grant's choice of antireform cabinet members. Later, Grant ostentatiously paraded in the questionable company of financial wheeler-dealers Jay Gould and Jim Fisk. He was not overly scrupulous in accepting their gifts and services. Adams looked on and sorrowed. A president should be more circumspect. What was Gould up to?

On Sept. 24, 1869—"Black Friday"—Gould unwillingly sold the $50,000,000 in gold that he had acquired in his almost successful attempt to corner the New York gold market. The financial panic that followed ruined hundreds of speculators and paralyzed the nation's economy for weeks. The public cried for indictment of the culprits who had engineered this fiasco. The House appointed Rep. James A. Garfield to head a congressional committee to investigate the fluctuations in the price of gold— the New York market.

[10] *Newsday*, November 9, 1973. By special permission of the author, Abraham Blinderman.

Adams now had a cause—finding the story behind the gold conspiracy. Like any investigative reporter, he was able to get "leaks" from important witnesses and talkative congressmen, but he waited until the completion of the hearings before writing his piece. As he documented more and more sordid details of the conspiracy, he came to agree with Rep. Garfield's declaration that "the abysses of wickedness . . . are opening before us." This is the story Adams reported.

Gould had bribed Abel R. Corbin, Grant's brother-in-law, and got him to have the pliable Gen. Butterfield appointed to a key post as assistant treasurer of New York City; he had vainly tried to bribe Grant's aide, Gen. Porter, and he had bought gold on speculation for Mrs. Grant (although without her knowledge).

Corbin was apparently able to convince Grant that the government should not sell its gold reserves, thereby keeping the price up for Gould. His polished presentation went like this: High gold prices would benefit western farmers who shipped their produce to eastern ports for export; prosperous farmers would insure a prosperous nation.

Perhaps it was Gen. Porter's suspicions of Gould that gave Grant second thoughts about Gould and Corbin; perhaps it was Gould's untimely correspondence with Grant. The President ordered Corbin to disassociate himself from Gould, and on Sept. 24 ordered the selling of government gold to break Gould's hold on the market. "Black Friday," with the financial ruin of so many Americans, was the result. But Corbin let Gould in on Grant's decision in time for Gould to sell his gold and escape bankruptcy.

All this tormented Adams. He knew that the trail of corruption led from Gould to the White House, but he thought Congress' Garfield committee would not dare probe all of the evidence because so many important people were involved. He was right. Neither the President nor his wife was called to testify. Gen. Butterfield resigned. Corbin continued to live in Washington although Grant never spoke to him again. And Jay Gould and Jim Fisk maintained their grip on the Erie, Fisk gleefully exclaiming of the investigation "that nothing is lost save honor."

Adams sorrowed over this attitude. The damage to the nation's morale was immeasurable; not one young man of promise remained in the government service. "All Boston, all New England, and all respectable New York . . . agreed that Washington was no place for a respectable young man." He despaired of the reform of political parties, writing that intelligent people are corrupted and vulgarized by political parties. But he had no alternative to the party system.

Since he felt in 1869–1870 that "every intelligent man about the government was prepared to go," he could not readily remain in Washington himself. He wrote his own political epitaph in his autobiography, "The Education of Henry Adams," an epitaph that contemporary politicians might read profitably:

"The Administration drove him and thousands of other young men into active enmity, not only to Grant, but to the system or want of system, which took possession of the President. Every hope or thought which had brought Adams to Washington proved to be absurd. No one wanted him; no one wanted any of his friends in reform; the blackmailer was the normal product of politics as of business."

And what of Rep. Garfield, whose investigation stopped short of thoroughness? After the hearings ended, he revealed that he had heard from the White House: "The President expresses himself under a good many obligations to me for the management of the gold panic investigation." Having failed to uncover the full extent of the Grant Administration corruption, he went on to become President himself.

Socratic dialogue

According to Blinderman, it was through Henry Adams' raising the right questions and then honestly answering them that Adams was able to arrive at his important decision regarding participation in party politics in his times. This question-and-answer process is a variation of the systematic form of inquiry first made famous by Socrates and so is identified with his name as *Socratic reasoning.* As exemplified by his student, Plato, in his *Dialogues,* Socrates opens up a chosen subject matter by asking key questions regarding the philosophic problems raised. In the Henry Adams article, Professor Blinderman begins with a quotation from *The Apology,* which is Plato's account of Socrates' last thoughts and words, as in obedience to the sentence passed upon him by his fellow Athenian citizens he drank the fatal cup of hemlock.

Here as illustrative of the Socratic method is a portion of another one of the *Dialogues* called "The Symposium," wherein Socrates in discussion with a friend, Agathon, poses crucial questions regarding the nature of love.

AGATHON & SOCRATES[11]

Now, Agathon my friend, it seems to me that you led off your discussion beautifully by saying that it is necessary first to show what the nature of Love is, and then to discuss his works. I thoroughly admire such a beginning. So tell me this about Love please, since the rest of what you

[11] Reprinted by permission of The University of Massachusetts Press from *The Symposium of Plato,* Brentlinger, ed., Groden, trans., Baskin, illust., © Copyright 1970 by The University of Massachusetts Press.

said about him was so beautiful and splendid—is Love such as to be the love of something, or of nothing? I'm not asking if it is the love of some mother or father—to ask whether Love is the love of a mother or father would be absurd—but as if I were asking about a father. Is a father the father of someone, or not? You should undoubtedly say to me, if you wanted to answer me properly, that it is of a son or daughter that a father is a father. Or wouldn't you?

Certainly, said Agathon.

And it would be the same for a mother?

They were in agreement about that as well.

But now then, continued Socrates, answer a few more, so that you get a better understanding of what I want. Let me ask you this: a brother—the thing itself, just as it is—is it the brother of someone or not?

He answered that it was.

Is it not, then, the brother of a brother or sister?

Yes.

So try, he went on, and tell me about Love. Is Love the love of nothing or of something?

Surely he is the love of something!

Now think, Socrates urged, of what this may be, and keep it to yourself; but tell me whether he desires this thing of which Love is the love or not?

Oh yes, Agathon replied.

Does he have the thing which he desires and loves, when he desires and loves it, or does he not have it?

He doesn't have it, I would guess, Agathon said.

Then consider, continued Socrates, beyond guessing, whether it isn't necessary for the desiring thing to desire what is lacking, and not to desire it if it isn't lacking? It seems marvelously clear to me, Agathon, that this is necessary. What about you?

It seems that way to me, too, he said.

Good. So, would anyone wish to be great when he was great? Or strong if he were strong?

That would be impossible, from what we've been saying.

Since they would not be lacking that which they were.

True.

For if he were strong, and still should want to be strong, said Socrates, or swift, and wanted to be swift, or healthy, and wanted to be healthy— since one generally thinks in that sort of situation, and in all of the same sorts of cases, that those who are of such and such a nature and possess those same qualities, want the things that they have (I'm inserting this so that we won't deceive ourselves), for these men, Agathon, if you think about it, it is imperative that they have everything, at a given moment, which they have, whether they wish it or not, and who, I ask you, would desire that? But whenever someone says "I am healthy, and I want to be healthy," "I am rich, and I want to be rich," or "I desire the very things I have," we shall say to him, "you mean, dear fellow, that possessing riches, health and strength, you want to possess them in the future, too, since as far as the present is concerned you have them, desiring it or not." But look, when you say "I desire my present belongings," do you think you're saying anything besides: "I wish that the things I have now will be provided for me in the future?" Wouldn't he agree?

Certainly, said Agathon.

Then Socrates went on, So there is a love of that which is not present for one, which one doesn't have, namely the existence of those things in the future, preserved, and provided always.

Absolutely, he answered.

Now such a person, and every other person who feels longing, longs for what is not at hand, for what he isn't himself, and for what he lacks, and these are the sorts of thing that desire is of, and Love?

Definitely, he said.

So come, urged Socrates, let us agree on what has been said. Is Love, first of all, anything but the love of things? And further, isn't it of those very things which it needs?

That's right, Agathon agreed.

Indeed, now think back to the things you said about Love in your oration. If you like, I'll remind you. I believe you spoke of the way that the deeds of the gods were initiated because of the love of beautiful things. For there couldn't be a love of ugly things. Didn't you say that?

Yes, I said it, replied Agathon.

And you spoke quite properly, my friend, asserted Socrates. And if this is the case, can Love be the love of anything but beauty, and not ugliness?

He granted that.

Then wasn't it agreed that he loves what he lacks and doesn't have?

Yes, he said.

Love, then, is wanting in beauty, and doesn't have it?

Necessarily.

But what have we here? Would you say that what was wanting in beauty and in no way possesses beauty was beautiful?

Obviously, it isn't.

Are you then still going to agree that Love is beautiful, if that's how it is?

And Agathon declared, I'm afraid, Socrates, that I didn't know what I was talking about.

Oh, but you spoke beautifully, Agathon, he assured him. But tell me a little more. Don't you think of what is good as being beautiful as well?

Yes, I do.

Then again—if Love is lacking in beauty, and the good is beautiful, he must be lacking in goodness as well.

Socrates! he exclaimed, I'm incapable of refuting you, so have it your own way!

The truth, lovely Agathon, Socrates said, you cannot refute, but Socrates is easily refuted.

In this dialogue we see that the Socratic art of question and answer requires that the questioner be willing to consider all alternatives and to examine each one carefully for its possible truth as the "right" answer to the perplexing problem under discussion.

Psychologically, the Socratic method is also an effective rhetorical device, for it at least appears to give all sides of the question their proper hearing. By taking up the viewpoints, one after the other, of the "other side," the writer—or speaker—gives the impression that he is seriously considering the points advanced by the opposition. He thus disarms much of the hostility probably already existing; he shows his fair-mindedness by conceding that there is much to be said for the opposing views. Furthermore, by assuming the role of a modest inquirer intent only upon "the truth," he gains the goodwill of all concerned.

For a modern example of this Socratic art wherein the question-and-answer dialogue is deliberately used for satiric effect, consider a representative effort by Russell Baker. To make his point in the brief space his daily column affords, he—like the famous Art Buchwald—deliberately sets up "a straw man" whose views on some controversial topic are so extreme that they are easily made ridiculous.

ENERGY CRISIS SOLVES EVERYBODY'S PROBLEMS AND MAKES IT EASY TO ANSWER ALL QUESTIONS[12]

by RUSSELL BAKER

Washington—Here are pressing questions about the energy crisis and answers supplied by the experts.

Q. What is the energy crisis?

A. The energy crisis is the finest all-purpose alibi in America today. If you can't deliver the goods, it is because of the energy crisis. If you want to raise prices, it is necessitated by the energy crisis. If you want to cancel a visit with your wife's relatives, tell them, "Sorry, it's the energy crisis." If your children bump into you leaving a pornographic movie house, just explain that it's the energy crisis.

---

[12] © 1973 by the New York Times Company. Reprinted by permission.

Q. Wasn't anybody smart enough to notice until right now that we were running out of oil?

A. Of course! Children of the 1930's—and they are running the government today—were aware of it. "What will happen when we have used up all the oil?" they used to say. "What a silly question!" their parents used to reply. "Before that can happen science will come up with something new to replace oil."

Q. Why hasn't science come up with something new to replace oil?

A. Because if it did, economic disaster would result. Oil companies would collapse. So would shipping and pipeline companies. Texas would become a disaster area and American taxpayers would have to put every sheik in Arabia on welfare. There would no longer be any reason to build the Alaska pipeline.

Q. If the people running the government knew the energy crisis was coming, why didn't they stop construction years ago on the interstate highway system and use the money to build railroads?

A. Because they knew the interstate highway system would be needed to help save gasoline when the energy crisis occurred. Without the interstate highways' capacity to move traffic at 70 miles an hour, it would be impossible to cut gasoline consumption by reducing the speed limit to 50 miles an hour.

Q. Instead of going on Daylight Saving Time to cut electricity usage a little at the end of the day, why not close down television after 9 o'clock so people will have to go to bed?

A. If television shut down at 9 P.M., it would be the end of the 11 P.M. TV news shows all over the country. These shows are vital to fighting the energy crisis because they are often sponsored by gasoline companies whose commercials advise the audience how to cut gasoline consumption.

Q. I have just bought a large car which uses a gallon of gasoline every 8 miles. Since the people running the government knew the energy crisis was coming, why didn't they tell the auto makers, so the auto makers wouldn't have made this car and sold it to me?

A. Because the people running the government were concerned about your safety. They did not want you to take your family onto turnpikes teeming with gigantic tractor-trailers unless you were all traveling in a vehicle much sturdier than the average tiny compact, particularly since your family includes three large children, two aging cats and a grandfather who is almost as big as Muhammad Ali.

Q. If I throw away my new big car and buy a new tiny compact car to help fight the energy crisis, where shall I put my three large children, two aging cats and oversized grandfather when I take advantage of my fantastically lower gas consumption to go on a family holiday?

A. Strap them on a bicycle rack attached to the back of your car. Alternatively, tell them they can't go along this time on the family vacation, and give them the all-purpose alibi: "Sorry, kids, gramps and cats, but there's an energy crisis on."

Q. *Why was the energy crisis begun at this time, just when I was finally beginning to get interested in Watergate?*

A. The government reasoned that since fewer and fewer people believed anything the government said anymore it should hold the energy crisis right away while there were still a few people left to believe in it.

Dialectic thinking

It was not until the eighteenth century that Socratic dialogue took on a new dimension in the form of reasoning now known as *dialectics*. It began with Immanuel Kant's efforts to open the old, lifeless medieval thesis-deduction system and let in new light and life. Kant wanted fresh ways of looking at man, society, and nature. The Kantian dialectic can be summed up in this brief and highly oversimplified form:

1. I have a *thesis* (a generalization, a judgment, a proposition), but a thesis is only the product of frail human minds.
2. That being true, I may as well consider that its opposite may be equally "true." I will call this contradictory view the *antithesis* and try to learn what this contrasting of opposites will do to give me insights into the problems with which I am dealing.

This systematized thesis-antithesis mode of intellectual inquiry took on an even greater dimension when another German philosopher, George W. F. Hegel, added a third possibility, the *synthesis*, which proposes that the "truth" may not lie in either the thesis or the antithesis but rather in the result of the clash between these extremes.

You can find this Hegelian dialectic in practice now almost anywhere. Without realizing it, you yourself may employ dialectic thinking to find suitable options and alternatives when confronted with a serious problem, as did the young man in the following anecdote.

On his first evening alone manning a "Life Line" suicide-call post, a volunteer responds to a telephone ring and hears a girl's despairful voice say: "Life's just a crock of crap and I can't take any more of it." After some nervous questioning, the shaken volunteer learns these details: The girl is strung out on drugs; her lover has kicked her out of his pad; she has no money, and she thinks she is pregnant. No, she cannot go home. Her father is dead and her mother is married to a man the girl cannot stand. Besides, she says, both are alcoholics. So why should she make the effort to keep on living?

First, as he has been coached, he tries to assure her that her condition is not helpless or hopeless and that he has excellent medical and counseling agencies to which he can refer her. She cuts him off and refuses to go to any such agency. While trying to think of other solutions, he, in emotional reaction to her "ingratitude," is tempted to tell her she does not really want any help. But finally, as a last resort, he remembers that one of the regulars on the "Life Line" staff had told him she would, if it were necessary, herself go to the address of a person who refused all other offers of help. He gives the caller this information and is relieved to hear this solution is acceptable. He makes the call and the visit is arranged.

This incident and the kind of thinking the young volunteer has been engaged in is "dialectic." It involves working toward a comprehensive viewpoint while trying to find and test for acceptability various aspects of a troublesome situation. We can see how he applied the Hegelian dialectic to the complex problem the caller posed for him. He presented first the thesis that the usual sources of medical and counseling services were available and would help the caller. When that offer was rejected, he was tempted to dismiss her with the antithesis that she really did not need or want his help. Then, finally, he found the synthesis, a happy compromise between the other two extremes and one which satisfied all concerned.

This Hegelian dialectic is at work in much of the decision making we are all engaged in every day, as, for example, in these conclusions:

THESIS: Everybody needs to learn to speak standard English.
ANTITHESIS: Nobody needs to learn to speak standard English.
SYNTHESIS: Whoever needs or wishes to speak standard English should be given every assistance.

THESIS: You only live once, so live it up!
ANTITHESIS: No, no! In this life you must prepare for Eternity!
SYNTHESIS: Well, I'll enjoy this life as much as I can but still not forget about "saving my soul."

THESIS: Women should enjoy equal rights with men in all respects. So urge your legislature to pass the constitutional amendment giving women these rights.
ANTITHESIS: No, women never have had and never should have equal rights with men. So urge a vote against it.
SYNTHESIS: Women should have equal rights with men in many things but

for their own good not in all. So a constitutional amendment is not what is needed.

Useful as such applications of Hegelian dialectics can be, they can also be mind blowing. Much of the underlying philosophies of the Absurd and Existentialism found in modern dramas, novels, poetry, and films are the results of this thinking. Above all, the dialectic is the one relied upon by Marx and Engels in arriving at the basic concepts underlying communist theory. We see an ironic result: the dialectic that once encouraged fresh inquiry and new ideas has ended up as the official "Dialectical Materialism" producing the worlds of Lenin, Stalin, Castro, and Mao, wherein societies are "planned" bureaucratic economies hostile to free inquiry and criticism.

Everyone is familiar with novels like George Orwell's *1984* and Aldous Huxley's *Brave New World* which project into grim futures the results of totalitarian state policies and practices, but few also know that both books are indebted to one written in 1919 by a Russian novelist, Evgenis Zamjatin, entitled *We*. How Zamjatin employed the Hegelian dialectic to keep his thinking free of Communist party doctrine can be seen in the following statement, wherein he proclaims himself an eternal "heretic" or rebel:

> Today is doomed to die, because yesterday has died and because tomorrow shall be born. Such is the cruel and wise law. Cruel, because it dooms to eternal dissatisfaction those who today already see the distant heights of tomorrow; wise, because only eternal dissatisfaction is the guarantee of unending movement forward, of unending creativity. He who has found the ideal today has already turned into a pillar of salt as was Lot's wife, has already grown into the earth and moves no further. The world lives only by heretics: Christ the heretic, Copernicus the heretic, Tolstoy the heretic. Our creed is heresy: tomorrow is infallibly heresy for the today which has crumbled into dust. Today negates yesterday, but tomorrow is the negation of negation: always the same dialectical path, which carries the world into infinity along a grandiose parabola. Thesis yesterday, antithesis today, and synthesis tomorrow.[13]

How much the Zamjatin kind of "heretic" and rebel continues to be a product of the Hegelian dialectic of free inquiry and critical analysis appears, as has already been mentioned, in the arts and literature of our times.

[13] From Alex M. Shane, *The Life and Works of Evgenis Zamjatin* (Berkeley: University of California Press, 1968), pp. 22–23.

FOCUS POINT

1. "Dialectic" is derived from the Greek term for "the art of discourse" and was the original name of *logic.*

2. Immanuel Kant devised the antithesis as a contrary to thesis in order to open ideas to questioning and examination.

3. George W. F. Hegel went one step further and posited the synthesis as a means of discovering other possibly valid concepts and insights.

4. This Hegelian dialectic was adopted by Marx and Engels in their criticisms of nineteenth-century capitalism.

5. Forms of the Hegelian dialectic have become essential features of "Dialectical Materialism" of the kind dominating the ideology of modern communistic states.

6. But the dialectic of Hegel also enables thinkers in capitalistic, democratic countries to find and explore new ideas and potentialities.

EXERCISES

1. Here are some possible dialectic outlines one can construct. Complete the missing statement as you think the dialectic form would state it.

    THESIS: All American novelists today thrive on the rage and love of violence they find in American cities.
    ANTITHESIS: No American novelists today thrive on the rage and love of violence they find in American cities.
    SYNTHESIS: _____

    THESIS: Some modern novelists write wholly about sexual violence and outrage.
    ANTITHESIS: _____
    SYNTHESIS: Some modern novelists may touch upon sexual violence and outrage.

    THESIS: _____
    ANTITHESIS: No author's style is affected by his outlook on life.
    SYNTHESIS: Some writers' styles are affected by their outlook on life.

2. What do you think of contemporary fiction? Has its attraction to violence affected films or have films of sadistic nature influenced the fiction? Select one recent novel you have read and discuss it in light (or in the "dark"!) of current tastes and styles.

Awareness and intuition

A novel sound or an unexpected silence, a movement of color or a whiff of fragrance—any vivid sense impression can startle one into giving it full attention. If it is interpreted as being pleasant and enjoyable, it gives rise to feelings of well-being and even happiness. On the contrary, at night on a too quiet street the sound of rapidly nearing footsteps behind one can change a friendly neighborhood scene into a nightmarish trap. Whatever the strong sense impression, the body is triggered into heightened awareness. One's whole being becomes alertly conscious while appropriate images flood the imagination with messages of warning or delight.

At the same time and mingled with those "messages" may be the sudden flashes of understanding we call *intuitions*. Without any apparent preparation we see meanings in the most commonplace of things—meanings that had never before been apparent. These mysterious visitations, these moments of enlightenment, may give us glimpses of the true reality of situations and of ourselves. Gifted poets and even scientists cherish and develop these moments of insight and depend upon them.

Such experiences are common to us all, even to the most unpoetic and unscientific of us, but usually we dismiss them—or try to—because they may be disturbing to and unsettling of our "ordinary self." It is such experiences, however, that the student-writer should learn to incorporate into his writing if he wishes to say something worth reading.

A prominent composition instructor has adapted the approaches suggested by Rollo May and Arthur Koestler, two well-known authors writing on "creativity," as a possible means of permitting students to avail themselves of such effective use of their experiences.

> These writers argue that if a student is to create, to "bring [something new] into birth" [Rollo May's word], he must learn to understand thoroughly his experiences, the data he has to work with—what May calls his "world." He must become intimately familiar with the details of those experiences, the possible relationships among facts, and the possible implications of those facts. He must then be willing to transform, reformulate, or recombine those experiences into new imagined forms. As May puts it, the creative person (including, presumably, a student seeking new

ideas) must engage in an intense "encounter," voluntarily, with his experiences or what he sees around him. "Genuine creativity is characterized by an intensity of awareness, a heightened consciousness."[14]

This desired quality of awareness, then, is a state of mind and feeling wherein one is highly conscious of his surroundings as these in their various ways affect his senses, emotions, and thoughts. It means deliberately cultivating and using the senses of sight, hearing, smell, taste, and feeling to note things which one has never before been aware of, at least consciously. In that state of heightened consciousness he may find himself thinking "creatively," if out of a welter of images and sensations there finally emerges some sense of discovery, a recognition of something "strange and spare" in the ordinary and the familiar. In short, awareness may well bring with it intuition.

The intuitive discoveries which may emerge from such moments also may arise from the practice called meditation. Meditation is any prescribed ritual in which aspirants of the various world religions deliberately seek a deeper understanding of nature, themselves, and whatever possible Transcendent Being they believe exists. In such meditation, some one "subject" or "topic" is chosen, perhaps quite deliberately, and in the mental-emotional process best known as "contemplation" the person meditating carefully allows his memory, imagination, and feelings to bring into his consciousness new concepts and awarenesses. It must be emphasized, however, that meditation is not daydreaming! Fruitful results can come from periods of meditation only if one has previously disciplined his mind and body in ways harmonious with the world view in which he believes.

Here is how one author describes this kind of experience.

Experiencing becomes deeper and more differentiated by our work in perception: the attuning of our sense organs and the recovery of their innate automatic reactiveness. We work on allowing more quiet in and around the eyes, on giving up the effort in looking and on "letting come" rather than "doing," so that what comes through vision can be received not by the eyes alone but by our totality, and one can truly say: "*I* see," or "*I* hear." We allow our eyes and ears, mouth, nose, hands, feet—our whole sensitized surface, antenna-like—just to be the entrance doors through which impressions, sensations, odors, tastes and sounds enter us, there to be received, absorbed and digested by our whole self. We practice sitting

[14] Richard L. Larson, "Discovery through Questioning: A Plan for Teaching Rhetorical Invention," *College English* 30 (November 1968): 127–128.

quietly, with eyes closed and becoming receptive to whatever sounds may reach us (slight stirrings, voices, wind or rain, music next door, street noises, etc.) *without trying to identify and label them immediately,* but letting them freely enter us and be experienced. Quietly allowing our eyes to open, without "looking," we receive impressions: the people in the room whose presence speaks to us in many ways; objects and plants; the play of color; light and shadow. . . .[15]

And here are two short accounts by well-known authors which exemplify some of these "awareness" processes and the originality they may produce. A third piece is a most practical article relating from a business executive's point of view the importance of awareness in the world of commerce and industry.

I JUST LOST MY TENSION AGAIN[16]
by JOHN THORPE

I walk around with no ideals or goals. I pass ripe blackberry bushes.

There's a man in me who would prove. He is right but little else. My knowledge of people was built up somewhere else. It was a heavy-handed preparation and it dies hard.

I blew money. I lost things. I got over the loud thing for awhile. Loud or quiet is about the same. It means you don't have anything to come on to people with. And you have to give up first.

I feel like everyone knows but me. I just sit there open-mouthed.

Yesterday I watched heavily environmental faces: half-closed faces with smiles that carry into the skull.

There are the people to hold in my arms. There is the street.

There's a laugh which indicates simply I drink and I'm too afraid to pay attention.

Then there's a lupine bush. It's somehow the fact I don't move alone.

My boots are starting to wear down on the side, they're lopsided so the heel juts out. It's the inhibition or physical flaw I feel before I hear talk.

---

[15] Charlotte Selver, "Report on Work in Sensory Awareness and Total Functioning," in *Explorations in Human Potentialities,* ed. Herbert A. Otto (Springfield, Ill.: Charles C Thomas, Publisher, 1966), p. 278.

[16] *The Paris Review,* 14, No. 53 (Winter 1972): 32. By permission of The Paris Review.

I did very little. I had a central character by virtue of that. Not as if I'd found a place they couldn't take away.

I did what I wanted. And I brought two children into this world. I respected the mystery and mastered nothing I'm aware of.

I squat here, looking at the moon, deciding to appear.

PARTNERS[17]

by RICHARD BRAUTIGAN

I like to sit in the cheap theaters of America where people live and die with Elizabethan manners while watching the movies. There is a theater down on Market Street where I can see four movies for a dollar. I really don't care how good they are either. I'm not a critic. I just like to watch movies. Their presence on the screen is enough for me.

The theater is filled with black people, hippies, senior citizens, soldiers, sailors and the innocent people who talk to the movies because the movies are just as real as anything else that has ever happened to them.

"No! No! Get back in the car, Clyde. Oh, God, they're killing Bonnie!"

I am the poet-in-residence at these theaters but I don't plan on getting a Guggenheim for it.

Once I went into the theater at six o'clock in the evening and got out at one o'clock in the morning. At seven I crossed my legs and they stayed that way until ten and I never did stand up.

In other words, I am not an art film fan. I do not care to be esthetically tickled in a fancy theater surrounded by an audience drenched in the confident perfume of culture. I can't afford it.

I was sitting in a two-pictures-for-seventy-five-cents theater called the Times in North Beach last month and there was a cartoon about a chicken and a dog.

The dog was trying to get some sleep and the chicken was keeping him awake and what followed was a series of adventures that always ended up in cartoon mayhem.

There was a man sitting next to me.

He was *whitewhitewhite:* fat, about fifty years old, balding sort of and his face was completely minus any human sensitivity.

His baggy no-style clothes covered him like the banner of a defeated country and he looked as if the only mail he had ever gotten in his life were bills.

Just then the dog in the cartoon let go with a huge yawn because the

[17] From *Revenge of the Lawn.* Copyright © 1963, 1964, 1965, 1966, 1967, 1969, 1970, 1971 by Richard Brautigan. Reprinted by permission of Simon and Schuster.

chicken was still keeping him awake and before the dog had finished yawning, the man next to me started yawning, so that the dog in the cartoon and the man, this living human being, were yawning together, partners in America.

WHEN YOU LOSE TOUCH WITH THE RANK AND FILE[18]
by RAYMOND DREYFACK

Management consultant Richard S. Buse, president of Patrick B. Comer Associates, Inc., Greensboro, N.C., tells about the executives of an 1,800-man plant who decided to set up maintenance standards and priorities. Industrial engineers made their study and recommendations. The maintenance crew was assembled. Starting on a certain date, it was told, here was how the department would be run.

Reaction was swift, results decisive: Wide-ranging anger and bitterness and an immediate slowdown.

The snafu jolted management into the action it should have taken in the first place. In a series of meetings, the importance and values of the new system were explained. Employees were convinced that paychecks wouldn't be adversely affected, that opportunities would increase. Then, workers were permitted to speak their minds and blow off steam.

This time the change was accepted; cooperation replaced hostility and anticipated gains were eventually realized. But the loss through failure to build an early pipeline to the ranks will never be recovered.

Failure to take the pulse of your people can be damaging indeed. Emily Halliday, office manager of Morgan Personnel Agency, Inc., which serves New York's brokerage industry, sees clogged pipelines as the cause behind innumerable employee resignations.

"Nine out of 10 complaints boil down to poor communications — management's inability to get to the roots of what motivates and demotivates people," she says.

Saul D. Astor, president of Management Safeguards, Inc., a New York City-based security firm, goes a step further. "Failure to gauge employee attitudes leads to morale breakdown. This makes it easy for weak-willed people to rationalize disloyalty and dishonesty," he states.

C. Howard Hardesty Jr., an executive vice president of Continental Oil Co., unhappily recalls one situation where line people tried hard to convey problems and gripes to a team of roving troubleshooters. The troubleshooters "listened to what the employees said, but they didn't

---

[18] From *Nation's Business* 61 (December 1973): 61–63.

really hear, so it never bubbled upwards," Mr. Hardesty says. "Listening isn't enough. It's the hearing that counts."

In this case, the failure to hear resulted in a lengthy work stoppage.

HOW TO KEEP IN TOUCH

A variety of strategies exist for getting accurate information on the attitudes of middle managers, supervisors and line personnel.

"Most important," Mr. Hardesty stresses, "is top management's need to identify the vastness of the task and to see it as a problem. Next step is to structure your organization with the problem in mind. As companies grow, it's in the nature of the beast for close contact to be lost. There's a tendency to overcentralize, set up too many tiers."

Kay C. Lambeth, president, Erwin-Lambeth, Inc., a Southern custom furniture maker, agrees. Asked: "How does a busy top executive find time to gauge employee feelings?" she replies: "You take the time. You realize that reading the pulse of your people is a number one priority."

One good way to get readings, Mr. Hardesty suggests, is through letters to employees. Conoco uses this device to tell people about major events, safety programs, systems changes. Personnel liaison experts then follow up by talking with employees on the job, listening to reactions, assessing responses. Some companies invite workers to take suggestions and grievances directly to the president. At the Cooper-Bessemer plant in Mt. Vernon, Ohio, a self-sealing letter form is put in each issue of the company publication. Letters must be signed—a safeguard against pranksters and cranks.

Nucor Corp., steel joist producer, uses periodic plant dinners as a major means of upward communication. "After dinner," notes F. Kenneth Iverson, president and chief executive officer, "wide-open discussion takes place with just one ground rule enforced—no personalities."

Informal meetings are particularly effective in getting supervisors to speak their minds, most executives agree. "It gives them a sense of belonging," Mr. Astor observes. "It's an excellent way to get problems and grievances out into the open."

He calls to mind one case where serious inventory shortages existed over a period of months. One day a seminar was set up to deal with the problem. Little else was done, yet the shortages dropped dramatically. Top management got the message. Employees needed simply to realize that management was aware of the problem and deeply concerned.

To demonstrate top executive concern, Conoco runs a motivation school. Employees are pulled off their jobs periodically to attend sessions which range from three days to a week. Problems are discussed, gripes hashed out. Consensus-type thinking is encouraged, credit and criticism avoided. When free expression is honestly sought, the company finds, people are quick to respond.

The program provides a forum for airing problems and complaints; at the same time it clues management in regarding important employee concerns.

CLEANING THE PIPELINE

Consultant Buse cites three ways to keep the pipeline clear:

1. Executive-run meetings with employees and supervisors.
2. Employee opinion surveys.
3. A functional open-door policy.

The three work best in combination, he stresses.

Meetings, Mr. Buse says, should be limited to 10 to 15 people, mixing job classifications and departments. They should last no more than 45 minutes. Specifics should be discussed; supervisors and line employees should be asked about their jobs, their problems and ideas for improvement.

When action is taken on problems and ideas that are aired, it convinces employees that management is sincere. Which, in turn, encourages frank communication.

Surveys are valuable, Mr. Buse reports, because they protect worker anonymity. "An opinion survey cuts through the hierarchy, gets right to the point. Often, what employees complain about verbally is merely symptomatic of far-removed, deep-seated problems."

Providing an open-door policy that is something more than lip service, he adds, requires strong management conviction and support. It implies an end to the time-worn concept of backing the foreman, right or wrong. "A bad foreman," the consultant contends, "can wreck an organization."

Management, he says, must get the idea across to employees that they have free access to higher management. At the same time, they're encouraged to talk over problems with their foreman first.

"Few presidents have time to rely exclusively on first-hand, person-to-person communication," notes New York City management consultant Henry O. Golightly, president of Golightly & Co. International, Inc. "Still, no president can afford to ignore this method. Nothing else he does will bring him as close to the rank and file."

By the nature of his job, he adds, the boss rarely hears the blunt, hard truth. Managers tend to paint a rosy picture. They don't actually lie, merely apply bright colors and ignore the dark. If you don't get into the thick of it yourself, the version you hear is apt to be distorted, he thinks.

Most top executives try to get around the office or plant whenever possible and talk directly to people. Nucor Corp.'s Mr. Iverson knows a surprising number of his 1,800 employees by name. Mrs. Lambeth likes to go through the furniture factory at least once a day. She touches base frequently with other members of the top team. If she can't make the rounds herself, the chairman or executive vice president usually takes over the task.

Following this policy sometimes uncovers oddball tribulations. Some time ago Mr. Iverson decided to outfit truck drivers with "snappy" uniforms. "Outside of our salesmen," he told them, "you're the only company representatives our customers see."

Eisenhower jackets, special shirts and ties were provided. Shortly after, Mr. Iverson received an anxious letter from a worker's wife. She was worried about the effect her husband's new look would have on the girls at the stops he made. At least get rid of the neckties, she pleaded.

The president's close relationship with his people enabled him to talk over the problem with the driver and arrive at a compromise solution. He agreed to wear the necktie when he drove his truck, but to leave it in his locker when he went home.

DO THEY MEAN WHAT THEY SAY?

How can you assess what you're told? There's no foolproof system. Says Erwin-Lambeth's Executive Vice President R. S. Powell: "You can't measure attitudes without applying judgment based on experience and intuition."

Patience, adds Chairman J. E. Lambeth Jr., is essential in reading attitudes accurately.

"Half truths resulting from impatience in getting the whole story create more misunderstanding than any other factor I know," he says.

Another key factor, says Conoco's Personnel Vice President A. B. Slaybaugh, is an executive's sour response to bad news. "If your people get the message that such news angers or irritates you, they're liable to think twice before leveling next time. Bad news, like any other information, should be dealt with positively and constructively."

However beneficial it may be to deal directly with people, realistically, most top executives are swamped with other high priorities. If such is the case, Mr. Hardesty notes, the executives should delegate person-to-person communication and keep in close touch with the delegates.

The personnel department, Mr. Slaybaugh believes, should be a top manager's right arm. "An executive should spend 70 per cent of his time, if he can, listening to people. If he can't, personnel should do it for him. A personnel manager's chief function is to listen—and hear."

How can you get people to tell you what they really feel?

Mr. Slaybaugh emphasizes the need for a positive approach to this business of problems and gripes.

"The trick," says Mr. Slaybaugh, "is to reward people for suggestions which improve any aspect of the operation. Recognition of some sort—a letter, money, a special commendation—should follow any good idea whether it directly saves money or not. Experience proves that if the climate is right for free expression, most employees will speak up."

"Dirty tricks" in reasoning and arguing

All errors or faults in reasoning go under the general term of "fallacies." They abound in arguments, especially in heated ones where every effort is being made to defeat the opponent holding an opposite view. One of the most likely places to find these fallacies at their deceptive best and worst is, of course, in advertising, where space and time limit the seller to very brief messages, thus tempting ad copywriters to exploit all manner of persuasive devices. But, in their ignorance, even the most honest and upright of people may be guilty of these same fallacies. Here are the major ones.

Use of emotion-arousing words ("purr" and "snarl" words)

Examples

The senator has strong *big money* support.
The senator is a *demagogue* who promises everybody everything.
His father liked the *finer* things of life.
His father was a *rounder*.

Begging the question: The point that is to be "proved" may suddenly be assumed to have been made, whereas nothing has really been offered as evidence except some repetition in perhaps slightly different language of the point to be established.

Example: "The mayor of our fair city has always said he would fight air pollution wherever he found it, and he has not changed his stand on that great issue which involves the health and well-being of all of us and our children. I have his letter here in hand promising to wage even a more vigorous campaign against pollution than ever. He deserves your support in the upcoming election for his outstanding record trying to clean up our air!"

To show how complex the explanations of these fallacies can be when given thorough examination, run through this one written by a student of argumentation.

ON BEGGING THE QUESTION AT ANY TIME[19]
by ROBERT HOFFMAN

In "Begging the Question, 1971" [ANALYSIS, 31.4 (1971], Richard Robinson suggests that the notion of begging the question is something of a muddle, for it is absurd to tell someone that his premise is true, that his conclusion follows from it, but that all the same his argument is bad because it "begs the question."

Perhaps we can get unmuddled as follows. An argument is *a set of propositions* of which one is claimed to follow from the other(s), which are regarded as providing evidence for the truth of that one. The least number of propositions an argument can comprise is two. Keeping this in mind, there are three possibilities to consider. (a) Here, begging the question consists in inferring the truth of the putative conclusion *not* from that of some *other* proposition, but from its *own* truth, posited as a premise. Accordingly, the same proposition is asserted twice, so the condition of there being at least two propositions is unsatisfied and there is no argument at all. When the putative argument does comprise two or more propositions, then either (b) the conclusion follows from some proposition *other* that itself, in which case the argument is valid and does not beg the question (though it may contain unnecessary premises), or (c) the conclusion follows *only* from itself posited as a premise, in which case the other premises are unnecessary and the putative argument, as in (a), is not an argument at all.

Thus, begging the question is a kind of defective reasoning, though not a kind of defective argument. It is the error of taking oneself to be presenting an argument when one is merely asserting the truth of some proposition.

Circular reasoning: Instead of dealing seriously with counterarguments or criticisms, the spokesman for a particular point of view may merely dismiss them as being "wrong" and keep coming back to his own view of the problem, which, he may admit, is also unsatisfactory.

Example: Here is one against gasoline rationing:

Making the coupons transferable and thus converting what would otherwise be a black market into a white one relieves some problems. Not only would it aid compliance, it would also reinstate the role of the market. A high trading value for the coupons would hold down driving. But we would fool ourselves by giving room to the hope that tradable coupons eliminate the problems of rationing. They would exacerbate the question

[19] From *Analysis* 32 (December 1971): 51.

who should get how much, because they are essentially a gift of money. They would shift bootlegging from the retail to the wholesale level. And if we like the white coupon plan because it employs the market principle, how about just relying on an uncontrolled price without rationing and without controls? The argument goes around in a circle, finding something wrong with every solution. It will be a choice among mounting evils, and the longer we can postpone and ultimately perhaps avoid it, the better.[20]

The appeal to questionable authority: A statement or testimonial by someone not qualified to give expert opinion may be cited as evidence.

Example: "You're worried about what's right and what's wrong about this situation? All you have to do is remember what John Mitchell said: 'When the going gets tough, the tough get going.'"

Argument by false analogy: Since an analogy is a form of argument which assumes that if two things are alike in several respects they must be virtually identical, a "false analogy" would be one wherein the points of difference between the two things are stronger than the points of resemblance.

Example: "The United States is on the brink of disaster. Remember the Roman empire fell when its armies were made up of professional soldiers, when its citizens cared only for bread and circuses, and when its religious beliefs decayed! Well, our armed forces today are largely made up of professionals, violent professional football games and crime films fill our TV screens, and our churches on Sunday remain more than half empty!"

Argumentum ad hominem: Instead of dealing with the vital issues of an argument or point of view, an unscrupulous opponent may instead attack the personal character and reputation of the one with whom he disagrees. This fallacy includes all forms of "character assassination" and "name calling" as well as attributing guilt through association.

Example: "You can't take his word for anything. He's got a criminal record. He was arrested for possession of drugs. Now don't try to tell me that only a quarter ounce of marijuana was found in his car! Wasn't he caught with two hippies as passengers?"

[20] From Henry C. Wallich, "Gasoline Rationing," *Newsweek*, 24 December 1973, p. 112.

Repeated affirmation: Instead of giving relevant evidence, the person under attack may merely continue to repeat his claims.

Example: "I tell you I'm not a crook! Every penny I've got I've earned legally. I'm innocent of all wrongdoing, and I can prove it. I will prove it. All attacks against me are lies, damned lies. I never took a dishonest cent in my whole life."

Verbal confusion: Language may be used to obscure unpleasant facts. This can also be called "circumlocution."

Example: "Good diplomats abhor outright lying. . . . They regard it as a sign of amateurism. Centuries of experience have gone into the building up of a pattern of acceptable circumlocution. There is a Chinese tale of a proud but mediocre chess-playing diplomat who one day lost three chess games in a row. A friend asked how he had done. The diplomat replied, 'Well, I didn't win the first game, and my opponent didn't lose the second. As to the third game, I asked him to agree to a draw, but he wouldn't.'"[21]

FOCUS POINT

1. Five kinds of thinking for writing
   a. Purposeful
   b. Daydreaming
   c. Indecisive
   d. Creative
   e. Meditative

2. Applied thinking
   a. Problem solving: the six-step "model"
   b. Deductive reasoning: the syllogism and enthymeme
   c. Original thinking
      i. Inductive reasoning
         (a) Socratic dialogue
         (b) Dialectical thinking
      ii. Intuition

[21] From William McGaffin and Erwin Knoll, *Anything but the Truth* (New York: G. P. Putnam's Sons, 1968), p. 64.

EXERCISES

1. Here are some general problem areas involving all manner of painful conflicts and solutions at cross-purposes. If one happens to hit you in a sore spot or suggests another problem you would like to try "solving," apply the six-step model of problem solving discussed in this chapter.
   a. What to do if—
      Your part-time job employer ("boss") is a real headache
      You wonder whether you have chosen the right field of study
      To register to vote you must identify with a political party
      You're the only boy (girl) in your family
      Your friends are older (younger) than you are
      You are at fault in an automobile accident
      Your roommate gives you a bad time
   b. There must be a better way to—
      Get an education
      Earn a living
      Get assignments done on time
      Live on a budget
      Finance college sport programs
      Identify those who really need help
      Make new friends
      Halt crimes locally
      Run a city

2. Read this criticism of a political science instructor written by a freshman and then answer the questions following it.

LEARNING IS AN EXPERIENCE

Dr. Poli Sci, you are boring me to death! I am told you are a dedicated teacher who loves students. Prove it. Take that dreary American Government class and put some "sock" into it. The way it is now, I might as well be learning how to speak a dead language or how to knit with my toes.

When I drag into the lecture hall, my mind, like Pavlov's dog, is conditioned. Immediately all senses slow down, interest dwindles, and the torturous phenomenon of the 50-minute lecture begins. As I was telling a friend the other day, when I am 5 minutes late for your class I really feel bad, because that means that I miss 5 minutes of a good nap. I know I'm not missing much, however, because on the days I have managed to stay awake I have noticed certain familiar teaching (?) methods. You always open your lecture with some lame apology for being late, being behind in the outline or whatever seems right for the day. I don't expect you to be infallible. You're not the pope, you know. Then comes the bearded lecture, straight from the yellowed notes. There are a few personal touches added, of course, such as reading from a textbook (which I have dutifully purchased) or rattling off some well-known quotation from your note memorization file. I also notice that if you do get off on some interesting tangent you promptly slap your hands, and retreat to the hallowed outline.

Obviously there is a crime being committed. Determining the criminal, however, is not as cut and dried as it seems. The students are at fault, too. It is our negligence that has allowed this farce to continue. We can't expect a professor to be actively involved in an education which we ourselves take passively. In fact our passivity probably amplifies lack of interest for a doctor of Political Science, who is teaching an introductory class.

I do think if you improve your attitude, then students will do the same. Restate your goal as a teacher frequently, and don't lose sight of who you are. To your students, among others, you are a valuable source of feedback to questions that arise in the course of discovery. You are also a living example that tedious facts can be conquered and that they can be useful. You are someone to be interacted with, not a side show to be stared at and forgotten when the hour's over.

I really feel like a dummy as I mechanically copy down your profound statements. Get me involved. Dare me to think and respond. When you make one of those erroneous statements like "Every president since 1900 has been a great president," say it with the kind of emphasis that provokes me. I don't want to be a sponge that merely soaks up information and squeezes it out on examination day. Please don't waste my time like that!

If I had this I would do things differently. I would require that the students do more than just memorize parts of the constitution which can be looked up in any eighth-grade history book. I would run my class like a democratic government. I'd be president and the students would be the congress. I would deliver one concise, well prepared State of the Union message each week and the other two days congress would be in committee. Each committee would investigate some aspect of government covered in the text and report to the joint session its findings. Since there is bound to be dissent in any organized government, I would ask that the Resistance outline a suitable course of action for themselves. If they couldn't think of something original, I would suggest term papers, or objective tests. And since grades are unavoidable, there could be a Supreme Court. There are real possibilities here. The judges could be sociology or political science majors (working on a term project), graders, or maybe even the dissenters.

From my point of view as an individual student, this type of class would be a great deal more appealing. But don't take my word for it. Find out how your students feel. Make an evaluation sheet for your classes to fill out. Obtain reactions to your class as it is, and concrete suggestions for improving it.

Prove that a democracy can be run effectively. Encourage your congress (students) to be specific. Make them define how you (the president) are to execute the laws of the classroom which they set up for you. You have the veto power, give your congress, at least, the power of legislation. From the propaganda I've been fed, I assume that in the USSR or Red China, a political science class would be taught by an authoritarian instructor, but what a way to teach democracy!

Questions:
   a. What is her problem? How does she make you feel it is one important to her?
   b. What kind of problem is it—*fact* or *change of policy*?
   c. How does she show she knows what she is talking about?
   d. What is her first logical "solution"?
   e. Does she offer any alternatives?
   f. Do you think she has found a solution that would work? From what she has said of him, could her instructor make it work?
   g. Has she sold you on her solution? Do you have a better one?

3. As an effort to be "creative" and "original," describe as accurately and vividly as you can a deliberate experiment in *awareness* as you have experienced it. You want to see more, hear more, and otherwise become more observant of things in a particular situation than you ordinarily might. Some suggestions:

Entering an automobile early in the morning
Riding to the campus on a bus
The first cup of coffee of the day
Waiting in a laundromat
Waiting for a late instructor to arrive
Waiting in a dreaded office
The atmosphere of a place of work
Coming home late at night
A dinner with friends
Sitting on a park bench

4. On the editorial pages of a local newspaper, find an editorial, a column, or a letter from a reader which you consider exhibits "dirty tricks" argumentation. Attach the clipping to your critical analysis of the article.

6

Development: Putting It All Together

Learning to write well is a gradual and complicated process: gradual because there is so much to be learned, and complex because all things one needs to know cannot be learned at one and the same time. It involves, as we have seen, mysterious thought and feeling processes which must be made, somehow, to work in harmony; it requires a working knowledge of sentence syntax and basic paragraphing, and above all it demands some richness of vocabulary and familiarity of how words can be made to work their magic.

In this chapter we shall try to draw all of these necessary features together, but again we must defer extensive discussion of other important aspects of effective writing—*style* and *rhetorical tone*—to still another chapter.

AIMS OF DISCOURSE

By now you are already familiar, surely, with the basic formula employed by academic scholars and professional authors alike in their respective kinds of periodicals. You know the general functions of the three basic parts of that composition model: the *introduction,* which attracts the reader's attention and leads into the topic or thesis to be discussed or argued; the *body,* which presents a chain of related paragraphs wherein significant points and their supporting details are presented; and, finally, the *conclusion*, the summing up or drawing to a climactic judgment.

These three functional parts appear in one form or another in almost all kinds of writing, such as the examples in the accompanying table grouped according to their basic purposes: *expressive*, having for its purpose the establishing of viewpoints and expressing intentions; *referential*, which is analytical and informative in purpose; *literary*, which intends to delight and instruct; and *persuasive*, which seeks to change opinion or move to action.

FOUR BASIC AIMS OF DISCOURSE

EXPRESSIVE	REFERENTIAL	LITERARY	PERSUASIVE
Of Individual	*Exploratory*	Short story	Advertising
Conversation	Dialogues	Lyric	Political speeches
Journals	Seminars	Short narrative	Religious sermons
Diaries	A tentative	Limerick	Legal oratory
Gripe sessions	definition of . . .	Ballad, folk song	Editorials
Prayer	Proposing a solution	Drama	
	to problems	TV show	
Of Social	Diagnosis	Movie	
Minority protests		Joke	
Manifestoes	*Scientific*		
Declarations of	Proving a point by		
independence	arguing from		
Contracts	accepted premises		
Constitutions of	Proving a point by		
clubs	generalizing from		
Myth	particulars		
Utopia plans	A combination of both		
Religious credos			
	Informative		
	News articles		
	Reports		
	Summaries		
	Nontechnical		
	encyclopedia		
	articles		
	Textbooks		

SOURCE: From James E. Kinneavy, "The Basic Aims of Discourse," *College Composition and Communication* 30 (December 1969): 302.

As shown here by Professor Kinneavy, the four "basic aims of discourse" are Expressive, Referential, Literary, and Persuasive. Different as these aims and their listed "examples" are, all of them are compositions sharing in one way or another the design model we have spelled out. What is more, whether it be a "utopian plan" or an "editorial," it also will draw upon the intellectual-emotional energies and modes discussed in our earlier attempts to show how composition topics grow out of observation of details and how such details lead the writer to his conclusions.

CLASSICAL STRUCTURE

Both the model and the means of developing a subject for a composition or a speech can be traced back to the Greeks and especially to Aristotle and, later, to the great Roman rhetorician, Cicero, who saw composition design from this point of view:

And since all the activity and ability of the orator falls into five divisions, I learned that he must first hit upon what to say; then manage and marshal his discoveries not merely in orderly fashion, but with a discriminating eye for the exact weight as it were for each argument; next go on to array them in the adornments of style; after that keep them guarded in his memory; and in the end deliver them with effect and charm. I had also been taught that before speaking on the issue, we must first secure the goodwill of our audience; the next we must state our case; afterwards define the dispute; then establish our allegations; subsequently disprove those of the other side; and in our peroration expand and reinforce all that was in our favor, while we weakened and demolished whatever went to support our opponents.[1]

The "five divisions" Cicero speaks of are *Exordium* (opening), *Partition* (statement of issues), *Argumentation* (evidence and reasoning), *Refutation* (attack on opponent's argument), and *Peroration* (summing up). Although this organizational structure was primarily designed for speeches to be given during debates on matters of state affairs—such as war, trade, crime, and public morality—it still provides a useful basic model for essays dealing with controversial questions of the kind listed in the above chart as "social" and "scientific."

[1] *De Oratore*, trans. E. W. Sutton and H. Rockham (Cambridge, Mass.: Harvard University Press, 1942), p. xxxi.

METHODS OF DEVELOPMENT

Whether you are writing an argument or merely trying to explain or explore an idea that has occurred to you, you will have to depend upon paragraph forms as your larger unit of expression after the sentence. Every paragraph has its own particular part to play in the development of that idea or the communication of the impressions associated with it. And just as we have seen the sentences in the paragraph work together, providing coordinating and subordinate ideas to support the statement made by the topic sentence, so also in the full-length theme or article each paragraph serves to support the main statement or thesis.

Think of every paragraph as one making its own distinct and special contribution to the whole by doing well its particular task. What these "tasks" can be has already been touched upon in the section dealing with paragraphs, but how they work together to "build" a composition can be seen if one understands all that paragraphs can do.

To begin with, here is a list of the various functions and types of information that can be provided in paragraphs:

Example or illustration	Process
Definition	Analysis
Comparison	Classification
Contrast	Description
Analogy	Anecdote

All of which can be summed up in yet another abstract term: *details.* Whether in the sentence or in the paragraph, the literary functions these words stand for make up the basics of communications, in *all* the media: newspapers, magazines, films, radio, and television broadcasts. Master them and the rhetorical tones described in the next chapter, and you can be well on your way to becoming an adept and resourceful writer.

Granted, it is one thing to be able to recognize these special functions at work in a paragraph and still another and more difficult challenge to write one yourself; but still, taking a close look at some models illustrating these paragraph tasks should be enlightening.

Process

Taking up the steps of a process, one after the other, in chronological and logical order is well illustrated in this excerpt from James Jones's novel about student revolt in Paris, *The Merry Month of May*. (The first paragraph is included to identify what is being done.)

> Place Maubert when we came out into it was still a mess. But it was being cleaned up, the burnt-out cars had disappeared, and a crew of Italian specialists were re-laying the paving stones ripped up by the student rioters. This was still back before somebody in the Government decided to replace the ripped-up paving stones with asphalt. We stopped a minute to watch them work.
>
> They were beautiful to watch. The men who laid the stones worked on their knees or else worked bent way over, swinging, at the waist. Each master stone-layer had two apprentice workers, one who kept him supplied with two creeping piles of the stones on his right and left which moved slowly forward with him as he worked. The other prepared and smoothed continually with a shovel the bed of sand on which the stones were laid, afterward throwing and sweeping in the sand that filled the minute spaces between the stones. Every so often the stone-supplier, usually a youth, would reject and throw out to the side a stone that was either too large, too small or too unevenly hewn. He would throw out about one stone in seven. But the stones he passed were not at all that evenly matched, and that was where the miracle came in. The master stone-layer, without ever bothering to look at it, would reach behind him for a stone, heft it, heft it maybe several times, toss it so that another face of the roughly squared stone came down in his palm, perhaps toss it again, looking quickly all the while at the six or seven available places in front of him for laying the next stone. Then he would place it, smoothing and adjusting with his other hand the already smooth sand under it—and it would fit. Occasionally he would heft a stone and then toss it aside and pick up another. They worked amazingly fast, 15 to 20 seconds to lay a stone. Inches away right beside them just beyond the tapes which protected them the reinstituted traffic whirred down the one-way Boulevard toward the river on the surface of paving stones that had already been replaced.[2]

As in the explanation of any process, Jones in this report of what his narrator noted as he watched has not only given the reader the essential materials and the kind of skilled workers required but also the fundamental principle essential to the whole process. In this one, that essential is the ability of the master artisan to decide swiftly which of the possible six or seven open spaces would be the best one for a particular stone handed him by his assistant. Given thus are items essential to all explanations of a process: the materials, the conditions for their use, the special skills of the workers, and the basic operating principle needed to be observed.

[2] James Jones, *The Merry Month of May* (New York: Delacorte, 1970), p. 144.

Description

Paragraphs of description require this same care in enumeration of details that make up a dominant impression, which may be spelled out or only suggested, as it is in this excerpt from *The Works of Love* by Wright Morris.

> Will Brady lived in the room at the front, over the screen door that slammed with a bang, in a room that was said to be suitable for Light Housekeeping. To get to this room he walked up the stairs, along the bright-green runner of roach powder, and at the top of the stairs he took the door on his left. It opened on a small room with two windows on Menomonee Street. The window on the left was cut off by the bed, but over the years and through many tenants one window in the street had proved to be more than enough. On a winter afternoon it might even be warm, as the slanting winter sun got at it, and be leaning far out one could look down on the street and see the park. An ore boat might be honking, or the sounds of the ice breaking up on the lake.
>
> Inside the room was a small gas plate on a marble-topped washstand, a cracked china bowl, a table, two chairs, a chest of drawers, an armless rocker, an imitation fireplace, and an iron frame bed. Over the fireplace was a mirror showing the head of the bed and the yellow folding doors. The bed was in the shape of a shallow pan with a pouring spout at one side, and beneath this spout, as if poured there, a frazzled hole in the rug.
>
> To get from the stove to the sink it was better to drop the leaf on the table and then lean forward over the back of the rocking-chair. On the shelf over the sink were four plates, three cups and one saucer, a glass sugarbowl, two metal forks, and one bone-handled spoon. On the mantelpiece was a shaving mug with the word *Sweetheart* in silver, blue, chipped red, and gold. In the mug were three buttons, a roller-skate key, a needle with a burned point for opening pimples, an Omaha street car token, and a medal for buying Buster Brown shoes. At the back of the room were the folding doors that would not quite close.[3]

In the first of these three paragraphs, in telling us about Will Brady the narrator gives us details of movement. We are taken up the stairs to the "door on his left" which is opened for us to see immediately the two windows. We not only are made to accompany Will Brady up to the room but are also made to visualize through sense-image words much of what Brady is experiencing. We hear the "bang" of the screen door and then see, perhaps even smell, the "bright-green runner of roach powder."

[3] Wright Morris, *Wright Morris: A Reader* (New York: Harper & Row, Inc., 1970), pp. 196–97.

We are likely to feel something of a claustrophobic sensation at seeing "the window on the left . . . cut off by the bed," just as we may feel the "warmth" of the "winter sun" and the sensation of "leaning far out" the window, and hearing the ore boat "honking."

The second paragraph well illustrates a more static scene, but the image of the bed "in the shape of a shallow pan with a pouring spout" ends as a most dynamic one. In the third paragraph, at the start we are again on the move, being taken into close examination of one object after the other, down to "a needle with a burned point for opening pimples"! Throughout this description of Will Brady's room we are deluged with minute details, but it is left up to us to form a generalization regarding them. In each paragraph we are asked to supply the topic-sentence idea, thereby making us feel immersed in the room details as if we were voyeurs. Yet this whole description is itself only detail in Morris' portrayal of the character and life of this "antihero," Will Brady.

Analogy is another dramatic way of making a point. It consists of relating two unlike things or situations by selecting the features they have in common. To be effective, however, the points of similarity must be stronger than those of difference between the two. Here is an analogy written by a student interested in a law enforcement career.

The open system of police organization, which is also found in the military, resembles an automatic sprinkler system. In the system you have a timing device which determines when the sprinklers are to be turned on; a valve which at the signal from the timer opens, allowing the water to pass to the sprinklers and then on to the lawn. After a prescribed length of time, the timer signals to shut the system off. What makes this an open system is the fact that it will continue to operate as it was originally programmed, irresponsive to the surrounding conditions. It might be pouring rain outside; nevertheless the sprinklers will come on, making it possible for the system to do more harm than good. Now most "modern" police departments operate exactly in this fashion. Orders or commands come down through the ranks to be carried out by the people on the street. These orders, or policies, are largely established on the basis of old concepts of "cops and robbers," which experience has demonstrated to be largely ineffective. What is wrong with this system is the lack of "feedback" from the officers actually doing their daily work.

Contrast

Whereas analogy stresses the similarity of things, *contrast*, an equally effective means of showing the implications of an abstract idea, relies upon revealing the differences. How well contrast serves to expand upon a general statement with dramatic detail can be seen in this observation made by Cecil Beaton, one of the arbiters of fashion in this century.

> Our pace of life has quickened so that women's features now reflect the frenzied, insecure age in which they live. Women's eyes used to be wistful. Today few possess serene eyes; they do not mind creases in their brows and often wear a frown on their foreheads. Young girls are proud of their high cheekbones and a flat hollow in their cheeks, whereas fifty years ago cheeks were fully rounded. Latterly the rather prehensile mouths have replaced the rosebud of yesterday. Whereas make-up was used only by *cocottes* in the Victorian and Edwardian heydays (ladies used to slap their cheeks and bite their lips before entering a ballroom to obtain a higher colour), any woman without lipstick today appears anaemic. Hair dyeing has become so general that it is not kept a guarded secret. Eyebrows, instead of being arched or wearing the old-fashioned startled look or the look of pained surprise, are slightly raised towards the outer edges, even acquiring a mongolian look. After twenty years of eyebrow plucking, eyebrows do not grow as thickly as they did.[4]

This paragraph of contrasts is only one of four taking up the general topic of how changing notions of beauty dictate what Beaton calls "physiological transformations." The other three contrasts with women of the last century deal with the "scraggy *decolletage*" (busts) of today versus "wonderful" ones of yesteryear, the "monumental" beauty of well-fleshed women versus the "thin, flat hips" of the present, and even the disappearance of "pudgy little hands with dimples and pointed fingers" to be replaced by the now woman who "holds her handbag . . . with her thumb sticking out at a tangent." It is apparent that to make striking use of contrast one must not only have a good fund of information regarding details, but also feelings strong enough on the subject to make the choice of language appropriate to the stance.

Example

The general and the abstract statement immediately becomes meaningful and concrete if it is followed by an *example*. Examples are specific instances which attest to the truth of the thesis or topic sentence or any other statement of judgment. Julian Bond, the well-known young

[4] Cecil Beaton, *The Glass of Fashion* (New York: Doubleday & Company, Inc., 1954), pp. 285–286.

black legislator from Georgia, wrote a "Foreword" for a recent book on black people and their chances for economic betterment in business. In this essay Bond ends one paragraph with a general statement and then begins a new one with a specific example.

> A dominating reality in American society is its racism and the implementation of effective programs and cures will not willingly be done for us.
>
> · For example, instead of more measures addressed to the real needs of Blacks, President Nixon has put forth Black capitalism. Here is a man who cannot help but know that capitalism has yet to solve the problems of white poverty, yet he offers a pitifully underfinanced public-relations gimmick as an answer to our needs. What we need is not Black capitalism but something more properly called "community socialism," that we may have profit for the many instead of the few; so that neighborhoods and communities shall have the major say in who gets what from whom. Black people need to find ways to control what we can. This includes our politics, our economy, and other aspects that give us a greater measure of control over our own destiny.[5]

Semanticists call this kind of pinning down abstractions to particular instances "coming down the abstraction ladder." It is a good protection against falling into the practice many beginning writers have of delivering nothing but generalizations, making wide sweeping statements, never trying to fit them to everyday situations or realistic problems. Students who discover the immediate interest that specific examples arouse also are happy to find that this likewise takes care of the problem of "finding enough words" for a composition assignment. As the Julian Bond excerpt shows, once an example has been provided, it opens up other ideas. For Bond moves on from his dissatisfaction with Nixon's "Black capitalism" proposal to "What we need is not Black capitalism but something more properly called 'community socialism' . . ." This is another abstract term that requires even more specific details than it receives.

Illustration

An *illustration* resembles an example, but it often takes the form of a short narrative or incident clarifying the point to be made. Since the illustration partakes of the nature of narrative, it may resemble a short story in structure and so have a main character who has encountered an

---

[5] Julian Bond, in *Black Business Enterprise,* ed. Ronald W. Bailey (New York: Basic Books, Inc., Publishers, 1971), p. x.

obstacle or difficulty that arouses some suspense in the reader. Like a short story, it may well work up to a climax, or intensity of interest, and then be immediately followed by a resolution of that conflict. The illustration as narrative appeals to the imagination and emotions of the reader and strives for empathy or identification. In these respects it is a powerful means of supporting a thesis or viewpoint, but its weakness as logical "proof" lies in the fact that a single instance showing the apparent working of some general rule does not establish the validity of that rule. What follows is a student essay relying upon an experience for an illustration which the student insists is authentic.

A FLASH OF DEJA VU

by LAURIE JANE BOXER

When I was 14 years old, I had a memorable spiritual experience which has influenced my thinking ever since.

I had gone to visit my father, who was then living in Rome, Italy. I had pictured Italy many times in my dreams, sleeping and waking, and I was curious to see how closely reality would resemble those images. I had done some travelling before this, from my home on the west coast to New York and Chicago to visit relatives, and I knew that it was often startling how a place never seemed like you thought it would look.

When my father met me at the airport I had already been through Italian customs and had re-claimed my baggage. I was surprised at how easy it had been to understand the few words of Italian that had been spoken to me—I had hardly needed the translations that followed when they learned my citizenship. I supposed that the phrase book I had glanced at on the plane had helped a lot. When I told my father this, he laughed and said, "You're lucky. I've been taking lessons for a year and I still can't understand anyone!"

We got a taxi-cab and my father gave the address of his pension. As soon as I heard the name of the street, I knew just where the cab would go. I played a game in my mind; the cab would come to a corner and I would guess which way it would turn. I was right every time. Places that we passed looked familiar to me. They awakened feelings that had been dormant for a long time, and I supposed it had to do with seeing my father after a long separation. But after awhile I did notice something that struck me.

These buildings that I was passing, these little plazas, fountains, streets, were all just like my dreams of Italy. There was none of the usual discrepancies between the dreams and the realities. This was *exactly* as I had pictured it.

When we finally arrived at the pension I recognized it, or thought I did. I pointed to a large grey stone building, a very old building that had been re-built many times from the look of the architecture. "That's it!" I cried out to my father. I knew this place, it was like coming home. But he stopped me, telling me that we were going to be living in the next building, a more modern building. I was a little put off by this and I still looked back at the other house as we started to climb the steps.

When I was shown to my room, however, the feeling returned stronger than before. I was filled with emotions that I couldn't have named. These feelings had to do with the room. I felt a great longing for something half-forgotten.

Suddenly I knew beyond a doubt that I had lived here before. The room was darkened, with the shutters closed to block out the afternoon sun. I stood before that window for a long time, knowing just what I would see outside. Finally I pulled back the curtains, loosened the latch on the shutters and looked out. Tears filled my eyes as I saw what I knew was a very familiar scene. There was the old stone bench, sagging from hundreds of years of use. I had sat on that stone bench, in good times and bad, and I had thought many deep thoughts about life and its meaning, sitting on that bench. Did I ever think that someday, in some other life-time, I would come back to have another look at that place? And there, unchanged, was the stone wall that I had climbed in the days when I laughed and played with . . . . the name was gone now, but I could so clearly remember those happy days.

Everything I saw from that window was known to me. I had lived here before.

As I was taking in all of these overwhelmingly familiar sights, the lady in charge of the pension came in to see how I liked my room. I told her it was wonderful, and that I especially liked the view from the window. "Oh yes," she said, "It is indeed a lovely little courtyard. This building was re-built after the last war, you know. At one time these two buildings were one large one. They are still both owned by the same man." So now I knew why the other house had seemed more familiar from the outside!

This experience led me to read about reincarnation and to discover that my feeling of "deja vu" was indeed a very common one. I have come to believe that I have lived many other lives. And I agree with Voltaire, who said, regarding this subject, "It is no more remarkable to be born twice than to be born once."

Classification

The ability to sort things out, to bring together related ideas, and to put aside those that are not relevant is of special value to the writer.

He relies upon the processes of *classification* and develops the habit of trying always to categorize experiences, people, and ideas. In seeking to bring similar ideas together in his mind, naturally he also engages in other forms of thinking, such as analysis and even invention. Through analysis he is able to examine in detail facts and theories for their bearing upon one another and then decide upon their appropriateness; he may even have to invent new categories.

How utilitarian this process of classification is can be seen in a visit to any supermarket, where you find canned goods, detergents, paper stocks, fresh vegetables, meats, dairy products, and all other merchandise most systematically shelved and displayed. Every stock clerk becomes expert in defining and classifying. Relying upon this order and arrangement, you, as a shopper, can immediately locate the products you wish to buy. Granted it's a big jump from being able to walk directly to canned sliced freestone peaches to being able to organize your thoughts for a composition—still the mental processes involved are not too unlike.

How classification becomes an important detail in a study of a literary work is well shown in this analysis of a famous novel:

> The use of crude language in *The Catcher in the Rye* increases, as we should expect, when Holden is reporting schoolboy dialogue. When he is directly addressing the reader, Holden's use of such language drops off almost entirely. There is also an increase in this language when any of the characters are excited or angry. Thus, when Holden is apprehensive over Stradlater's treatment of Jane, his *goddams* increase suddenly to seven on a single page (p. 39).
>
> Holden's speech is also typical in his use of slang. I have catalogued over a hundred slang terms used by Holden, and every one of these is in widespread use. Although Holden's slang is rich and colorful, it, of course, being slang, often fails at precise communication. Thus, Holden's *crap* is used in seven different ways. It can mean foolishness, as "all that David Copperfield kind of crap," or messy matter, as "I spilled some crap all over my gray flannel," or merely miscellaneous matter, as "I was putting on my galoshes and crap." It can also carry its basic meaning, animal excreta, as "there didn't look like there was anything in the park except dog crap," and it can be used as an adjective meaning anything generally unfavorable, as "The show was on the crappy side." Holden uses the phrases *to be a lot of crap* and *to shoot the crap* and *to chuck the crap* all to mean "to be untrue," but he can also use *to shoot the crap* to mean simply "to chat," with no connotation of untruth, as in "I certainly wouldn't have minded shooting the crap with old Phoebe for a while."
>
> Similarly Holden's slang use of *crazy* is both trite and imprecise. "That drives me crazy" means that he violently dislikes something; yet

"to be crazy about" something means just the opposite. In the same way, to be "killed" by something can mean that he was emotionally affected either favorably ("That story just about killed me.") or unfavorably ("Then she turned her back on me again. It nearly killed me."). This use of *killed* is one of Holden's favorite slang expressions. Heiserman and Miller are, incidentally, certainly incorrect when they conclude: "Holden always lets us know when he has insight into the absurdity of the endlessly absurd situations which make up the life of a sixteen-year-old by exclaiming, 'It killed me.' " Holden often uses this expression with no connection to the absurd; he even uses it for his beloved Phoebe. The expression simply indicates a high degree of emotion—any kind. It is hazardous to conclude that any of Holden's slang has a precise and consistent meaning or function. These same critics fall into the same error when they conclude that Holden's use of the adjective *old* serves as "a term of endearment." Holden appends this word to almost every character, real or fictional, mentioned in the novel, from the hated "old Maurice" to "old Peter Lorre," to "old Phoebe," and even "old Jesus." The only pattern that can be discovered in Holden's use of this term is that he usually uses it only after he has previously mentioned the character; he then feels free to append the familiar *old*. All we can conclude from Holden's slang is that it is typical teenage slang: versatile yet narrow, expressive yet unimaginative, imprecise, often crude, and always trite.[6]

This kind of weighing and considering, of selecting and discarding elements that do belong together and those that do not, makes Professor Costello's inquiry into Holden's speech illuminating. The fact that Costello has, as he says, "catalogued over a hundred slang terms used by Holden" indicates also the time and care that classification can entail. So do not get discouraged and give up too soon when asked to try to sort out your own ideas and experiences in preparing to write a composition. Classification takes patience and real effort to bring matters into focus so that one can see points of similarity and difference and then go on to draw relevant conclusions.

FOCUS POINT

1. The three organizational parts of a composition—introduction, body, and conclusion—are derived from the classical "Five Divisions": *Exordium* (opening), *Partition* (statement of issues), *Argumentation*

---

[6] Donald P. Costello, "The Language of *The Catcher in the Rye*," *American Speech* XXXIV (October 1959): 91.

(evidence and reasoning), *Refutation* (attack on opponent's argument), and *Peroration* (summing up).

2. Paragraphs of details include the following means of opening up and developing an idea:

Example or illustration	Process
Definition	Analysis
Comparison	Classification
Contrast	Description
Analogy	Anecdote

3. These *details* are essential in writing all the basic forms of discourse.

TOPICS FOR DISCUSSION AND WRITING

1. Assume you are writing a composition which seeks to establish this thesis or conclusion: "I now think that one particular change yet needs to be made, and it is this one: (name the desired change) ."
Now to support that assertion, write at least one paragraph doing one of the following:
   a. *Describing* a typical scene or place that needs such change.
   b. *Comparing* or *contrasting* present viewpoints or practices with new policies or practices that should take their place.
   c. Telling in story form an actual experience you have had which *illustrates* why you believe this change is necessary.
   d. *Classifying* types of people or behavior you object to because these need to change.
   e. *Explaining* a process, a formula, or a method that has served you well.
   f. *Defining* the situation or problem you would have changed—what is its *general* nature and what are its *specific* characteristics that distinguish it from others of this kind? (A "shorthand" example: an economic *recession* is [in general terms] a period of low employment and limited activity in sales of all kinds [now moving toward the specific] which differs from a *depression* in that a *recession* is neither so severe nor so long-lasting.)

2. Write a critical report on a *type* of movie that appeals to you or disgusts you, but in your composition devote most of your attention

to one particular film seen recently that best embodies the features you admire or dislike. (You may wish to examine this type of film for its moral quality, its artistic skill or lack, its stereotypes or originality, etc.)

REWRITING YOUR PAPER

"We learn to write by rewriting" is a truthful observation if by "rewriting" we mean careful and critical examination and the willingness to revise according to clearly seen principles. Necessary for profitable rewriting is a strong desire, even determination, to improve: feelings involving self-respect and honest pride. And certainly good rewriting demands that one know the techniques and skills that characterize effective work.

That much being understood, we can go on to propose some general steps and means of improving that first draft which you have finally managed to hammer out but rightly fear can stand considerable improvement.

1. Let your work "cool off." Put it aside for at least several hours so that when you reread it your mind is not "plugging in" details that you have thought of but have not actually put down on paper. When you return to it then, you will be closer to the situation of your reader, who does not have the benefit of all the ideas you did not use and knows only what you have told him.
2. Read it aloud to yourself, imagining that you are reading it to your classmates, at least one of whom is going to say "What did *that* sentence mean?" Of course, you are going to find weak points of one kind or another. (Nobody is perfect, especially in a first draft.) Note them for revision.
3. Examine the whole thing for general organization. Does the "body" really have enough evidence in it to support the thesis of your "introduction" or the viewpoints or recommendations of your "conclusion"?
4. Now try to outline it, using as much as possible the standard outline form. (If you have worked from an earlier outline sketch, note how your essay follows or veers from that outline. You never felt you had to follow that outline slavishly, did you?)

A standard outline form

I. Introduction including a thesis statement or central purpose
II. First major point supporting the thesis or purpose
    A. First minor fact or idea supporting or illustrating this major point
        1. First detail amplifying "A"
        2. Second detail amplifying "A"
            a. Detail supporting "2"
            b. Detail supporting "2"
    B. Second minor point or idea supporting the first major point
        1. _____
        2. _____
III. Second major point supporting thesis or purpose
    A. _____
    B. _____
IV. Third major point
    A. _____
        1. _____
            a. _____
            b. _____
    B. _____
V. Conclusion

_____

5. Do your paragraphs relate to the outline so that each one deals with a specific aspect of your subject?
6. How are these paragraphs developed; by what kinds of details studied in this chapter?
7. Now consider the sentences in the paragraphs.
    a. Are they all "complete"? Does each make sense by itself?
    b. Do they relate to the topic sentence (whether stated or implied) of *this* paragraph as coordinate or subordinate details?
    c. Do they lack necessary transitions or connections?
    d. How about their punctuation? Would some be better joined together? Divided up?
8. Examine your choices of language. Why did you use *that* word?
    a. Is the language appropriate to your stance?
    b. Is it economical and not redundant?
9. For further improvement of your style, consult Chapter 7.

7

Rhetoric and Style

From all that has been said so far about language in general, dialects in particular, sentence and paragraph forms, and logic, it should come as no surprise to anyone to be told that he or she already has a distinctive *style* of self-expression and also a practicable knowledge of *rhetoric*. For anybody today who remains alive and functioning certainly is skilled in at least one dialect that is "correct" and that, therefore, enables him to be highly communicative in the social group with which he identifies. He can "speak the language," dress in the mode, and socially behave in fashions approved of by his peers; he may even be accepted as an innovator or "creator."

What is more, he may have learned to function equally well in other social groups. Should a black, a Chicano, or an Indian, for example, so desire and have the opportunities, he can learn to adopt any number of dialects and life styles as well as the value systems that govern those social classes. Through training and/or education, it is possible to become adept and, therefore, accepted in trades and professions each of which has its own vocabulary (jargon), its own governing traditions, and its own social patterns — in short, its own style.

And any person thus having an appropriate speaking or writing style also has, knowingly or unknowingly, acquired skills in rhetoric. He has learned *how* to use language and the specific psychological strategies necessary to help him cope with the problems in communication everyone faces in any given society. Whatever their eccentricities, individuals when they are "on the job" speak and act in the appropriate style:

attorneys as practitioners of law, teamsters as truck drivers, accountants as business-record analysts, clergymen as ministers, and teachers as instructors. Housewives also speak and act as such in their homes and at PTA meetings, students do the same in classrooms, and even drug pushers on city streets have their own style. All have a variety of styles and a considerable range of verbal strategies aimed at persuading others.

In fact, whatever our style of "roles" and "games" in life, all of us become so confirmed in them that we tend to be blind to the "styles" of others. We even think our "picture" of the world is the only reality and that anyone who disagrees with it is "wrong" and "unreal." Thus, consciously or unconsciously, we use rhetoric to keep our narrow visions intact and to attack all who even appear to threaten what we think we stand for.

Style thus reflects the *image* a person has of himself, or the one he would like to have. And just as individuals have such identifiable styles and rhetorical patterns, so do great nations. The United States under the Richard M. Nixon administration certainly had a deplorable "image" both at home and abroad because of White House "styles" of scandals and political rhetoric. The Soviet Union's style and rhetoric regarding its famous novelist, Alexander Solzhenitsyn, who has revealed the barbarism prevalent in the Stalin era, has not been able to improve its social image. And meanwhile the reports of journalists on the People's Republic of China under Mao and the rhetoric of his famous "Red Book" reveal tremendous efforts to mold a whole new society modeled on a "workers'" life style.

ETHICS AND RHETORIC

The two closely related terms, "style" and "rhetoric," can be most important to all speakers and writers, for we are affected by what they signify and how they operate, even though we may not be aware of them as words. Because they are so closely related they are difficult to define and distinguish. But as "the art of persuasion," rhetoric has had a long tradition. In its origins with Plato, Aristotle, and Cicero, the study of rhetoric was always identified with "what is good and true." Those trained speakers and writers who valued "winning" or scoring a point more than they did the common good of society were scornfully labeled "sophists" and their arguments "sophistries." In its traditional best meaning, rhetoric is the art of establishing confidence and trust in the *voice* of the writer so that the reader-audience will identify with him in the cause or purpose he wishes them to act upon or accept. Central to the following discussion of rhetoric is the notion of an honest man, thinking clearly, presenting his logically developed argument, with an intent to move other men to his way of thinking.

As in so many instances, we begin by invoking Aristotle, even in this era of swift and compelling change that sometimes appears to seek the defoliation of the past. Rhetoric, he tells us, is the faculty of observing the available means of persuasion. That persuasion grows out of the personal character of the rhetorician, who is capable of instilling a certain attitude in the audience and whose language provides a proof or an apparent proof for the point he wishes to argue. He is a man who sincerely believes that he knows the truth about something and who desires to secure that truth among members of his audience and throughout his entire community. To do so, he must be sharply aware of the intricacies of the human mind; he must also have a conception of what is right and what is good; in addition, he must have the will to reason painstakingly and the ability to think logically; and finally, he must be aware of the inclinations and desires of his audience without himself being disposed to pander to those among it.

In the broadest sense, then, rhetoric has to do with knowing about argumentation. It is only in the narrower and more restricted sense that it has anything to do with the ornamentation and polish that cling to the surface of a written or spoken text. There is an ethical foundation to rhetoric, and the configurations of language that ultimately give the statement its outward form owe their existence to the security of that foundation. The rhetorician's chief devices are the sharpness of his mind and his eye, the genuineness of his consideration for the audience, the sincerity of his character, and the authenticity of his convictions. If ornamental polish or elegantly asserted style do exist in an effective sample of rhetoric, it is there only because the speaker or writer has discovered the means of effective persuasion, whereupon he could then invent techniques of getting his argument across to his audience convincingly. The eloquence of his words, the structure and cadence of his sentences, and the pattern and unity of his organization—not necessarily important in themselves—depend fundamentally upon his awareness that he is a man striving to persuade other men, and to persuade them with justification. Students should make that initial assumption about the rhetorician and his art, regardless of how our understanding of the term rhetoric has shifted since Aristotle's time.[1]

[1] From Christopher Katope and Paul Zolbrod, *The Rhetoric of Revolution* (New York: The Macmillan Company, 1970), p. 192.

RHETORICAL STANCE

Putting all of these features together, we can group them under the general heading of "rhetorical stance," meaning by "stance" an emotional or intellectual attitude. Stance is the term first given popularity by Wayne C. Booth, who regards it as "the available arguments about the subject itself, the interests and peculiarities of the audience, and the voice, the implied character of the speaker. I should like to suggest that it is this balance, this rhetorical stance, difficult as it is to describe, that is our main goal as teachers of rhetoric."[2] Stance thus includes everything that goes into the makeup of one's mental-emotional attitudes in preparation for speaking or writing in order to inform others, to persuade them to think or act in a desired manner, or to give them delight and pleasure by appealing to their imagination and feelings.

Rhetoric, then, cannot be considered apart from style, which is the term given for the means whereby such desired effects upon the reader-audience are attained. All writing and speaking to any purpose, therefore, involves some choice of styles, and anyone who has read extensively as well as attentively has a wide variety of styles he can draw upon to produce the particular results he wants. Naturally, he will settle upon one that is in harmony with his temperament and tastes. A Neil Simon, whose talents run to comedies like *Barefoot in the Park*, would not easily turn to writing tragedies, nor would an Arthur Miller, whose tragic view of life is reflected in dramas like *The Death of a Salesman*, readily choose light comedy. Yet it is possible, as the works of William Shakespeare attest, for a genius to master many literary styles and forms, just as an artist like Picasso could move from one school, or style, to another and even create his own unique forms.

STYLE AND INDIVIDUALITY

The implication of these statements is that every writer deserving to be read tries in his work to find the right form, the right tone, the right language for that particular work so as to make it bear his own personal stamp. As Walter Pater, the great English stylist, explained decades ago in his famous essay, "Style," this kind of artistic conscientiousness and

[2] From "The Rhetorical Stance," *College Composition and Communication* 14 (October 1963): 141.

responsibility to one's best self is part of style, even when one is trying not only to write good imaginative literature but also to present a fact:

> The line between fact and something quite different from external fact is, indeed, hard to draw. In Pascal, for instance, in the persuasive writers generally, how difficult to define the point where, from time to time argument which, if it is to be worth anything at all, must consist of facts or groups of facts, becomes a pleading—a theorem no longer, but essentially an appeal to the reader to catch the writer's spirit, to think with him, if one can or will—an expression no longer of fact but of his sense of it, his peculiar intuition of a world, prospective, or discerned below the faulty conditions of the present, in either case changed somewhat from the actual world. . . . For just in proportion as the writer's aim, consciously or unconsciously, comes to be the transcribing, not of the world, not of mere fact, but of his sense of it, he becomes an artist, his work *fine* art; and good art (as I hope ultimately to show) in proportion to the truth of his presentment of that sense; as in those humbler or plainer functions of literature also, truth—truth to bare fact, there—is the essence of such artistic quality as they may have. Truth! there can be no merit, no craft at all, without that. And further, all beauty is in the long run only *fineness* of truth, or what we call expression, the finer accommodation of speech to that vision within. —[WALTER PATER, *"Style"*]

No one has argued this point of the individuality of writing styles better than Louis T. Milic, and he does so on the basis of these assumptions:

1. A writer's style is the expression of his personality.
2. A writer must write in his own style.
3. A writer can be recognized in his style.
4. No writer can truly imitate another's style.
5. The main formative influences on a writer are his education and his reading.
6. A writer's language is governed by the practice of his time.
7. Language changes gradually with time.[3]

Many acute readers find special pleasure in trying to glimpse "the voice" in what they read:

[3] Louis T. Milic, "Against the Typology of Styles," in *Essays on the Language of Literature*, eds. Seymour Chatman and Samuel R. Levin (Boston: Houghton Mifflin Company, 1967), p. 443.

I have found by spontaneous experience more and more that even the aesthetic pleasure of a poem depends for me on the fineness of the personality glimpsed between its lines; on the spirit of which the body of a book is inevitably the echo and the mould. — [F. L. LUCAS, *The Decline and Fall of the Romantic Ideal*]

A man's sense of the world dictates his subjects to him, and this sense is derived from his personality, his temperament, over which he has little control and possibly none, except superficially. It is not a literary problem. It is the problem of his mind and nerves. These sayings are another form of the saying that poets are born not made. A poet writes about twilight because he shrinks from noon-day. He writes about the country because he dislikes the city, and he likes the one and dislikes the other because of some trait of mind or nerves; that is to say because of something in himself that influences his thinking and feeling. So seen, the poet and his subject are inseparable. — [WALLACE STEVENS, *The Necessary Angel*]

SPECIAL RHETORICAL TONES

Like that of everyone else, it is true, your writing style is personal and individual and may even be distinguished from the styles of others. It reveals the richness or the poverty of personality, the command or the lack of literary skills. It also wins or loses for you the reactions you desire from your readers on occasions. For whenever words go down on paper, some form or other of what we have so far described as rhetoric begins to be built into the composition, and makes those words, intended specifically or not, to have some direct, immediate effect upon whoever reads them. And one of the most important features of rhetoric is tone, which has already been touched upon several times but now deserves fuller treatment by itself.

Tone can be defined as the character and temperament of the voice that the observant reader "hears" as he takes in what is being said. In the analysis of poetry, this tone, this voice may be called the *persona*; in fiction, it is the *narrator*. Tone sounds with the mood and state of mind the writer sustained while bringing his work to its conclusion. It is the quality present in work that makes readers say to themselves things like: "This guy's great!" "That's telling them off!" "What a bore!"

Parody

To illustrate this matter of uniqueness of styles, perhaps nothing serves better than the rhetorical strategy of *parody*. By approximating as closely as possible the way an author will typically react, think, and express his views in some given situation, the parodist ridicules the style while sedulously aping it. Parody thus involves exaggeration of characteristic mannerisms, vocabulary range, approach to subject, and degree of distance ordinarily maintained between himself and his reader-audience.

Here is how William Safire, a columnist for the *New York Times*. took off six of his fellow daily columnists whose distinct styles may be found in newspapers across the country. To really appreciate the originality of the styles being parodied, try comparing one or the other with a recent example of the columnist's work.

HOW IT (ANYTHING) LOOKS DEPENDS ON WHERE YOUR WINDOW IN THE IVORY TOWER IS LOCATED[4]

by WILLIAM SAFIRE

Washington, 1862—President Lincoln announced today his intention to free the slaves in those states still in the rebellion as of Jan. 1, 1863. White House aides referred to the press handout as an "Emancipation Proclamation" and characterized it as a "major statement." A fictional roundup of comment:

by a MARY MCGRORY

So the word finally crashed through the barrier erected by his "secretaries," Nicolai and Hay, to the wise-cracking warrior that cartoonists have come to know and love as "The Big Baboon," that the Civil War is not being fought about preservation of the Union after all, but about the abolition of slavery. It's about time.

Lincoln's name may be on the document, but the real authors are Wendell Phillips and William Lloyd Garrison, who were out marching in the streets while Honest Abe was doffing his stove-pipe to the gang who tried to tag "Copperhead" on the people who believe in peace and human freedom . . .

by an EVANS AND NOVAK

At a stormy, secret Cabinet meeting two months before the Emancipation Proclamation, Postmaster General Montgomery Blair—the only man with political savvy still close to the increasingly isolated and morose President—warned Lincoln that the move could spell disaster for candidates in the midterm elections.

By polling bellwether-beaten districts chosen for us by psephologist Oliver Scammonberg, we find four border states—Maryland, Kentucky, Delaware, and Missouri—are still loyal and highly necessary to the Union cause. But they are slaveholding states. At the urging of vote-conscious Blair, Lincoln watered down his edict to apply only to Confederate states.

Even so, proslavery sentiment in the North is likely to cause a political whiplash. Barring bombshells, insiders say anti-Lincoln forces will sweep New York, Pennsylvania, Ohio, Indiana and Illinois, all states Lincoln carried years ago.

by a WILLIAM BUCKLEY

The rodomontade accompanying the White House statement—"Emancipation Proclamation" has a mouth-filling quality—obscures one of the *recherche* ironies of this administration. Here is a President freeing slaves (on paper, at least) and at the same time imprisoning thousands of his countrymen unlawfully, denying them the basic Anglo-Saxon right to habeas corpus. Can we expect to hear a mighty roar from liberal abolitionists on that issue, sensitive as they are to the cause of human freedom? As Gen. Nathan Bedford Forrest said only last week, "I told you twice, goddammit, no."

Although the assault by central government on private property is troubling, the constitutional principle of the equal creation of men must control, which is why conservatives can support the restoration of certain muniments, if not the aureate rhetoric, of this "proclamation. . . ."

by a C. L. SULZBERGER

One must assume that the primary reason for Mr. Lincoln's Emancipation Proclamation was to influence the government of England not to enter America's Civil War on the side of the South. Antislavery sentiment among England's workingmen is high, and no British leader, much as he would like to encourage a Southern victory that would enhance England's dominance, can afford to oppose it.

Thus the emancipation is seen by observers here in Ulan Bator, strategic nerve center of Outer Mongolia, as a diplomatic-military masterstroke. . . .

by an ART BUCHWALD

Now that emancipation is here, everybody wants to be a slave. My friend, Simon J. Legree, who has just become a management consultant to Little Eva Industries, thinks now that slavery is on the way out, nostalgia for it will grow. "Chains and flogging turned a lot of people off for awhile," says Simon. "But now they're coming to see the advantages: No taxes, no responsibilities, no jury duty. . . ."

by a JAMES RESTON

The trouble with Mr. Lincoln's proclamation is that it deals with the politics of the problem and not the problem itself.

The President, in seeking a compromise, has freed the slaves in only those states in which his government has no power to enforce emancipation, and has not freed the slaves in those states where his government does have the power to enforce it. That's why the mood pervading this capital today is somewhat cynical, holding that the proclamation is a lot of weak talk, and this is especially difficult for the wives.

The problem has not lent itself to a political solution, which is why we're fighting a Civil War. "Preservation of the Union," a worthy goal, is a political abstraction. Slavery is another matter—a profound moral issue—and it can no longer be ducked, compromised about or postponed. Mr. Lincoln will soon have to take an unequivocal moral stand.

As the yet-unborn Walter Lippmann will one day write, "...

To a great extent it is tone that often serves to stylize a composition, for as Kenneth Burke points out, we always adopt a mode of "telling" which serves what we feel is our need and which thereby also "stylizes" what we say.

But let us try out a hypothetical case. Suppose that some disaster has taken place, and that I am to break the information to a man who will suffer from the knowledge of it. The disaster is a *fact*, and I am going to *communicate this fact*. Must I not still make a *choice of stylization* in the communication of this fact? I may communicate it "gently" or "harshly," for instance. I may try to "protect" the man somewhat from the suddenness of the blow; or I may so "strategize" my information that I reinforce the blow. Indeed, it may even be that the information is as much a blow to me as it is to him, and that I may obtain for myself a certain measure of relief from my own discomfiture by "collaborating with the information": I may so phrase it that I take out some of my own suffering from the information by using it dramatically as an instrument for striking him. Or I may offer a somewhat similar outlet for both of us, by also showing that a certain person "is to blame" for the disaster, so that we can convert some of our unhappiness into anger, with corresponding relief to ourselves.

Now, note that in every one of these cases I have communicated "the fact." Yet note also that these are many different *styles* in which I can communicate this "fact." The question of "realistic accuracy" is not involved; for in every case, after I have finished, the auditor knows that the particular disaster, about which I had to inform him, has taken place. I have simply made a choice among possible styles—*and I could not avoid such a choice.* There is no "unstylized" feature here except the disastrous event itself (and even that may have a "stylistic" ingredient, in that it might be felt as more of a blow if coming at a certain time than if it had come at a certain other time—a "stylistic" matter of timing that I, as the imparter of the information, may parallel, in looking for the best or worst moment at which to impart my information).[5]

What Burke is saying is important, for it reveals the complex of feelings and impulses that come before a word is uttered or put down on paper. Before he can begin communicating even a plain fact, we see, the writer or speaker can hardly avoid making choices in the manner and tone he deems most appropriate to the situation. These "choices" are, in turn, determined, as Burke also says, by the *motives* (feelings, interests, hopes, fears, desires, etc.) prompting him to make those choices and thereby also ultimately shaping the style of what is said:

The motivation out of which he writes is synonymous with the structural way in which he puts events and values together when he writes; and however consciously he may go about such work, there is a kind of generalization about these interrelations that he could not have been conscious of, since the generalization could be made by the kind of inspection that is possible only *after the completion of the work.*[6]

FOCUS POINT: RHETORIC AND STYLE

1. Rhetoric calls for a dialect appropriate to the audience.

2. Style reflects the image a person has of himself.

3. All writing and speaking to any purpose involves some choice of styles to find the right form, tone, and language in order to inform, move, or amuse a particular audience.

4. Tone is the character and temperament of the writer's voice as the observant reader "hears" it.

[5] Kenneth Burke, *The Philosophy of Literary Form* (New York: Vintage Books, 1957), p. 109.

[6] Ibid.

TOPICS FOR DISCUSSION AND WRITING

1. Imagine you have been asked by the local officials of a most deserving charity to write a letter appealing to college-age students for financial support or donation of voluntary labor.

2. In defense of some campus cause, program, or undertaking, write a letter to the editor of your campus newspaper wherein your stance clearly shows your awareness of the situation and its importance to the college community.

How various rhetorical tones can be traditional, even be ancient, and yet lend themselves to individual voices most effectively—whatever their *motives*—is a study always surprising for what one can learn from it. Let us begin with a tone you may have thought (before reading Burke) had no personal "sound" at all.

News report

The following brief news item deserves close reading.

SEARCH ABANDONED

North Bend, Wash. (UPI)—The search for two young girls buried by a thunderous snow avalanche Sunday was called off after the extreme threat of more slides kept rescue workers holed up in a ski lodge all day Monday.

Shortly before the search was cancelled until better weather moved into the area, a sheriff's deputy said relatives of the girls "have pretty much given up hope" that their daughters would be found alive.

There it is, a typical news "story" written by a reporter using the "inverted pyramid" design of beginning with the essential who—what—when—where—why information and then adding as many details as space in the column will allow. In two one-sentence paragraphs, both together totaling only 71 words, we are given the "facts," including even a partial quotation of a deputy sheriff's report of the family's assessment of the situation.

Does the "story" have a style apart from its standard formulaic design? Does it have a special tone?

It does, indeed have a tone—an *objective* one almost brutally detached from all of the emotions inherent in the tragic situation. The reporter gives only the external events—the search called off by rescue workers "holed up in a ski lodge all day Monday." Yet the whole first sentence sketches enough details to engage the imagination of compassionate readers: how terrifying the sound and sight of the "thunderous snow avalanche" must have appeared to the "two young girls" enjoying a Sunday ski outing on the slopes; how the rescue workers "holed up" in the ski lodge must feel as they look out the lodge windows at the fresh storm preventing further probing with 25-foot long sticks for those girls buried two days before by that sudden "thunderous snow avalanche"; and how the rest of the family must regard the scene, leading them to say much more than the brief summary of the deputy's words tells us.

Had the reporter vividly communicated these emotional aspects, however, he could not have maintained the dispassionate objectivity favored by newsmen, and the result would probably have been sentimentalization.

Sentimental narrative

Empathy and *pathos* are traditional terms for emotions aroused in audiences or readers. Empathy occurs when the audience-reader "feels with" the character who is central to the story; it happens to us when we unconsciously join in the action we are witnessing or reading about by crying out or using "body English" to help the character with whom we identify. We may find ourselves embarrassed after shouting "Look out!" in the middle of a moving picture performance when our hero is about to make a fatal blunder. Pathos is the name of the emotion we feel for those "innocent bystanders" of sad events who really are in no way responsible for their own downfalls. The kind of narrative called "sentimental" commonly arouses a related quality of emotion, *bathos*, and even seeks to arouse it for its own sake—to "bathe" in it.

Incidents wherein people innocent of any but the most forgivable of mistakes suffer anguishing afflictions make up the traditional fare of sentimental literature. In such narratives the virtuous undergo, at least for a time, a succession of heartbreaking losses and mishaps while evil incarnate appears to triumph. It is a world of only two values: the good and the bad, and the "good" must be rewarded either by prosperity and/or a sure place in heaven.

Sentimentalism has been defined as "a harmonizing of the true, the good, and the beautiful, which is at the same time a harmonizing of self-love and self-approval with benevolence,"[7] an apt description of what it means to be "moved to tears." The writer governed by motives requiring him to fashion language patterns that will so move his readers thus seeks to create characters doing good deeds in a world of good intentions with which readers are happy to identify because they feel they are such fine souls themselves. It is this aspect that William Van O'Connor stresses in his definition: "The sentimentalist inclines to express greater emotion than the occasion warrants and to find satisfaction merely in indulging his feelings. The sentimental poet achieves his effects by narrowly selecting detail that will intensify the emotional impact, by treating an experience more seriously than it deserves."[8]

Almost anywhere one opens to a page in Oliver Goldsmith's *The Vicar of Wakefield,* one finds a passage exemplifying the sentimental tone. Goldsmith wrote it as a "potboiler" to keep from starving in his garret on Fleet Street, the scribbler's row of London. See if you can detect the rhetorical means this prolific eighteenth-century author employed to "move" his readers.

CHAPTER XXII. OFFENSES ARE EASILY PARDONED WHERE THERE IS LOVE AT BOTTOM

The next morning I took my daughter behind me, and set out on my return home. As we travelled along, I strove, by every persuasion, to calm her sorrows and fears, and to arm her with resolution to bear the presence of her offended mother. I took every opportunity, from the prospect of a fine country through which we passed, to observe how much kinder heaven was to us than we were to each other, and that the misfortunes of nature's making were very few. I assured her that she should never perceive any change in my affections, and that during my life, which yet might be long, she might depend upon a guardian and an instructor. I armed her against the censures of the world, showed her that books were sweet unreproaching companions to the miserable, and that if they could not bring us to enjoy life, they would teach us to endure it.

The hired horse that we rode was to be put up that night at an inn by the way, within about five miles from my house, and as I was willing to

---

[7] Alan Dugald McKillop, *The Early Masters of English Fiction* (Lawrence, Kans.: University of Kansas Press, 1956), p. 88.

[8] *Sense and Sensibility in Modern Poetry* (Chicago: University of Chicago Press, 1948), p. 131.

prepare my family for my daughter's reception, I determined to leave her that night at the inn, and to come for her, accompanied by my daughter Sophia, early the next morning. It was night before we reached our appointed stage; however, after seeing her provided with a decent apartment, and having ordered the hostess to prepare proper refreshments, I kissed her and proceeded towards home. My heart caught new sensations of pleasure the nearer I approached that peaceful mansion. As a bird that has been frighted from its nest, my affections out-went my haste, and hovered round my little fire-side with all the rapture of expectation. I called up the many fond things I had to say, and anticipated the welcome I was to receive. I already felt my wife's tender embrace, and smiled at the joy of my little ones. As I walked but slowly, the night waned apace. The labourers of the day were all retired to rest; the lights were out in every cottage; no sounds were heard but of the shrilling cock and the deepmouthed watchdog, at hollow distance. I approached my little abode of pleasure, and before I was within a furlong of the place, our honest mastiff came running to welcome me.

It was now near mid-night that I came to knock at my door; all was still and silent; my heart dilated with unutterable happiness, when, to my amazement, the house was bursting out in a blaze of fire and every aperture was red with conflagration! I gave a loud and convulsive outcry, and fell upon the pavement insensible. This alarmed my son, who, perceiving the flames, instantly waked my wife and daughter, and all running out, naked, and wild with apprehension, recalled me to life with their anguish. But it was only to objects of new terror; for the flames had, by this time, caught the roof of our dwelling, part after part continuing to fall in, while the family stood, with silent agony, looking on as if they enjoyed the blaze. I gazed upon them and upon it by turns, and then looked round me for my two little ones; but they were not to be seen. O misery! "Where," cried I, "where are my little ones?" — "They are burnt to death in the flames," says my wife calmly, "and I will die with them." That moment I heard the cry of the babes within, who were just awaked by the fire, and nothing could have stopped me. "Where, where are my children?" cried I, rushing through the flames and bursting the door of the chamber in which they were confined. "Where are my little ones?" — "Here, dear papa, here we are," cried they together, while the flames were just catching the bed where they lay. I caught them both in my arms and snatched them through the fire as fast as possible, while just as I was got out, the roof sunk in. "Now," cried I, holding up my children, "now let the flames burn on, and all my possessions perish. Here they are, I have saved my treasure. Here, my dearest, here are our treasures, and we shall yet be happy." We kissed our little darlings a thousand times, they clasped us round the neck, and seemed to share our transports, while their mother laughed and wept by turns.

I now stood a calm spectator of the flames, and after some time, began to perceive that my arm to the shoulder was scorched in a terrible manner. It was therefore out of my power to give my son any assistance, either in attempting to save our goods or preventing the flames spreading to our corn. By this time, the neighbours were alarmed, and came running to our assistance; but all they could do was to stand, like us, spectators of the calamity. My goods, among which were the notes I had reserved for my daughters' fortunes, were entirely consumed, except a box with some papers that stood in the kitchen and two or three things more of little consequence, which my son brought away in the beginning. The neighbours contributed, however, what they could to lighten our distress. They brought us clothes and furnished one of our outhouses with kitchen-utensils; so that by day-light we had another, tho' a wretched, dwelling to retire to. My honest next neighbour and his children were not the least assiduous in providing us with everything necessary and offering whatever consolation untutored benevolence could suggest.

When the fears of my family had subsided, curiosity to know the cause of my long stay began to take place; having therefore informed them of every particular, I proceeded to prepare them for the reception of our lost one, and tho' we had nothing but wretchedness now to impart, yet to procure her a welcome to what we had. This task would have been more difficult but for our recent calamity, which had humbled my wife's pride and blunted it by more poignant afflictions. Being unable to go for my poor child myself, as my arm now grew very painful, I sent my son and daughter, who soon returned, supporting the wretched delinquent, who had not courage to look up at her mother, whom no instructions of mine could persuade to a perfect reconciliation; for women have a much stronger sense of female error than men. "Ah, madam," cried her mother, "this is but a poor place you are come to after so much finery. My daughter Sophy and I can afford but little entertainment to persons who have kept company only with people of distinction. Yes, Miss Livy, your poor father and I have suffered very much of late; but I hope heaven will forgive you."
During this reception, the unhappy victim stood pale and trembling, unable to weep or to reply; but I could not continue a silent spectator of her distress; wherefore assuming a degree of severity in my voice and manner, which was ever followed with instant submission, "I entreat, woman, that my words may be now marked once for all: I have here brought you back a poor deluded wanderer; her return to duty demands the revival of our tenderness. The real hardships of life are now coming fast upon us; let us not therefore increase them by dissention among each other. If we live harmoniously together, we may yet be contented, as there are enough of us here to shut out the censuring world and keep each other in countenance. The kindness of heaven is promised to the penitent, and let ours be directed by the example. Heaven, we are assured, is much more pleased to view a repentant sinner, than many persons who have supported a course of undeviating rectitude. And this is right; for that single effort by

which we stop short in the down-hill path to perdition is itself a greater exertion of virtue than an hundred acts of justice.

Both the incident and the language that narrates it are clearly designed to arouse sympathetic emotions in the readers. Here is a noble and forgiving father bringing back to her home the "lost" daughter who has been living in shame in the city. And what misfortune does he encounter just when his generosity and paternal love should be rewarded by "heaven"? His house ablaze and his other children awaiting his rescue! Then though badly burned and homeless, he retains his stern but charitable paternal character, reconciles the family to "the unhappy victim," and restores all to "our former serenity."

Goldsmith's language abounds with terms and expressions meant to suggest Christian forbearance, charity, and acceptance of daily ills without complaint against Providence. The tone of trust and faith has made this idealized picture of the noble poor a moving one for millions of readers over the past two centuries. In almost every line one finds expressions such as these:

"O misery!"	"joy of my little ones"
"honest mastiff"	"the down-hill path to
"my poor child"	perdition"
"to ease the heart"	"my heart dilated with
"a repentant sinner"	unutterable happiness"
"our good neighbours"	"the rapture of expectation"
"untutored benevolence"	"censures of the world"
"kindness of heaven"	"I hope heaven will forgive
"tender embrace"	you"

Goldsmith's sympathetic readers would agree with the father, the Vicar who narrates this story, that "books were sweet unreproaching companions to the miserable, and that if they could not bring us to enjoy life, they would teach us to endure it." Reading such sentiments, they would feel the kind of virtuous benevolence and self-approval our definitions of sentimentalism specify.

A question: Now that you may be feeling benevolent and warmhearted about such simple, good people, can you recognize their descendants as characters the daily TV "soap opera" series such as "As the Earth Turns," "Days of Our Lives," "All My Children," "Guiding Light," and "Doctors"? And what are the lingering influences upon novels and films like Eric Segal's *Love Story?*

EXERCISES

1. Select one of the following "news" items, and by using your imagination enlarge upon the basic facts of the news account and try to
write a "sob sister" report, wherein you seek to arouse very sympathetic feelings in your readers for the "victims." The tone should be
"sentimental," but take care! It is only too easy to go over the line
into the maudlin or totally absurd.

   a. *Rathdrum, Idaho* (AP)—Where proof is lacking, rumors fly. And Kootenai
   County authorities say they continue to receive new reports that missing
   Ron and Rita Marcussen are the victims of a cult murder.

   The young couple was last seen Nov. 19, and clues to their where-
   abouts have been nearly nonexistent. But rumors of satanic killings intensify and authorities are concerned.

   "This is getting completely out of hand, completely warped out of
   proportion," said county Chief Criminal Deputy Harry Button. "It's out
   and out fantasy. These stories are thick in the area, and in Spokane, and
   people are terrorized for no reason. I could go on for hours about how sick
   these rumors make me feel."

   But others accept them. Spokane County Sheriff William J. Reilly
   wants people to stop spreading the stories because they are untrue and
   "getting out of hand." Button says the "whispering campaign" must stop.

   "We've got people absolutely terrified," he said. "They're afraid to go
   out at night. They lock their doors. They jump at trees. It's horrible."

   b. *Washington*—President Nixon Friday reacted to the criminal indictment
   of seven former aides by urging the public to presume them innocent
   unless proven guilty.

   "The President is confident that all Americans will join him in recognizing that those indicted are presumed innocent unless proof of guilt is
   established in the courts," said deputy press secretary Gerald L. Warren.

   c. *Moscow* (AP)—The Soviet Union announced on Friday "successful completion" of a new series of missile tests that Western experts believe included the firing of a new rocket with multiple warheads.

   The missiles were fired from the Soviet Union into the North Pacific
   in a program that began Feb. 19. The original announcement said the tests
   would continue until March 10. But a Soviet news agency report said the
   firing had been completed. No explanation was given.

   d. *London* (AP)—Bernadette Devlin, one-time queen of the barricades in
   Northern Ireland, lost her place in the British Parliament on Friday, defeated by an extreme Protestant.

She was first elected for the Mid-Ulster district in April, 1969, after vaulting into prominence as a heroine of the Northern Ireland Roman Catholics in their fight against the British province's Protestant majority.

At 22, she was the youngest Member of Parliament. Her sharp tongue in Northern Ireland debates and the birth of an illegitimate daughter won her frequent headlines.

She married Michael McAlaskey, a school teacher two years her junior, on her 26th birthday last April 23. By then she had dropped from the front pages.

Campaigning as Mrs. McAlaskey, she was beaten into third place in a four-way contest taken by Joe Dunlop. Dunlop, representing Protestant hardliners, polled 26,044 votes. Ivan Cooper of the Catholic-based Social Democratic party came next with 19,372.

Mrs. McAlaskey, crusading as an independent advocating a Socialist united Ireland, got 16,672 votes.

e. *Jacksonville, Fla.* (AP)—When her husband died last year, 85-year-old Rosa Owens had to sell her home for $1,050 to pay for the funeral.

The state then refused to give Mrs. Owens welfare, saying she had violated regulations by selling the property for less than its assessed value of $2,885.

Mrs. Owens appealed and Thursday a three-judge federal panel ordered the Florida Division of Family Services to put the Jacksonville woman on welfare and pay her what she should have drawn since last May.

f. *Washington*—The nation's birth rate declined sharply again in 1973, indicating that the trend to smaller families shows no signs of tapering off.

With the exception of a two-year interval, the birth rate has been declining steadily ever since the post-war baby boom ended in the mid-1960s.

Both the birth rate and a more precise measurement called the fertility rate are now at the lowest point since the U. S. government began gathering reliable statistics early in this century.

The absence of any signs that the decline is slackening continues to surprise demographers.

"It's a continuation of what we've been seeing, but it's still a surprise to everyone who studies this phenomenon," said Charles Westhof, professor of demographic studies at Princeton University and former director of the U. S. Commission on Population.

"You would think that there would be an upturn at some point, especially now when the children of the baby boom are in the child-producing years.

"But it's not happening. What you're getting now, in fact, is an absolute decline in the number of babies being born, not just a reduction in the rate."

Most authorities attribute the continuing decline to a combination of new attitudes—a desire for fewer children, greater acceptance of abortion, and more widespread use of contraceptives.

Lately, there has been speculation that economic conditions may have a substantial effect on the birth rate and economic bad times tend to encourage couples to have fewer children.

g. *Ann Arbor, Mich.* (AP)—A Ku Klux Klansman, stricken with terminal leukemia, held a deathbed news conference and said he bombed 10 school buses in Pontiac in August, 1971.

Elmer Tackett, 54, said he set and lit dynamite fuses that destroyed the buses the day before a court-ordered school desegregation busing plan was to go into effect.

Tackett, a motel manager, held the news conference in his room at the University of Michigan Hospital at the urging of his attorney. His statement was recorded by a court stenographer.

He admitted being a member of the Ku Klux Klan at the time of the bombing and said he carried out the job on the instructions of an anonymous caller with the aid of a masked accomplice whom he could not identify.

Five other men were convicted in federal court last year of conspiracy to bomb the buses. All are serving prison sentences.

Tackett, a Kentucky-born former coal miner, said doctors have given him two weeks to live. He said he made the statement about the bombing "to clear my conscience."

He was hopitalized four weeks ago. A doctor diagnosed his illness as leukemia last January.

He said the five convicted men did not participate in the actual bombing. "There was only one man who had anything to do with the bombing—that was me," he said.

Tackett said he bombed the buses because he opposes school busing, adding, "I would do it (the bombing) a dozen times."

h. *Vancouver, Wash.*—Police Friday continued their search for the driver of a hit-and-run vehicle which killed a wheelchair patient Wednesday night.

Killed was Harold Joseph Gable, 53, who lived alone near the scene of the accident on Fourth Plain Boulevard.

Gable was struck apparently on his way to a nearby market. He was traveling west against traffic, next to the curb. The area does not have sidewalks.

Gable's smashed wheelchair was reported by a passing motorist. Police found the body about 40 feet away, against the side of a building.

Self-assured, personal voice

There are times when the occasion, the subject matter, and the writer's own state of mind require that he speak out in his own voice and to do so he unabashedly adopts the first person pronoun—*I*. It is natural, then, even expected, that he explain, argue, describe, and relate whatever he wants to say in his own characteristic *persona*. Instead of remaining detached from his subject, he candidly expresses his opinions, likes, and dislikes. For example, in place of an impersonal statement such as this one: "The American oil companies must share the blame for the big jump in fuel prices and should not try to appear innocent in their institutional advertisements," an indignant syndicated columnist like Tom Wicker of the *New York Times* will make his criticism personal in this manner: "To begin with, and whatever the effect on newspaper and television profits, I, for one, point the finger of fault at pious, self-serving, devious, mealy-mouthed, self-exculpating, holier-than-thou, positively sickening oil company advertisements in which these international behemoths depict themselves as poverty-stricken paragons of virtue embattled against a greedy and ignorant world."— [20 February 1974]

There is no mistaking that personal disgust and anger as an outspoken highly individual statement. Nor can you mistake the stoical sincerity of the Ram defensive tackle, Merlin Olsen, in speaking of the injuries such a professional athlete must expect to endure:

> "I played 12 games in 1970 with a bad knee," said Olsen, "and I kept aggravating it. I knew it required an operation—both for torn ligaments and cartilage.
>
> "My feeling was that as long as I could operate efficiently, and I didn't take a horrible shot on the knee, I wasn't going to hurt myself worse by playing.
>
> "I knew the risks and was willing to assume them. I wouldn't have asked the Ram medical staff to assume them for me. I never used pain killers because I wanted to be conscious of the pain level. I didn't want to be hit and not know I had torn it more severely.
>
> "I think you reach a point of concentration in a game where you leave the conscious part of pain behind you, anyway, so you can concentrate on playing. The injury hurt me before the game, or at halftime, or when I was sitting on the bench, but rarely on the field."
>
> He found this to be true in the last game of the 1971 season, against Pittsburgh.
>
> "I got stepped on just before the end of the first half," Olsen said. "My hand was gashed open so I could see three of the bones. The pain was terrible. When we went in at halftime, I asked the doctors how long it would take to stitch it up. They said probably 45 minutes. I told them we didn't have 45 minutes.
>
> "So they taped it up and layered it with some gauze to absorb the blood. Afterwards, it took 40–45 stitches to close the wound.

"But I was only conscious of the hand a couple of times in the second half. I realized I'd lost some power in it. But as soon as I decided to play, the pain level dropped out of sight. I don't know if it was a form of self-hypnosis."

Then came the 1971 Pro Bowl.

"I was hit directly on the kneecap and my knee bent the wrong way about 15 degrees," said Olsen. "The minute that contact was made I could feel things starting to tear.

"I tried to get the foot out of the ground and couldn't. I couldn't stop my momentum, either. I was like slow motion. I could feel each muscle and ligament popping. Once I was on the ground, the pain was about as intense as anything I've ever felt. But the pain was with me only about 30 seconds. Then it was gone—totally.

"When I went in at halftime the doctors examined me. They'd pick up my foot and the knee would stay right on the table. I got off the table and went into the shower and the knee collapsed backward on its own. A couple of coaches were standing there and they turned white and almost passed out."[9]

Such "in character" language and point of view are features also of the voice of the *essayist*. Now do not let the term throw you, as it does some students when they are first asked to write "an essay" and do not realize that whenever anyone writes about a personal experience, an impression, a discovery of some kind, or an evaluation of life, nature, or human nature he is writing an essay. Traditionally, the essayist "speaks" in the first person and gives the impression that he is conversing intimately with readers who appreciate his sharing of experiences and ideas with them. The essayist tries his best, of course, to ensure holding the interest of his readers by taking pains to make his language as attractive as his subject matter.

The tone of the essay has often been described as a kind of "genial egotism," meaning that the author does not hesitate to disclose his own singular viewpoints, tastes, and experiences. As a genre of writing, the essay dates back to Michel de Montaigne, the sixteenth-century Frenchman who recorded his everyday observations and impressions. As the selection appearing below from his *Autobiography* shows, he did not seek to argue or to prove anything; he merely offered to share his novel discoveries with others who might find his insights and even his idiosyncrasies of language and style worth perusing. As he shaped the genre, the essay differs from diary or journal entries, which ordinarily lack the conciseness and polish of the essay. It can be said of any essayist who

[9] Dwight Chapin, "Painful Truth," *LA Times-Washington Post Service*, 20 February 1974.

deserves the readership he has garnered that he is "a real character," perhaps not the best of companions if met in person, but one who in print fascinates and disturbs with the unashamed frankness and vigor of his thoughts and feelings.

WHAT I FIND IN MY ESSAYS[10]

When I lately retired to my house I resolved, as far as I could, to meddle in nothing, but pass in peace and privacy what little time I had to live. It seemed to me I could not better gratify my mind than by giving it full leisure to dwell in its own thoughts and divert itself with them. And I hoped that, with the passage of time, it could do this with greater ease as it became more settled and ripe.

But the contrary was the case. Like a horse broke loose, it gave itself a hundred times more rein. There rose in me a horde of chimeras and fantastic creatures, one upon another, without order or relevance. To contemplate more coolly their queerness and ineptitude I began to put them in writing—hoping in time to make my mind ashamed of itself. A mind that has no set goal loses itself. To be everywhere is to be nowhere. No wind serves the man bound for no port.

I never set pen to paper except when an overdose of idleness drives me to it, and never anywhere but at home. My library is situated in a corner of my house; and if anything comes into my head to look up or write there, lest I forget it in walking across the courtyard—for I have no retention at all—I must commit it to the memory of someone else. So my book is built in scraps and intervals, often interrupted by long months of absence.

I have no sergeant to whip my ideas into rank—except chance itself. Sometimes they come trooping in single file, and sometimes by brigades; and as they come I line them up. I want the reader to see my natural and ordinary gait for the stagger it is.

I have sometimes been urged to write the events of our time by persons who fancy I view them with an eye less blinded by passion than others, and more particularly because fortune has given me intimate access to the leaders of our various parties. But they do not consider that to purchase even the glory of Sallust I would not spend the pains, and that there is nothing so contrary to my style as continuous narrative.

I am forever cutting myself short for lack of breath. My ability to compose or elucidate anything is worthless. I am more ignorant than a child of the phrases and even the very words to express the commonest things. This is why I have undertaken to say only what I know how to say,

[10] From *The Autobiography of Michel de Montaigne*, edited and translated by Marvin Lowenthal. Copyright 1935 and renewed 1963 by Marvin Lowenthal. Reprinted by permission of Alfred A. Knopf, Inc.

fitting my subject to my powers. Besides, my freedom of speech is so unbridled I would likely publish opinions that both reason and my own better judgment would condemn as indiscreet and unlawful.

Our judgment is a tool of all work. In my *Essays* I try it out on every occasion. If it is a subject I do not understand, even so I essay. I take soundings of the ford; and if it is too deep for me, I stay on shore. The knowledge our judgment gives us that we can proceed no farther is a virtue on which it prides itself. Sometimes, in an idle and frivolous subject, I see if my judgment can't supply it with body and give it a prop. Again, I exercise it on a worthy theme that has been tossed about by a thousand hands and where it can walk in the paths of others. In this case, its work is to select the best route.

But I have an apish nature. When I used to write verses (I did so only in Latin) they plainly showed the last poet I had read. Therefore I am loath to write on well-known topics for fear I'll handle them at another's expense.

I take the first subject chance offers me. They are all equally fertile for my purpose: a fly will serve. I do not intend to treat them exhaustively; for I never see the whole of anything—and neither do they who promise they will show it to us. Everything has a hundred angles and facets: I take up one, perhaps to give it merely a lick, again to lift the skin a bit, and sometimes to pinch it to the bone. I give a stab, not as wide but as deep as I can; and, very often, I like to turn a thing over in an unfamiliar light.

By tossing my ideas about—samples cut from the cloth and pieced together without pattern or promise—I am bound neither to answer for them nor to stick to them. I can drop them when I please; and return to my doubt and uncertainty, and to my dominant form, which is ignorance.

When I write I gladly do without the company or recollection of books, lest they hinder my style. Also, in truth, because the good authors take the heart out of me. I am of the same mind as the artist who painted cocks most vilely and used to forbid his lads to allow a live cock to enter his workshop. But I can scarcely do without Plutarch. No matter what you treat of, he is always at your elbow holding out to you an inexhaustible store of riches. I am vexed to be so tempted: I hardly ever finger him without stealing a wing or a leg.

It suits me, too, to write at home, in a rude countryside where there is no one to aid or correct me. I hardly know a man hereabouts who understands the Latin of his Paternoster, or as little if not less of French. I myself speak a somewhat different French in Paris than in Montaigne.

I might have done better elsewhere, but my work would have been less my own. And its principal aim and virtue is to be nothing but myself. I readily correct accidental errors, in which I abound, as I speed carelessly on. But the blemishes that are natural and common to me would be a sort of treason to remove.

When someone tells me, or I tell myself: "You overflow with metaphors—this is of Gascon vintage—that is a dubious phrase (I reject nothing which is current on the streets of France, for the man who would correct usage by grammar is a simpleton)—there's an ignorant opinion—now you go too far—here you fool too much—men will think you mean in earnest what you say in jest"—to all this I reply: "Do I paint myself to the life? It's enough. I am doing what I proposed. The man who knows me will meet me again in my book, and the man who knows my book will meet it again in me."

But what annoys me is that my mind usually strikes off its deepest and subtlest thoughts, and those that please me best, when I least expect them and am least prepared—on horse, in bed, or while at meals—but chiefly on horseback, where my brain is most active. And they will suddenly vanish before I can find means to put them down.

When I dream, I promise to remember my visions (for I am apt to dream that I dream); but next morning, while I can recall their general tinge—gay, sad, or strange—the harder I try to recapture them, the deeper I plunge them in oblivion. I find the same with the ideas that pop accidently into my head. I retain nothing but a vague image of them—just enough to torment me into a fruitless chase.

Watching the method of a mural-painter I have working for me, I was taken with the desire to imitate him. He selects the best place in the center of a wall to paint his picture, which he finishes with all his craft. The empty space around it he fills in with grotesques, fantastic figures whose only charm is their variety and extravagance.

And what are the essays I scribble if not grotesque and far-fetched creatures, lacking save by chance all order, continuity, and proportion? In this respect I follow my painter nicely. But I fall far short in the better and greater part of his task. I have not the ability even to dare undertake a rich and polished picture executed with the proper art.

Some writers are so ridiculous as to run a mile out of their way for a fine word. For my part, I would rather wrench a sentence to make it fit my thought than go a step from the road to look for the right expression. Words are made to follow and wait upon us. If the French won't come, let the Gascon serve. I want my subject to capture and inflame the imagination of my listener so he will have no time to remember the words. When I see a noble expression, I do not exclaim: *'Tis well said,* but *'Tis well thought.*

Fine minds set off a language not by introducing novelties, but through putting it to more vigorous and varied use by bending it to their own purpose. They do not create words, but enrich their meanings. The rarity of this talent may be seen from the many scribblers about us. They are brave enough not to follow the common highway, but their lack of discretion ruins them. Their writings show nothing but a pitiful delight in new and strange styles which, instead of enhancing, degrade their subjects. Provided they can plume themselves out in a new phrase, they are indifferent to what they say. To take up a new word they discard an old one, which often has more vitals and strength. A thousand poets drone on prosaically. But the best prose shines with the luster, vigor, and boldness of poetry, and not without a spark of its fire.

Whenever I take up my pen, I owe a sacrifice to the Graces, as Plutarch says of someone, in order to conciliate their favor. For they desert me throughout. Polish and beauty are wanting. When I choose a lively theme, it is to follow my own bent, which is enemy to all grave and ceremonious wisdom; it is to enliven myself and not my style—if I may call that a style which is a formless ungoverned speech, a popular jargon. I speak on paper as I do to the first person I meet. And I see well enough that I sometimes overdo it; and by trying to avoid affectation, I fall into it by a contrary route.

The titles of my essays do not always embrace their content. Often they denote it merely by a sign. It is the careless reader who loses track of the subject, not I. There will always be hid in a corner some word which, however hard to find, will not fail to bring him back.

I wander with indiscrimination and riot. My style and my mind are vagabonds together. You must play the fool a little, if you would not be thought wholly a fool.

I want my subject-matter to mark its own divisions: to show in itself where it begins, breaks off, rejoins, and ends, without my interlacing it with stitches and transitions made for dull ears—and without explaining my own explanations. Who doesn't prefer not to be read at all than read by drowsy, inattentive eyes?

If I can't arrest my reader by the weight of what I write, it is something, perhaps, if I can do it by my intricacy. "Yes, but he will repent afterwards that he ever bothered with you!" True—but still he will have bothered.

The numerous chapters into which I clipped the first part of my book seemed to me to dissolve the attention of my reader before it was aroused. On this account I have lengthened the later ones. The reader who is not willing to give an hour is not willing to give anything.

The stories I borrow I leave to the conscience of those I took them from. My conclusions are my own and depend upon reason, and every reader is free to add his own examples. If he knows of none, let him be wary of concluding that none exist—human experience is strangely rich and varied.

In the subjects I handle, which are our manners and behavior, imaginary examples are as pat as real ones, provided they are within the realm of possibility. Whether they actually occurred in Paris or Rome, to John or Peter, does not matter so long as human beings might have experienced them. I use the shadow as well as the substance of things.

Some authors propose to give an account of only those things that have happened; my purpose, if I can achieve it, is to tell what could happen. Yet in the examples I draw from what I myself have heard, read, said, or done, I have forbidden myself to alter even the most trivial circumstance.

My conscience does not falsify so much as a dot: what my ignorance may do, I cannot say.

No doubt I often speak of things that are better handled by masters of the subject, and with more truth. I merely give an essay of my natural faculties, and not of what I have acquired. If you catch me in a mistake, you will not embarrass me. I am not undertaking to be responsible to others in my writings when I am not responsible for them to myself—or even satisfied with them. The man who is in search of information should fish for it in waters where it swims. There is nothing I profess so little to provide.

I offer reflections of my own, in which I seek to disclose not things— but myself. As for the things, I may know them some future day, or perhaps I knew them once and will again if I can stumble on the passage where I found them.

Let no one, therefore, stress the matter I write, but the turn I give it. In what I borrowed, let them judge if I knew how to choose. I often make others say for me what I cannot say so well myself. I don't count up my borrowings: I weigh them. And they are almost all from such famous authors that they reveal their source without my explanation.

Sometimes I deliberately omit to mention the author in order to baffle those hasty critics who hurl themselves on everything, but particularly on living authors who write in our common speech—which seems to give everyone the right to criticize and to despise the works themselves as common. I want to see them give Plutarch a poke on my nose, and tear into Seneca when they think they are tearing into me.

I shall indeed be glad to have my feathers plucked by the hands of sound and clear judgment. For I hold myself responsible if I stumble over my own feet. Many faults escape our own eyes; and weak judgment consists, not in failing to detect them, but in refusing to admit them when pointed out to us.

While I have yielded to the public taste in sprinkling myself with quotations, I do not propose they shall totally drown me. Had I followed my own opinion, I would have spoken only with my own voice. Without pains or learning, I can borrow from the books about me in the room where I write a dozen such patchers and darners, gentlemen whom I hardly bother to glance at. I need no more than the introductory treatise of some German to stuff me with quotations, and head me for a neat reputation by gulling a silly world.

These hasty puddings of banality, by which so many people take a short cut to knowledge, are of no use except in subjects of the same dough. They serve to show off our learning, but not to instruct us.

I have seen books made of things neither studied nor understood. The author divides the research of its subjects among several of his learned friends, and preens himself on having furnished the plan, and the industry to wrap together this bundle of undigested fodder. Anyhow, the paper and ink are his. This is to buy or borrow a book, not to make one. It is to show the world not that he can write a book, but—lest there be any doubt—that he cannot.

I do the contrary. Among so many things to borrow, I am glad if I can steal something and change and disguise it for some new end, even at the risk of having it said I am ignorant of its true purport. We who love nature and reality think there is greater honor in originality than in learning.

As for the rest, I add to my first impressions, but I never correct them. For my purpose is to study the progress of my ideas, and leave each as it was born. I wish I had begun sooner, so I could have better observed the course they took. Then, too, I believe that if a man thinks he can do better, he should put it in a new book and not adulterate the old. For myself, I fear to lose by the alteration. I have grown older since the first publication of my *Essays* in 1580, but I doubt if I have grown wiser. Finally, anyone who knows my laziness will believe me when I say I would rather write as many more essays again than chain myself down to revising those I've already written.

Their favorable reception has given me more confidence than I expected. Praise is always pleasing, though the common judgment rarely hits the mark. If I am not mistaken, the worst writings of my time have won the greatest applause. Many a man has been a miracle in the world's eye, in whom his wife and page have seen nothing notable. Few men have been admired by their valets. In my country of Gascony, they think it droll to see me in print. The farther off I am read, the more I am esteemed. I have to buy my publishers here in Guienne; elsewhere they buy me.

When I hear anyone dwell on the language of my essays I would rather he held his peace. He is not so much exalting the style as belittling the sense; and the more indirectly it is done, the deeper it stings. Yet I am much deceived if anyone else furnishes stuff more worth pondering— whether, well or badly done, any other writer has poured so much matter on paper, or, at least, spread it as thick. To give fuller measure, I include only the starting-points: if I had expanded them I would have multiplied my volume many times over. How many stories I have strewn up and down my pages, which say nothing—but which, if you question them closely, would yield enough to produce an infinity of essays.

Neither my stories nor my quotations are always meant to serve as an example, an authority, or an ornament. Sometimes I do not regard them for the mere use I make of them. They often carry, beyond what I say of them, the seed of a richer and bolder thought. They carry a subtler undertone— both for myself, who do not wish to speak more explicitly, and for those who can catch my tune. I have my own reasons, perhaps, for saying things by halves, for speaking confusedly and awry.

What I find tolerable in my writings are only so in comparison with worse things which I see well enough received. So far from pleasing me, when I review them they disgust me. I have an idea in mind, a certain vague image which shows me, as in a dream, a better line that I can hew to. I don't know how to grasp or exploit it—and even then, the idea is mediocre.

As to my natural parts, of which these are the essays, they bend under the burden. My imagination and judgment grope in the dark. When I go as far as I can, tripping and stumbling, I glimpse ahead more and wider land wrapped in an impenetrable cloud.

When I want to judge someone else, I ask him how far he is pleased with his own work. I want none of these pretty excuses: "I did it only as a pastime—it didn't take me an hour—I've never looked at it since." Well then, say I, put it aside, and give me one which is indeed yourself—one you are willing to be measured by.

There should be a law against useless and impertinent scribblers, as against vagrants and idlers. If there were, I and a hundred others would be banished from the kingdom. I do not say this in jest. Scribbling seems to be a symptom of a diseased world. We never wrote so much as since our civil wars began. And when did the Romans so much as on the verge of their decline? Besides, the refinement of our wit makes no one wiser in government. These idle books get born because people don't attend to their proper business, but leap at the chance to divert themselves from it.

But I am less a writer of books than anything else. My business is to shape my life—this is my one trade and calling. The man who has any worth in him should show it in his daily manners and speech, his love affairs and his quarrels, in play, in bed, at table, and in the management of his business and house. The man who writes a good book while sitting in torn breeches should first mend his breeches. Ask a Spartan whether he would rather be a good orator or a good soldier—but don't ask me, for I would rather be a good cook if I didn't already have one. Good God, how I would hate to be thought a pretty fellow with my pen, but an ass at everything else! A servant I employed to write under my dictation imagined he had garnered a rich booty by filching a number of my essays, choosing those which pleased him most. I am consoled to think he will gain no more than I have lost.

If I had chosen to write learnedly, I would have written sooner, when I was nearer to my studies and had more brains and better memory. He who commits his old age to the press is a simpleton if he thinks to squeeze from it anything but dreaming, dotage, and drivel. In aging, the mind grows constipated and thick.

I, however, deliver my learning in thin driblets—but my ignorance in pomp and state. I write of nothing but nothingness itself—not of science but of unlearnedness. And I have chosen the years when my life—which is what I propose to paint—lies all before my eyes.

The rest to come has to do with death. And if I babble when I meet it, as others do, I'll likely give an account of my loquacious departure.

This frank, personal voice was first introduced to England by Francis Bacon, and became in the eighteenth century an early forerunner of the modern magazine through Joseph Addison and Richard Steele's ability to catch the popular ear. In the United States it was Henry David Thoreau in his famous *Walden* who, as he did for so many other things, made perhaps the best statement justifying the egotistical "I" as quoted and commented upon here by Taylor Stoehr:

> In most books, the *I*, or first person, is omitted; in this it will be retained; that, in respect to egotism, is the main difference. We commonly do not remember that it is, after all, always the first person that is speaking. I should not talk so much about myself if there were anybody else whom I knew as well. Unfortunately, I am confined to this theme by the narrowness of my experience. Moreover, I, on my side, require of every writer, first or last, a simple and sincere account of his own life, and not merely what he has heard of other men's lives; some such account as he would send to kindred from a distant land; for if he has lived sincerely, it must have been in a distant land to me. Perhaps these pages are more particularly addressed to poor students. As for the rest of my readers, they will accept such portions as apply to them. I trust that none will stretch the seams in putting on the coat, for it may do good service to him whom it fits.

What one immediately senses with Thoreau is less a tone than a voice—a particular stance in the world, though not exactly vis-à-vis an audience. He establishes himself here as a somewhat eccentric figure, confident of his subject (himself and his experiment at Walden Pond), assured of an audience (but not much involved with it—a "they" rather than a "you"). Sometimes the self-confidence may seem brittle (in its pervasive irony), or the voice will squeak with overtones of insistence that suggest a man writing to convince himself or to hide a further truth he fears; but for the most part Thoreau's "I" is an integrated ego, steady enough to make public what ordinarily is kept private, to offer the whole self to others. The insistent voice, overriding tone, enforces a certain distance from these others. The effect is *noblesse oblige*.[11]

FOCUS POINT: THE PERSONAL ESSAY

1. It is conversational in tone.

2. In a kind of "genial egotism" the author tells of his personal tastes, experiences, and outlook on life.

[11] "Tone and Voice," *College English* 30 (November 1967): 152.

3. He speaks in the first person, "I."

4. He may lead the reader from subject to subject but will always keep the same mood and remain in character of the *persona* with whom he begins.

TOPICS FOR DISCUSSION AND WRITING

1. From what he writes, what kind of person do you judge Montaigne to have been? What evidence supports your judgment? Is it possible for someone in our times to think and act as he says he did? Why or why not? How does he compare with an essayist like Henry David Thoreau, the author of *Walden?*

2. Since the essay form generally relies upon communicating the writer's mood as he looks back on incidents of his life and discovers some meaning in them, you may find the essay an interesting form with which to experiment. Here are some suggestions that may lead you to recall moments that, as you now think of them, have some significance they did not have when you first experienced them.
   a. Times when I wished I had good neighbors
   b. Corner grocery stores I have known
   c. Movies I used to like
   d. Bicycles (skates, cars, etc.) I have had and what I learned from them
   e. Types of people and their pets I have known
   f. Characters you meet in every summer camp
   g. Athletic coaches (ministers, teachers, scout leaders, etc.) who left their mark on me
   h. Books that turned me on to reading
   i. First times I would (would not) like to repeat

3. In his revealing, "confessional" essay, Montaigne recounts many decisions and choices he made in developing his writing habits and outlook as an essayist. Since you may find his views helpful in your own development as a student-writer, how did he stand on questions like the following?
   a. Is the mind naturally given to clear, orderly thinking?
   b. What does he mean when he says, "No wind serves the man bound for no port"?
   c. Did he find writing narrative easy?
   d. Is he usually cautious in his speech?

e. Was he much influenced by other writers and by what they had to say?
f. Where could he write best—at home or in some strange place?
g. Was he conscious of giving himself away in his writing?
h. Where did he get his best ideas—sitting at his desk or in his daily living routine?
i. Did he worry if he could not find the exact standard French language word he needed? What does he mean: "If the French won't come, let the Gascon serve"?
j. Should writers constantly be on the watch for new words to use in their work?
k. Does he tell the truth when he says, "I speak on paper as I do to the first person I meet"?
l. What is his favorite subject matter?
m. Is it his main purpose to give pleasure or to inform?
n. How "ethical" is he about using the language and books of other authors? Does he have any favorite authors?
o. How much is he given to rewriting his essays?
p. Of which is he more proud—his style or his thoughts?
q. If his main business, as he says, "is to shape my life," why does he spend so much time writing essays?
r. Is he proud of his literary work?

Tone of protest

Among the many angry voices of black leaders and authors of the late 1960s, there were few, if any, that did not ring with confidence in their protests against racial injustice and social inequality and with certainty of the audiences they were addressing. Leaders and authors like Malcolm X, Eldridge Cleaver, LeRoi Jones (Imamu Amiri Baraka), James Baldwin, Ralph Ellison, and activists like Huey P. Newton and Stokely Carmichael expressed facts, fears, and hopes shared by millions. Like the "Soledad Brothers" of the early 1970s they exhibited highly individual styles in adapting rhetorical strategies and tones in their citing of histories of persecution, in appealing for support, and in harshly attacking authority figures of what was called The Establishment. None has ever hesitated to use the pronoun "I" indicative of possession of an "integrated ego." They "found" themselves in their language and rhetoric and were themselves first persuaded of the "truth" of their messages before they could successfully communicate their messages to others.

Although no one of these well-known figures can speak for them all or do more than suggest the complexity and richness of their individual styles and voices, one of the "Tales" by Imamu Amirir Baraka (LeRoi Jones), the distinguished dramatist and poet, serves very well to indicate the strength and firmness of an "I" that Thoreau would have admired.

Jones gives his first person narrator, the "I" of "Heroes Are Gang Leaders," a strong sense of irony, portraying him as a man who sees that people and situations are seldom what they appear to be. Viewing other people and his experiences with them from this point of view may make him quietly laugh, but it is a bitter laughter bordering on despair. As the narrator confesses in the ambiguous opening sentences, his "concerns" have an "ironic tone" because he has observed that no matter what people say and feel they generally fail to do anything about it.

Yet although he admits he learns from people, is "taught" by them despite their inconsistencies, he says they do little to change him basically. He has learned "you can pick up God knows what from God knows who," and then goes on to tell us of his experience in a New York hospital and what ironic facts it taught him. His deliberate use of sentence fragments suggests the jarring contradictions of life as he sees it.

If jagged sentence fragments are a strong feature of his style, so are his figures of speech, which add to the rhetorical tone of irony. It is appropriate, then, to take up here some matters concerning figures of speech before we turn to Jones's tale.

Figures of speech

Imagination comes into play every time a person needs to put into words some of what he is feeling or thinking, for since words are only symbols themselves and are *not the things they stand for*, they do not *of themselves* convey the reality they are meant to represent. For example, when in the opening sentence of the second paragraph Jones says, "Sitting in a hospital bed on First Avenue trying to read, and being fanned by stifling breezes off the dirty river," each of us will respond to those words in different ways. We must because we ourselves are not "sitting in a hospital bed on First Avenue"; we are only reading a "voice" making a statement in printed words—and an incomplete, fragmentary statement at that! Yet if we read with any attention at all, we make in our minds some kind of picture or scene suggested by those words, and the "hospital bed" will resemble one we have seen in some hospital, perhaps even one we have spent some time in ourselves and so have vivid memories to draw upon to round out that picture in our imagination.

This need to communicate the *quality* of an experience such as the pain, surprise, fear, beauty, or shock characterizing that experience leads a person to make comparisons. Various kinds of comparisons have names familiar to all who know something about the *figures of speech.* A *figure* is any unusual or novel patterning of words or phrases. The most common of these figures are the following which all involve some form of comparison:

ALLUSION: The reference to historic or literary names, characters, or incidents. Example: He was no Shakespeare.

SIMILE: One thing is likened to another but different thing by the use of *like, as, as if, as though,* etc. Example: He swam like a porpoise.

METAPHOR: One thing is *directly* identified with another and dissimilar thing with no use of *like, as, as if,* etc. Example: She stood there, a statue of icy reproach.

PERSONIFICATION: An inanimate object, an abstraction, or an animal is considered to have human qualities. Example: The icy hand of Fear gripped him.

METONYMY: The use of the name of one object or quality for that of another to which it is related. Example: He was hitting the jug pretty heavy at the time.

SYNECDOCHE: The use of the part for the whole or the whole for the part. Example: She played first chair in the symphony orchestra.

HYPERBOLE: The use of exaggerated or extravagant terms to heighten an effect. Example: He was so hungry that with his eyes he devoured every last cake, cookie, pie, and bun in the bakery window.

PARADOX: An apparently self-contradictory statement but one nevertheless true. Example: She dieted so daintily that without half trying she gained only 5 pounds.

OXYMORON: The combining of words with apparently contradictory meanings. Example: a spendthrift miser, dismal happiness, a fierce lamb.

HEROES ARE GANG LEADERS[12]

by LEROI JONES

My concerns are not centered on people. But in reflection, people cause the ironic tone they take. If I think through theories of government or prose, the words are sound, the feelings real, but useless unless people can carry them. Attack them, or celebrate them. Useless in the world, at

[12] Reprinted by permission from *Tales* copyright © 1967, Grove Press Inc.

least. Though to my own way of moving, it makes no ultimate difference. I'll do pretty much what I would have done. Even though people change me: sometimes bring me out of myself, to confront them, or embrace them. I spit in a man's face once in a bar who had just taught me something very significant about the socio-cultural structure of America, and the West. But the act of teaching is usually casual. That is, you can pick up God knows what from God knows who.

Sitting in a hospital bed on First Avenue trying to read, and being fanned by stifling breezes off the dirty river. Ford Maddox Ford was telling me something, and this a formal act of teaching. The didactic tone of *No More Parades*. Teaching. Telling. Pointing out. And very fine and real in its delineations, but causing finally a kind of super-sophisticated hero worship. So we move from Tarzan to Christopher Tietjens, but the concerns are still heroism. And what to do to make the wildest, brightest, dispersal of our energies. In our not really brief flight into darkness. Either it is done against the heavens, sky flyers, or against the earth. And the story of man is divided brusquely between those who know the sky, and those who know only the earth. And the various dictators, artists, murderers and ministers, can come from either side. Each Left and Right, go right up to the sky, and the division is within their own territory. Lindberghs and Hemingways, Nat Turners and Robespierres. What they do is gold, and skyward, from whatever angle, they fly and return to an earth of mistakes. So Christopher Tietjens being made a cuckold, and trying vainly to see through mist and shadows down to Sylvia's earth. She called so furiously for him to fall. My friend, Johnny Morris, fighting off the Ku Klux Klan only to return from those heights to the silent hallway of some very real shack and watch some fool wrestle with his wife. Various scenes complete each other with desperate precision.

Sitting there being talked to by an old Tory, fixed and diseased by my only life. And surrounded, fortunately enough, by men like myself, who are not even able to think. Wood alcohol drinkers, dragged in from the Bowery, with their lungs and bellies on fire. Raving logicians who know empirically that Christianity can only take its place among the other less publicized concerns of men.

Sixty-year-old niggers who sit on their beds scratching their knees. Polacks who have to gurgle for the rest of their lives. Completely anonymous (Scotch-Irish?) Americans with dark ratty hair, and red scars on their stomachs. They might be homosexuals watching me read Thomas Me-an, and smelling the mystery woman's flowers. Puerto Ricans with shiny hair and old-fashioned underwear shirts, eating their dinner out of Mason jars.

And we are all alive at the same time. Contemporaries in that sense. (Though I still think myself a young man, and am still in love with things I can do.) Of the same time and source. Inheritors of so many things we will never understand. But weighted with very different allegiances, though if I am silent for a long time I hope we all believe in a similar reality. That I am not merely writing poems for Joel Oppenheimer or Paul

Blackburn . . . but everything alive. Which is not true. Which is simply not true. Our heroisms and their claims are fictitious. But if we are not serious, if we do not make up a body of philosophy out of which to work we are simply hedonists, and I am stretching the word so that it includes even martyrs. Flame freaks.

In the bed next to mine was a man, Kowalski, a very tall Polish man with a bony hairless skull, covered with welts and scratches. He had drunk paint remover and orange juice. He was the man who gurgled now, though he kept trying to curl his lips and smile. But I was hoping he would find out soon what a hopeless gesture that was, and stop it. I wanted to say to him, "Why don't you quit fucking around like that? It's certainly too late to be anybody else's man now. Just cut that shit out." With his weird colored teeth hanging below his lip, cutting the smile into strips of anguish.

He would eat my fruit when I offered it, or the nuts a rich lady gave me. Since I was not merely a "poor man" or a derelict, but a writer. That is, there was a glamorous reason I was in this derelict's ward. Look at my beard, and all the books on the table. I'm not like the rest of these guys. They're just tramps. But I'm a tramp with connections.

He would talk too, if I didn't watch him. He would gurgle these wild things he found in the tabloids. And point out murders and rapes to me, or robberies where everybody got away clean. He described the Bowery to me like it was a college, or the Village, or an artist's colony. An identical reality, with the same used up references . . . the same dishonesties and misplaced loyalties. The same ambition, naturally. Usually petty and ravaging. Another cold segment of American enterprise, and for this reason having nothing at all to do with their European counterparts, beggars . . . whom I suppose are academic and stuffy in comparison. Bums have the same qualifications as any of us to run for president, and it is the measure of a society that they refuse to. And this is not romanticism, but simple cultural observation. Bums know at least as much about the world as Senator Fulbright. You better believe it.

But one day two men came into our ward. A tall red-faced man, like from his neck up he had been painted by Soutine, or some other nut. The other man, was lost in his gabardine suit, like somebody who was not even smart enough to be rich. When I looked up from my book at them, I thought immediately what a stupid thing to think about people that they were cops. Although, of course, that is just what they were: cops. Or detectives, since they were in "plain" clothes, which is as hip as putting an alligator in a tuxedo. Very few people would make a mistake, except say those who would say it was a crocodile. That is, zoology majors.

The alligators came right down the aisle to Kowalski's bed; the little baggy one carrying a yellow pad on a writing board. They had been talking to each other very calmly and happily about something. Probably about man-eating tigers or the possibility of whores on Mars. But their faces quickly changed and reset when they got to the end of the row, and stood before my derelict's bed. "Hey," the red-faced man said, "Hey," at

Kowalski who was sleeping or by now pretending to sleep, "Hey, you Kowalski?" He shook the old man's shoulder, getting him to turn over. Kowalski shook his head in imitation of sleep, frowned and tried to yawn. But he was still frightened. Probably confused too, since I'm sure he'd never expected to see cops in a place the Geneva Convention states very specifically is cool. In fact he wiped his eyes convinced, I'm certain, that the two police officers were only bad fairies, or at worst, products of a very casual case of delirium tremens. But, for sure, the two men persisted, past any idea of giggling fantasy.

"Hey. You Kowalski?"

The old man finally shook his head slowly yes, very very slowly, yes. Pulling his sheets up around his neck like a woman or an inventive fag, in a fit of badly feigned modesty. The cops looked on their list and back at Kowalski, the tall one already talking. "Where'd you get the stuff, Kowalski? Huh?" The derelict shrugged his shoulders and looked cautiously toward the window. "We wanna know where you got the stuff, Kowalski, huh?" Finally, it must have dawned on the derelict that his voice was gone. That he really couldn't answer the questions, whether he wanted to or not, and he gurgled for the men, and touched his throat apologetically. The red cop said, "Where'd you get the stuff, Kowalski, huh? Come on speak up." And he put his head closer to the bum's, at the same time shaking his shoulder and finally, confronted by more gurgles, took the derelict's pajama shirt in his fingers and lifted the man a few inches off the bed. The little toady man was alternately watching and listening, and making checks on his yellow pad. He said, "Comeon," once, but not very viciously; he looked at me and rubbed his eyes. "Comeon, fella."

The large cop raised his voice as he raised Kowalski off the bed, and shook him awkwardly from side to side, now only repeating the last part of the question, "Huh? Huh? Huh?" And the old bum gurgled, and began to slobber on himself, his face turning as red as the policeman's, and his eyes wide and full of a domesticated terror. He kept trying to touch his throat, but his arms were bent under his body, or maybe it was that he was too weak to raise them from where they hung uselessly at his side. But he gurgled and turned redder.

And here is the essay part of the story. Like they say, my *point of view.* I had the book, *No More Parades,* all about the pursuit of heroism. About the death and execution of a skyman, or at least the execution, and the airless social compromise that keeps us alive past any use to ourselves. Chewing on some rich lady's candy, holding on to my ego, there among the elves, for dear god given sanctified life. Big Man In The Derelict Ward. The book held up in front of my eyes, to shield what was going on from slopping over into my life. Though, goddamn, it was there already. The response. The image. The total hold I had, and made. Crisscrossed and redirected for my own use (which now sits between the covers of a book to be misunderstood as *literature.* Like neon crosses should only be used to advertise pain. Which is total and final, and never really brief. It was all

I had. Like Joe Friday, or César Vallejo, in a hopeless confusion of wills and intents. To be judged like Tietjens was or my friend in the hallway watching his wife or breaking his fingers against an automobile window. There is no reasonable attitude behind anything. Nuns, passion killers, poets, we should all go out and get falling down drunk, and forget all the rules that make our lives so hopeless. Fuck you Kowalski! Really, I really mean it. St. Peter doing his crossword puzzle while they wasted another hopeless fanatic. It fits, and is more logical than any other act. Ugly Polish tramp).

Till finally I said, "That man can't speak. His voice is gone."

And the tall man, without even looking, wheezed, "And who the fuck asked you?"

It is the measure of my dwindling life that I returned to the book to rub out their image, and studied very closely another doomed man's life.

This "tale" resembles an essay more than it does a short story for the reason that although it deals with a series of incidents in a chronological order, the plight of Kowalski serves only to confirm and illustrate the philosophic conclusion Jones has reached in reflecting on the novel he has been reading. The incident is little more than an *anecdote* illustrating the point which Jones wishes to make.

Throughout, we find the unabashed first person narrator making effective poetic use of figures of speech. Here are some of them:

Similes

"He described the Bowery to me like it was a college, or the Village, or an artist's colony."

"A tall red-faced man, like from his neck up he had been painted by Soutine, or some other nut."

"The other man, was lost in his gabardine suit, like somebody who was not even smart enough to be rich."

"which is as hip as putting an alligator in a tuxedo."

"Pulling his sheets up around his neck like a woman or an inventive fag, in a fit of badly feigned modesty."

Metaphors

"And what to do to make the wildest, brightest, dispersal of our energies. In our not really brief flight into darkness."

"What they do is gold, and skyward, from whatever angle, they fly and return to an earth of mistakes."

"their lungs and bellies on fire."
"Flame freaks."
"The alligators came right down the aisle to Kowalski's bed. . . ."
"to shield what was going on from slopping over into my life."

Metonymy

"cutting the smile into strips of anguish."

Synecdoche

"another cold segment of American enterprise."

Hyperbole

"The other man was lost in his gabardine suit. . . ."
"Talking . . . probably about man-eating tigers or the possibility of whores on Mars."

Oxymoron

"the little toady man"
"his eyes wide and full of domesticated terror."

Allusion

"Sitting there being talked to by an old Tory. . . ."
"Lindberghs and Hemingways, Nat Turners and Robespierres. . . ."
"a place the Geneva Convention states very specifically is cool."
"St. Peter doing his crossword puzzle. . . ."

Urbane tone

Such then is the style of LeRoi Jones seen in this particular "tale": a style rich in rhetorical ironies and poetic in figurative speech. His voice is defiantly personal, unashamed in its self-revelation.

Among the many voices which distinguish the *essay* is also the kind represented by Hilaire Belloc, the precise, restrained, urbane critic and observer who exemplifies in his writing Swift's definition of style as "proper words in proper places." In the following passage from his book on his friend Gilbert Chesterton, another modern brilliant essayist,

Belloc neatly analyzes in personal, appreciative terms Chesterton's skill in the stylistic use of parallelism.

I have said that parallelism was the weapon peculiar to Chesterton's genius.

His unique, his capital, genius for illustration by parallel, by example, is his peculiar mark. The word "peculiar" is here the operative word. Many have precision, though few have his degree of precision. Multitudes, of course, are national in their various ways. No one whatsoever that I can recall in the whole course of English letters had his amazing— I would almost say superhuman—capacity for parallelism.

Now parallelism is a gift or method of vast effect in the conveyance of truth.

Parallelism consists in the illustration of some unperceived truth by its exact consonance with the reflection of a truth already known and perceived.

A truth may be missed by too constant a use, so that familiarity has dulled it; or by mere lack of acquaintance with it (the opposite danger); or by the repeated statement of it in false and imperfect forms. When the truth has been missed, it is recalled and fixed in the mind of the hearer by an unexpected and vivid use of parallelism.

Whenever Chesterton begins a sentence with, "It is as though," (in exploding a false bit of reasoning,) you may expect a stroke of parallelism as vivid as a lightning flash. Thus if some ass propounds that a difference of application destroys the validity of a doctrine, or that particulars are the enemies of universals, Chesterton will answer: "It is as though you were to say I cannot be an Englishman because I am a Londoner," or "It is as though you were to say that I cannot be an Englishman because I travel," or "As though you were to say Brown and Smith cannot both be Englishmen because one of them talks West Country and the other North Country."

This invaluable instrument of exposition, parallelism, you will find enshrined in metaphor; and in metaphor (or in its parent, simile) Chesterton also excelled. But he was at his greatest and most forcible when he fully developed the method through open and *explicit* parallelism.

He introduces it in more than one form; with the phrase I have just quoted, "It is as though," or more violently, the phrase "Why not say while you are about it," followed by an example of the absurdity rebuked.

For instance, to one who said all concealment was falsehood, he would reply: "Why not say, *while you are about it,* that 'Wearing clothes is a falsehood?' "

Sometimes he would use the form, "What should we think of a person who might say?" Sometimes he left out exordium altogether and merely stated the parallelism without addition. Always, in whatever manner he launched the parallelism, he produced the shock of illumination. He *taught*.

He made men see what they had not seen before. He made them *know*. He was an architect of certitude, whenever he practised this art in which he excelled.

The example of the parable in Holy Writ will occur at once to the reader. It is of the same origin and of similar value. The "parable" of the Gospels differs only from pure parallelism in the artifice of introducing a story in order to capture the reader's mind. But in essence a parable is the same thing as a parallelism.

Let us remark in conclusion that parallelism is of particular value in a society such as ours which has lost the habit of thinking. It illustrates and thereby fixes a truth or an experience as a picture fixes a face or land-scape in the mind.

It is (alas!) unlikely that this invaluable instrument will be so used again by any other; but Chesterton has used it to perfection and in abundance.

It permeated not only his vigorous expository prose, but still more his private conversation. How well I recall the discussions upon all affairs, of art, of politics, of philosophy, in which this genius of his appeared! All he advanced as argument was lit up by the comparison of an unknown by a known truth; of something half hidden by something fully experienced among us all.

Parallelism was so native to his mind; it was so naturally a fruit of his mental character that he had difficulty in understanding why others did not use it with the same lavish facility as himself. . . .

I know what I am talking about. Over and over again I have myself attempted to make something clear to my fellows by sharp, exact and re-vealing parallel. I have always had to seek long before I found anything approaching what I needed and the thing itself I never found. I have never been able to form a parallel which could satisfy my desire for illustration; and even metaphor, in which my contemporaries abound, I have, by a sort of instinct, avoided: perhaps because I was not competent therein: perhaps from scorn.

For it must be noted that metaphor lends itself to abuse. I remember the good laugh which Chesterton and I had together over the opening words of a politically-minded Anglican Bishop speaking on some tawdry public occasion. The prelate had been badly bitten, probably in youth (perhaps in the days of Cecil Rhodes, William Stead and the more valuable Mahan), by Oceanic visions. He opened his speech, which was almost a sermon, with the phrase, "Let us strengthen while we loosen the bonds of Empire."

We both heard these words together and they became deathless in each of our memories, as the example of how to talk nonsense which will go down.

Thus, if England were attacked by a savage foe determined to annihilate her commerce and destroy her wealth, and a Dominion were to open the ball by proclaiming its neutrality in the war, that would be an excellent result of what we have been doing for the last lifetime: strengthening the bonds of Empire by loosening them. We shall probably have a complete example of it in the near future.[13]

EXERCISE

Somerset Maugham, the author of the well-known novel *Of Human Bondage,* once said he could write about anyone of whom there was a little bit in him (in other words, of anyone he could imagine himself being). Maugham meant we all have "sides" to our character and are capable of playing many roles in a lifetime, giving each one an appropriate voice and life style. Assume a voice and role you find challenging, and using the first person pronoun "I," relate an incident wherein the narrator learned something worth knowing about human nature. Here are some suggestions:

1. An employer justifies to himself why he let a good employee go, but comes to realize that perhaps he made a mistake.
2. You are an athletic coach having a much needed talk with a star or a potential star on your team. You are afraid he may quit, sign a professional sports contract, or flunk out.
3. You have just sighted what you feel very sure must be a genuine UFO, and as objectively as you can under the circumstances you are trying to write a report of what you are witnessing.
4. You are a political figure trying to explain to a hostile constituent why you have voted as you have on a highly controversial measure.
5. A parent makes every effort to convince a son or a daughter that there need be no "generation gap" between them on a particularly sensitive issue.

Tone of allegory

Telling a lively story to "preach a lesson" is an ancient but still very effective way of making a point. Basically it depends for its appeal to readers upon the ringing sincerity or depth of feeling of the author and, of course, upon his narrative skill in veiling the underlying mean-

[13] Hilaire Belloc, *On the Place of Gilbert Chesterton in English Letters* (New York: Sheed & Ward, 1940), pp. 36–43.

ings of his story. One of the most famous of successful allegories is John Bunyan's *The Pilgrim's Progress,* written while Bunyan sat in a small town English jail under sentence for having preached to the public without having a proper ministerial license. As the subtitle—"In the Similitude of a Dream"—plainly declares, Bunyan is employing the popular device of a dream to veil the teachings the narrative illustrates.

The introductory poem proclaims "This book is writ in such a dialect/ As may the minds of listless men affect" and bids the reader "O then come hither,/ And lay my book, thy head, and heart together." We include part of the poem to show how deliberately John Bunyan tried to engage his readers by making various appeals to them. The first episode with its famous opening follows.

> This book will make a traveller of thee,
> If by its counsel thou wilt ruled be;
> It will direct thee to the Holy Land,
> If thou wilt its directions understand:
> Yea, it will make the slothful active be,
> The blind also delightful things to see.
> Art thou for something rare and profitable?
> Wouldst thou see a truth within a fable?
> Art thou forgetful? Wouldst thou remember
> From New Year's day to the last of December?
> Then read my fancies, they will stick like burrs,
> And may be, to the helpless, comforters.
> This book is writ in such a dialect
> As may the minds of listless men affect;
> It seems a novelty, and yet contains
> Nothing but sound and honest gospel strains.
> Wouldst thou divert thyself from melancholy?
> Wouldst thou be pleasant, yet be far from folly?
> Wouldst thou read riddles, and their explanation?
> Or else be drowned in thy contemplation?
> Dost thou love picking meat? Or wouldst thou see
> A man i' th' clouds, and hear him speak to thee?
> Wouldst thou be in a dream, and yet not sleep?
> Or wouldst thou in a moment laugh and weep?
> Wouldst thou lose thyself, and catch no harm,
> And find thyself again without a charm?
> Wouldst read thyself, and read thou knowest not what,
> And yet know whether thou are blest or not,
> By reading the same lines? O then come hither,
> And lay my book, thy head, and heart together.—

> [JOHN BUNYAN]

THE PILGRIM'S PROGRESS
IN THE SIMILITUDE OF A DREAM

As I walked through the wilderness of this world, I lighted on a certain place where was a den, and I laid me down in that place to sleep; and as I slept I dreamed a dream. I dreamed, and behold, I saw a man clothed with rags, standing in a certain place, with his face from his own house, a book in his hand, and a great burden upon his back. I looked, and saw him open the book, and read therein; and as he read, he wept and trembled; and not being able longer to contain, he brake out with a lamentable cry, saying, What shall I do?

In this plight therefore he went home, and refrained himself as long as he could, that his wife and children should not perceive his distress; but he could not be silent long, because that his trouble increased. Wherefore at length he brake his mind to his wife and children and thus he began to talk to them: O my dear wife, said he, and you the children of my bowels, I your dear friend am in myself undone by reason of a burden that lieth hard upon me; moreover, I am for certain informed that this our city will be burned with fire from heaven; in which fearful overthrow, both myself, with thee my wife and you my sweet babes, shall miserably come to ruin, except (the which yet I see not) some way of escape can be found, whereby we may be delivered. At this his relations were sore amazed, not for that they believed that what he said to them was true, but because they thought that some frenzy distemper had got into his head. Therefore, it drawing towards night and they hoping that sleep might settle his brains, with all haste they got him to bed. But the night was as troublesome to him as the day; wherefore, instead of sleeping, he spent it in sighs and tears. So, when the morning was come, they would know how he did; and he told them, Worse and worse. He also set to talking to them again, but they began to be hardened. They also thought to drive away his distemper by harsh and surly carriages to him; sometimes they would deride, sometimes they would chide, and sometimes they would quite neglect him. Wherefore he began to retire himself to his chamber, to pray for and pity them, and also to condole his own misery; he would also walk solitarily in the fields, sometimes reading, and sometimes praying, and thus for some days he spent his time.

Now I saw, upon a time when he was walking in the fields, that he was (as he was wont) reading in his book, and greatly distressed in his mind; and as he read he burst out, as he had done before, crying, What shall I do to be saved?

I saw also that he looked this way and that way, as if he would run; yet he stood still, because, as I perceived, he could not tell which way to go. I looked then, and saw a man named Evangelist coming to him and asked, Wherefore dost thou cry? He answered, Sir, I perceive by the book in my hand that I am condemned to die, and after that to come to judgment; and I find that I am not willing to do the first, nor able to do the second.

Then said Evangelist, Why not willing to die, since this life is attended with so many evils? The man answered, Because I fear that this burden that is upon my back will sink me lower than the grave, and I shall fall into Tophet. And, Sir, if I be not fit to go to prison, I am not fit (I am sure) to go to judgment, and from thence to execution; and the thoughts of these things make me cry.

Then said Evangelist, If this be thy condition, why standest thou still? He answered, Because I know not whither to go. Then he gave him a parchment roll, and there was written within, Fly from the wrath to come.

The man therefore read it, and looking upon Evangelist very carefully said, Whither must I fly? Then said Evangelist, pointing with his finger over a very wide field, Do you see yonder wicket gate? The man said, No. Then said the other, Do you see yonder shining light? He said, I think I do. Then said Evangelist, Keep that light in your eye, and go up directly thereto: so shalt thou see the gate; at which, when thou knockest, it shall be told thee what thou shalt do.

So I saw in my dream that the man began to run. Now he had not run far from his own door, but his wife and children, perceiving it, began to cry after him to return; but the man put his fingers in his ears, and ran on, crying, Life! Life! Eternal Life! So he looked not behind him, but fled towards the middle of the plain.

The neighbors also came out to see him run; and as he ran, some mocked, others threatened, and some cried after him to return. Now among those that did so there were two that resolved to fetch him back by force. The name of the one was Obstinate, and the name of the other Pliable. Now by this time the man was not a good distance from them; but, however, they were resolved to pursue him, which they did, and in little time they overtook him. Then said the man, Neighbors, wherefore are you come? They said, To persuade you to go back with us. But he said, That can by no means be; you dwell, said he, in the City of Destruction (the place also where I was born), I see it to be so; and dying there, sooner or later, you will sink lower than the grave, into a place that burns with fire and brimstone: be content, good neighbors, and go along with me.

OBST. What, said Obstinate, and leave our friends and our comforts behind us!

CHR. Yes, said Christian (for that was his name), because that *all* which you shall forsake is not worthy to be compared with a *little* of that that I am seeking to enjoy; and if you will go along with me, and hold it, you shall fare as I myself; for there where I go is enough and to spare. Come away, and prove my words.

OBST. What are the things you seek, since you leave all the world to find them?

CHR. I seek an inheritance incorruptible, undefiled, and that fadeth not away, and it is laid up in heaven, and fast there, to be bestowed at the time appointed on them that diligently seek it. Read it so, if you will, in my book.

OBST. Tush, said Obstinate, away with your book. Will you go back with us or no?

CHR. No, not I, said the other, because I have laid my hand to the plough.

OBST. Come then, neighbor Pliable, let us turn again, and go home without him. There is a company of these crazed-headed coxcombs that, when they take a fancy by the end, are wiser in their own eyes than seven men that can render a reason.

PLI. Then said Pliable, Don't revile. If what the good Christian says is true, the things he looks after are better than ours. My heart inclines to go with my neighbor.

OBST. What! more fools still? Be ruled by me, and go back. Who knows whither such a brainsick fellow will lead you? Go back, go back, and be wise.

CHR. Come with me, neighbor Pliable; there are such things to be had which I spoke of, and many more glories besides. If you believe not me, read here in this book; and for the truth of what is expressed therein, behold, all is confirmed by the blood of him that made it.

PLI. Well, neighbor Obstinate, said Pliable, I begin to come to a point; I intend to go along with this good man, and to cast in my lot with him. But, my good companion, do you know the way to this desired place?

CHR. I am directed by a man whose name is Evangelist to speed me to a little gate that is before us, where we shall receive instruction about the way.

PLI. Come then, good neighbor, let us be going.

Then they went both together.

As this sampling of allegory shows, nothing means what it appears to on the surface. The city to be burned is really the earth on Judgment Day; the "book" is, of course, the Bible; the "light" is the insights of faith, and the "wicket gate" is evidently the door of salvation. Similarly, the characters are the personifications of abstractions: "Obstinate" resists being persuaded to accept salvation, and "Pliable"—like his name —is willing to go along with Christian for the time being. It is Bunyan's didactic purpose veiled under an exciting story that once made his book one found in every Protestant home. And this same attractive power of masquerade continues to make allegory an appealing device to writers even today.

Tones of satire and irony

To make someone or something appear ridiculous or to arouse feelings of contempt or disparagement in others has always been the general purpose of *satire*. It can be as gentle as mild irony or as devastating as sarcastic invective, but whether seeking only to incite gentle though painful smiles and laughter or totally to discredit and destroy, satire is always on the attack in a war that sees the enemy as at least associated with Evil, if not Evil itself. Satire is available as a weapon both to the reformer who wants changes and to the traditionalist who desires only continuance of the status quo.

Satire thus is a genre having many voices, but basic to some of them is the mocking tone of irony, a term having a wide range of meanings:

> In seeking to define irony or distinguish its several kinds one can quite legitimately look at it from many different angles. But it is precisely this that explains the chaos which the terminology of irony presents. One has only to reflect for a moment upon the various names that have been given to "kinds" of irony—tragic irony, comic irony, irony of manner, irony of situation, philosophical irony, practical irony, dramatic irony, verbal irony, ingénu irony, double irony, rhetorical irony, self-irony, Socratic Irony, Romantic Irony, cosmic irony, sentimental irony, irony of Fate, irony of chance, irony of character, etc.—to see that some have been named technique, or the function, or the object, or the practitioner, or the tone, or the attitude. . . .
>
> The more familiar kind of irony is Simple Irony, in which an apparently or ostensibly true statement, serious question, valid assumption, or legitimate expectation is corrected, invalidated, or frustrated by the ironist's real meaning, by the true state of affairs, or by what actually happens. . . . Simple ironies always function quite openly as correctives.[14]

In satire, then, the ironist may even be the loving parent who gently scolds a child with *simple irony* by saying, "You're a great one, aren't you, causing your mother all this trouble?" when she is not at all displeased with what the child has done. Or the ironist may be the athletic coach deliberately using *verbal irony* to shame and arouse his players by addressing them with sarcasm: "What a bunch of wonders you guys were out there! No one ever saw anything like you! Such brilliant execution of plays! Such impenetrable defenses! And what team spirit! Just keep it up during the next half and you'll go down on the record books,

[14] D. C. Muecke, *The Compass of Irony* (London: Methuen & Company Ltd., 1969), pp. 4, 23.

all right, but as the lousiest, most gutless bunch of would-be athletes that ever put on a uniform!"

The ironic language of the ironist thus is generally either inflated or impoverished, tending to go to extremes and involving the absurd, featuring diction that may be full of slang and trite expressions or extremely witty. With this language the ironist assumes the role and voice of the *vir bonus*—the good, honest critic who is out to correct or to defend what he thinks is needful of his ministrations. He may be a Horace or a Juvenal in ancient Rome ripping into the vices and excesses of his day or a modern columnist like Arthur Hoppe resorting to satiric *high burlesque* to attack a political target of our time as in this piece:

GENESIS, REWRITTEN TO READ IN THE NEW AMERICAN STYLE[15]

by ARTHUR HOPPE

In the beginning, the Lord created the Administration.

And the land was without form, and void. The Lord said, Let there be law and order. And, lo, there was law and order. And it was good. And that was the end of the first year.

And the Lord said, Let the troubled waters be divided. That part which was in heaven, he called Fiscal Responsibility. The other part, he called Spendthrift Democrats. And that was the end of the second year.

And the Lord said, Let there be an end to permissiveness and mollycoddling; and it was so. And that was the end of the third year.

And the Lord said, Let there be peace. And he rained down fire and destruction. And, lo, there was peace. And that was the end of the fourth year.

And the Lord said, Let there be no more inflation. And that was the end of Phases I, II and III.

And the Lord said, Let there be Assistants in our image. And he formed Assistants from the dust of advertising agencies in his own image. And the Lord said unto them, Be fruitful and multiply and have dominion over every living thing that moveth upon the earth. And it was so.

And the Lord saw everything that he had made, and behold, it was very good.

Now the Lord planted The Garden of the White House, sowing therein the seeds of power and they flourished. And the Lord put his Assistants there. And he commanded them, saying, Of every tree of the garden thou mayest freely eat. But of the tree of knowledge of good and evil, thou shalt not eat of it.

But the serpent of power was more subtle than any beast of the field. And it whispered to the Assistants, saying, Eat of the forbidden tree, for then your eyes shall be opened, and ye shall be as gods, knowing good and evil.

And they did eat, and their eyes were opened, and they knew they were naked; and they sewed press releases together, and made themselves aprons, which became known as the Great Cover Up.

And when the Lord asked them if they had eaten of the forbidden tree, each blamed the other. And they offered up unto the Lord a goat named Dean in sacrifice. But the Lord was not appeased. And he drove them from the garden, saying, for dust thou art, and unto dust shalt thou return.

And so it came to pass that Mitchell begat Haldeman who begat Ehrlichman who begat Stans who begat Chapin who begat Liddy who begat Hunt, McCord and five Cubans, who begat . . . For, lo, multitudes got begatted.

Now the Watergate was open. Leaks, rumors and investigations flooded forth to cleanse the earth. And many cursed the Lord.

But one loyal servant, Spiro, found grace in the eyes of the Lord for his righteousness. And the Lord commanded him, saying, "Make thee an Ark of State and take thee all surviving creatures of my Administration, two by two, and all files, original and duplicate, so that they may survive the flood.

And for three long years, the Ark tossed on the troubled waters until at last it splintered on a mountaintop. And all aboard perished, crying, Lord, Lord, why hast thou forsaken us whom thou created in thine own image?

Now it was then that the heavens parted and a voice of thunder replied: Well, at least they won't have me to kick around anymore.

Closely allied to irony in satire is *wit*, which as the following definition suggests, has also its range of voice and tone effects to contribute in the defense or attack of any cause or situation. In the seventeenth century, wit was identified with either judgment or fancy, or with both at once. Wit, as judgment, suggests decorum of style, elegance, good taste, restraint, gentlemanly wit, and raillery—all that is usually labeled neoclassical. Wit, as fancy, suggests the more irrational, fanciful, sophistical, and whimsical elements: the invention of original comparisons, the use of paradox and antithesis; it stresses novelty and surprise.[16]

How this kind of highly civilized wit as judgment can do the work of satire in attacking social institutions can be seen in the writings of two

[16] Thomas H. Fujimura, *The Restoration Comedy of Wit* (New York: Barnes and Noble, 1968), p. 33.

novelists who have aimed their witty shafts at higher education in England. In the first selection, Thomas Love Peacock wittily describes the poor quality of the education received by the "hero" of *Nightmare Abbey* (1818).

When Scythrop grew up, he was sent, as usual, to a public school, where a little learning was painfully beaten into him, and from thence to the university, where it was carefully taken out of him; and he was sent home like a well-threshed ear of corn, with nothing in his head: having finished his education to the high satisfaction of the master and fellows of his college, who had, in testimony of their approbation, presented him with a silver fish-slice, on which his name figured at the head of a lauda-tory inscription in some semi-barbarous dialect of Anglo-Saxonized Latin.

Peacock's adoption of a mock serious tone and an elegant style to state the absurdities of the youth's university education is characteristic of his wit. Notice the balance in the opening of the sentence presented as *antithesis* (elements parallel in structure but opposite in meaning): "where a little learning was painfully beaten into him, and from thence to the university, where it was carefully taken out of him. . . ." That such "education" should have given "high satisfaction," to any of his instructors is ridiculous, a fact which the "silver fish-slice" with its poor Latin inscription underscores.

Our second novelist is one of the great satirists of this century, Evelyn Waugh, and in his *Decline and Fall* (1956) he also levels witty, ascerbic shafts at English university officialdom.

PRELUDE[17]

Mr. Sniggs, the Junior Dean, and Mr. Postlethwaite, the Domestic Bursar, sat alone in Mr. Sniggs's room overlooking the garden quad at Scone College. From the rooms of Sir Alastair Digby-Vaine-Trumpington, two staircases away, came a confused roaring and breaking of glass. They alone of the senior members of Scone were at home that evening, for it was the night of the annual dinner of the Bollinger Club. The others were all scattered over Boar's Hill and North Oxford at gay, contentious little parties, or at other senior common rooms, or at the meetings of learned

[17] From Evelyn Waugh, *Decline and Fall* (Boston: Little, Brown & Company, 1956), pp. 227–237.

societies, for the annual Bollinger dinner is a difficult time for those in authority.

It is not accurate to call this an annual event, because quite often the Club is suspended for some years after each meeting. There is tradition behind the Bollinger; it numbers reigning kings among its past members. At the last dinner, three years ago, a fox had been brought in in a cage and stoned to death with champagne bottles. What an evening that had been! This was the first meeting since then, and from all over Europe old members had rallied for the occasion. For two days they had been pouring into Oxford: epileptic royalty from their villas of exile; uncouth peers from crumbling country seats; smooth young men of uncertain tastes from embassies and legations; illiterate lairds from wet granite hovels in the Highlands; ambitious young barristers and Conservative candidates torn from the London season and the indelicate advances of debutantes; all that was most sonorous of name and title was there for the beano.

"The fines!" said Mr. Sniggs, gently rubbing his pipe along the side of his nose. "Oh, my! the fines there'll be after this evening!"

There is some highly prized port in the senior common room cellars that is only brought up when the College fines have reached £50.

"We shall have a week of it at least," said Mr. Postlethwaite, "a week of Founder's port."

A shriller note could now be heard rising from Sir Alastair's rooms; any who have heard that sound will shrink at the recollection of it; it is the sound of the English county families baying for broken glass. Soon they would all be tumbling out into the quad, crimson and roaring in their bottle-green evening coats, for the real romp of the evening.

"Don't you think it might be wiser if we turned out the light?" said Mr. Sniggs.

In darkness the two dons crept to the window. The quad below was a kaleidoscope of dimly discernible faces.

"There must be fifty of them at least," said Mr. Postlethwaite. "If only they were all members of the College! Fifty of them at ten pounds each. Oh, my!"

"It'll be more if they attack the Chapel," said Mr. Sniggs. "Oh, please God, make them attack the Chapel."

"I wonder who the unpopular undergraduates are this term. They always attack their rooms. I hope they have been wise enough to go out for the evening."

"I think Partridge will be one; he possesses a painting by Matisse or some such name."

"And I'm told he has black sheets in his bed."

"And Sanders went to dinner with Ramsay MacDonald once."

"And Rending can afford to hunt, but collects china instead."

"And smokes cigars in the garden after breakfast."

"Austen has a grand piano."

"They'll enjoy smashing that."

"There'll be a heavy bill for to-night; just you see! But I confess I should feel easier if the Dean or the Master were in. They can't see us from here, can they?"

It was a lovely evening. They broke up Mr. Austen's grand piano, and stamped Lord Rending's cigars into his carpet, and smashed his china, and tore up Mr. Partridge's sheets, and threw the Matisse into his water jug; Mr. Sanders had nothing to break except his windows, but they found the manuscript at which he had been working for the Newdigate Prize Poem, and had great fun with that. Sir Alastair Digby-Vaine-Trumpington felt quite ill with excitement, and was supported to bed by Lumsden of Strath-drummond. It was half-past eleven. Soon the evening would come to an end. But there was still a treat to come.

Paul Pennyfeather was reading for the Church. It was his third year of uneventful residence at Scone. He had come there after a creditable career at a small public school of ecclesiastical temper on the South Downs, where he had edited the magazine, been President of the Debating Society, and had, as his report said, "exercised a wholesome influence for good" in the House of which he was head boy. At home he lived in Onslow Square with his guardian, a prosperous solicitor who was proud of his progress and abysmally bored by his company. Both his parents had died in India at the time when he won the essay prize at his preparatory school. For two years he had lived within his allowance, aided by two valuable scholarships. He smoked three ounces of tobacco a week—John Cotton, Medium—and drank a pint and a half of beer a day, the half at luncheon and the pint at dinner, a meal he invariably ate in Hall. He had four friends, three of whom had been at school with him. None of the Bollinger Club had ever heard of Paul Pennyfeather, and he, oddly enough, had not heard of them.

Little suspecting the incalculable consequences that the evening was to have for him, he bicycled happily back from a meeting of the League of Nations Union. There had been a most interesting paper about plebiscites in Poland. He thought of smoking a pipe and reading another chapter of the *Forsyte Saga* before going to bed. He knocked at the gate, was admitted, put away his bicycle, and diffidently, as always, made his way across the quad towards his rooms. What a lot of people there seemed to be about! Paul had no particular objection to drunkenness—he had read rather a daring paper to the Thomas More Society on the subject—but he was consumedly shy of drunkards.

Out of the night Lumsden of Strathdrummond swayed across his path like a druidical rocking stone. Paul tried to pass.

Now it so happened that the tie of Paul's old school bore a marked resemblance to the pale blue and white of the Bollinger Club. The difference of a quarter of an inch in the width of the stripes was not one that Lumsden of Strathdrummond was likely to appreciate.

"Here's an awful man wearing the Boller tie," said the Laird. It is not for nothing that since pre-Christian times his family has exercised chief-tainship over uncharted miles of barren moorland.

Mr. Sniggs was looking rather apprehensively at Mr. Postlethwaite.

"They appear to have caught somebody," he said. "I hope they don't do him any serious harm."

"Dear me, can it be Lord Rending? I think I ought to intervene."

"No, Sniggs," said Mr. Postlethwaite, laying a hand on his impetuous colleague's arm. "No, no, no. It would be unwise. We have the prestige of the senior common room to consider. In their present state they might not prove amenable to discipline. We must at all costs avoid an *outrage*."

At length the crowd parted, and Mr. Sniggs gave a sigh of relief.

"But it's quite all right. It isn't Rending. It's Pennyfeather—some one of no importance."

"Well, that saves a great deal of trouble. I am glad, Sniggs; I am, really. What a lot of clothes the young man appears to have lost!"

Next morning there was a lovely College meeting.

"Two hundred and thirty pounds," murmured the Domestic Bursar ecstatically, "*not* counting the damage! That means five evenings, with what we have already collected. Five evenings of Founder's port!"

"The case of Pennyfeather," the Master was saying, "seems to be quite a different matter altogether. He ran the whole length of the quad-rangle, you say, *without his trousers*. It is unseemly. It is more: it is inde-cent. In fact, I am almost prepared to say that it is flagrantly indecent. It is *not* the conduct we expect of a scholar."

"Perhaps if we fined him really heavily?" suggested the Junior Dean.

"I very much doubt whether he could pay. I understand he is not well off. *Without trousers*, indeed! And at that time of night! I think we should do far better to get rid of him altogether. That sort of young man does the College no good."

Two hours later, while Paul was packing his three suits in his little leather trunk, the Domestic Bursar sent a message that he wished to see him.

"Ah, Mr. Pennyfeather," he said, "I have examined your rooms and notice two slight burns, one on the window sill and the other on the chim-ney piece, no doubt from cigarette ends. I am charging you five-and-sixpence for each of them on your battels. That is all, thank you."

As he crossed the quad Paul met Mr. Sniggs.

"Just off?" said the Junior Dean brightly.

"Yes, sir," said Paul.

And a little farther on he met the Chaplain.

"Oh, Pennyfeather, before you go, surely you have my copy of Dean Stanley's *Eastern Church?*"

"Yes. I left it on your table."

"Thank you. Well, good-bye, my dear boy. I suppose that after that reprehensible affair last night you will have to think of some other profession. Well, you may congratulate yourself that you discovered your unfitness for the priesthood before it was too late. If a parson does a thing of that sort, you know, all the world knows. And so many do, alas! What do you propose doing?"

"I don't really know yet."

"There is always commerce, of course. Perhaps you may be able to bring to the great world of business some of the ideals you have learned at Scone. But it won't be easy, you know. It is a thing to be lived down with courage. What did Dr. Johnson say about fortitude? . . . Dear, dear! *no trousers!*"

At the gates Paul tipped the porter.

"Well, good-bye, Blackall," he said. "I don't suppose I shall see you again for some time."

"No, sir, and very sorry I am to hear about it. I expect you'll be becoming a schoolmaster, sir. That's what most of the gentlemen does, sir, that gets sent down for indecent behaviour."

"God damn and blast them all to hell," said Paul meekly to himself as he drove to the station, and then he felt rather ashamed, because he rarely swore.

Irony abounds in this opening section of Waugh's novel. The situation itself is ironic in that it is a poor, decent theological student who is bounced out of school because he was the victim of holiday high jinks played on him by savage but privileged alumni, whose outrageous conduct was gleefully condoned by college officials delighted at the alcoholic beverages the fines incurred by these alumni would buy. Nor does the young victim himself receive any sympathy from the author; the final sentence with its pitiful curse, which was immediately followed by shame, condemns the youth for his supine attitude throughout.

Wit and irony infuse the language everywhere and nowhere more brilliantly than in the second paragraph with its description of the returning alumni and the highlight event of "the last dinner" when "a fox had been brought in in a cage and stoned to death with champagne bottles. What an evening that had been!" This last exemplifies *irony through apparent praise,* wherein what appears to be approval is, of course, just its opposite. Likewise the details of destruction supporting the ironic judgment "It was a lovely evening" lead to the equally satiric "But there was still a treat to come," which refers to the upcoming attack on the theological student.

Another ironic remark further excoriates all concerned: "Next morning there was a lovely College meeting." Words like "indecent" and "flagrantly indecent" applied to the youth who had been stripped of his trousers by one of the "illiterate lairds from wet granite hovels in the Highlands" only make more savage the ridicule, and underscore the disgust which drives the wit of this novelist.

TOPICS FOR DISCUSSION AND WRITING

1. Since the basis of all irony and satire is the belief, or stance, of the ironist and the satirist that he has a clear view of the "truth" of a situation, in any attempt to be satirical it is important that one first have some convictions. If you cannot always be certain you know what is right, you may at least clearly see what is wrong or false about an existing troublesome situation. This somewhat philosophical attitude underlies all successful strategies and devices of ridicule and sharp criticism arousing laughter.

   Our society today offers many targets for such attacks. Here are some possible areas inviting satirical treatment. Select one for your own try or substitute an area of your own. Single out a particular aspect, official, or figure that you consider representative of what is badly in need of reform. Do not be afraid to exaggerate what you consider the hypocrisy or absurdity of the situation you are attacking.

Professional sports	Fashions in clothes
College sports	Hair fashions
High school sex education	Employment prospects
"Terrible" movie films	Increased fees and tuition
Nauseating TV programs	The latest fad
Cost and quality of food	Nostalgia for the past
Abortion	Styles of marriage
Popular music stars	Local politicians
Disc jockey freaks	National elections
Bicycle lanes and traffic	Impossible examinations

2. Why not try your hand at *parody*? It requires the ability to mimic the pet expressions and general outlook of the target subject. As much as possible, too, parody to be successful demands capture of the "tone" characteristic of the one being taken off. The usual method is to choose the kind of subject matter that the thing parodied would naturally contain pronouncements on; then, by employing this typical phraseology make the subject matter twist off

into the ridiculous. (Examples of parodies abound in periodicals like *Mad, National Lampoon,* and *Punch.*) Possible targets are:

The set speech of a political figure much in the news
The Ten Commandments brought up to date
A high school commencement address by a "solid citizen"
A professional athlete trying to be modest
The "sermon" of a traffic court judge
A cigarette company president defending his company's sale campaigns
A salesman's "line" in persuading a prospect to sign on the dotted line

Mannered styles and tones

Some authors develop writing styles that at first appear unique and require readers who have fostered a special taste for such oddities or elegances of word patternings, tonal expressions, and perhaps esoteric subject matter. Authors working in such veins must expect readers to discover them and establish their reputations. Like artists such as Modigliani and Van Gogh, some authors may have long to wait for recognition and acceptance. Many may never enjoy more than a small circle of admirers whose ardent appreciation must make up for the neglect of the multitudes. Yet the works of a T. S. Eliot and an E. E. Cummings can burgeon into considerable popularity, as may a James Joyce of *Ulysses* and *Finnegan's Wake* fame, a Virginia Woolf of *Jacob's Room,* a William Faulkner of *The Sound and the Fury,* or more recently a William Burroughs of *The Naked Lunch.*

Nearly all new writers who come to be recognized as masters are innovators who open fresh fields of subject matter and perhaps also introduce new writing techniques. From these sources come such literary movements as Romanticism, Realism, Naturalism, Symbolism, Expressionism, Dadaism, Existentialism, Social Realism, and Absurdism along with such techniques as "slice of life" description, stream of consciousness, and interior monologue.

In time, these once novel techniques and approaches become more or less commonplaces for ambitious young writers, who learn to see life through the language and forms of earlier masters. This is dramatically evidenced by those two great Russian novelists of our time, Boris Pasternak and Alexander Solzhenitsin, who have acknowledged their indebtedness to Leo Tolstoy.

Yet not all of these stylistic innovations become rhetorical successes. For every Zola, Hemingway, Faulkner, Sartre, or Beckett there are numerous other authors whose styles partake of the unique but are perhaps not great direct influences upon other writers. Yet their work exhibits further possibilities of the English language as a means of expressing personal views and impressions. Their prose may be considered by some critics to be too "precious," too "mannered," and, therefore, "artificial," but it still will have its admirers.

Ronald Firbank is such an author. Here is an excerpt from one of his novels, *The Flower Beneath the Foot.* In this passage the highly eccentric Countess is being observed from afar by the Count through his telescope.

> But the inclination to focus the mundane and embittered features of the fanatic Countess, as she lectured her boatmen for forgetting their oars, or, being considerably superstitious, to count the moles on their united faces as an esoteric clue to the Autumn Lottery, waned a little before the mystery of the descending night.
>
> Beneath a changing tide of deepening shadow, the lifeless valleys were mirroring to the lake the sombreness of dusk. Across the blue forlornness of the water, a swan, here and there, appeared quite violet, while coiffed in swift, clinging, golden clouds the loftiest hills alone retained the sun.
>
> A faint nocturnal breeze, arising simultaneously with the Angelusbell, seemed likely to relieve, at the moon's advent, the trials to her patience of the Countess Yvorra: "who must be cursing," the Count reflected, turning the telescope about with a sigh, to suit her sail.
>
> Ah poignant moments when the heart stops still! Not since the hour of his exile had the Count's been so arrested.
>
> From the garden Peter's voice rose questingly; but the Count was too wonderstruck, far, to heed it.
>
> Caught in the scarlet radiance of the afterglow, the becalmed boat, for one brief and most memorable second, was his to gaze on.[18]

If your first reaction on scanning this prose is to cry out, "Crap!" you would no doubt find many agreeing with your judgment. Some more restrained and descriptive critics might respond with adjectives like "bombastic," "turgid," "inflated," and "pretentious." They also might complain about ambiguities in the opening sentence occasioned by the apparently dangling participial phrase "being considerably superstitious" and the equally floating infinitive phrase "to count the moles. . . ."

---

[18] "The Flower beneath the Foot," in *Ronald Firbank: Fire Novels* (Norfolk, Conn: New Directions Books), p. 222.

Who was "superstitious"? Who was "to count the moles"? And while they might frown upon the excessive use of *epithets* (adjective-noun phrases) such as "the descending night," "changing tide," "deepening shadow," "the lifeless valleys," "blue forlornness," "the loftiest hills," "the scarlet radiance," and "swift, clinging, golden clouds," they would note that this little incident does have a pleasing ironic tone. For the situation described is comic. As the Count raptly spies on the Countess and time stands still for him, his lover, Peter, is calling him from the garden. It is quite a hilarious mixture of flamboyant description, exotic syntax, and ludicrous characterization!

Another recent "curiosity" of style and tone has been the four-volume work by Lawrence Durrell called *The Alexandria Quartet*. As with all such mannered styles spectacular for both their language patternings and their exotic subject matter, this work has received what critics like to describe as "mixed reactions." It has been both roundly condemned and fulsomely praised. But sample it for yourself as another exhibit of the possibilities our language has in serving the purposes of narrative. This is a scene from *Justine*. Marginal notes call attention to some of the rhetorical figures.

I am recalling now how during that last spring (forever) we walked together at full moon, overcome by the soft dazed air of the city, the quiet *[personification] [simile]* ablutions of water and moonlight that polished it like a great casket. An aerial lunacy among the deserted trees of the dark squares, and the long dusty roads reaching away from midnight to mid-*[simile]* night, bluer than oxygen. The passing faces had *[metonymy]* become gem-like, tranced—the baker at his machine making the staff of tomorrow's life, the *[metaphor]* lover hurrying back to his lodging, nailed into a *[metaphor]* silver helmet of panic, the six-foot cinema posters borrowing a ghastly magnificence from the moon which seemed laid across the nerves *[simile]* like a bow. *[metaphor]*

We turn a corner and the world becomes a pattern of arteries, splashed with silver and deckle-edged with shadow. At this far end of Kom El Dick not a soul abroad save an occasional obsessive policeman, lurking like a guilty wish in *[simile]* the city's mind. Our footsteps run punctually as *[simile]* metronomes along the deserted pavements: two men, in their own time and city, remote from the *[simile]* world, walking as if they were treading one of the lugubrious canals of the moon. Pursewarden is speaking of the book which he has always wanted to write, and of the difficulty which besets a city-man when he faces a work of art.

simile
personification

"If you think of yourself as a sleeping city for example . . . what? You can sit quiet and hear the processes going on, going about their business; volition, desire, will, cognition, passion, conation. I mean like the million legs of a centipede

simile

carrying on with the body powerless to do anything about it. One gets exhausted trying to cir-

metaphor

cumnavigate these huge fields of experience. We are never free, we writers. I could explain it much more clearly if it was dawn. I long to be musical in body and mind. I want style, consort.

metaphor
simile
personification

Not the little mental squirts as if through the ticker-tape of the mind. It is the age's disease, is it not? It explains the huge waves of occultism lapping round us. The Cabal, now, and Balthazar. He will never understand that it is with God we must be the most careful; for He makes such a powerful appeal to what is *lowest* in human nature — our feeling of insufficiency, fear of the

synecdoche
metaphor
metaphor

unknown, personal failings; above all our monstrous egotism which sees in the martyr's crown an athletic prize which is really hard to attain. God's real and subtle nature must be clear of distinctions: a glass of spring-water, tasteless, odourless, merely refreshing: and surely its appeal would be to the few, the very few, real contemplatives? As for the many it is already included in the part of their nature which they least wish to admit or examine. I do not believe that there is any system which can do more than pervert the essential idea. And then, all these attempts to circumscribe God in words or ideas. . . . No one thing can explain everything: though everything can illuminate something. God, I must be still drunk. If God were anything he would be an art. Sculpture or medicine. But the immense extension of knowledge in this our age, the growth of new sciences, makes it almost impossible for us to digest the available flavours

metaphor

and put them to use."[19]

[19] Lawrence Durrell, *Justine* (New York: E. P. Dutton & Co., Inc., 1961), pp. 139–140.

How such sophisticated and elegant prose can become a means of analyzing a style and thereby perhaps add to the richness of one's own style has been shown by Phyllis Brooks of the University of California at Berkeley. She has successfully employed the method of *paraphrase* to acquaint student writers with the practicable values of learning how to work from models. She vividly explains how paraphrase works in helping students learn, for example, how to use parallel structure:

PARALLELISM PLUS REFERENCE[20]

Parallel structure is one of the trickiest ideas to explain and to teach. Errors in coordination, errors in apposition often have their roots in some misunderstanding of the *balance* of a sentence. Students can laugh at sentences like "He went to the White House in trepidation and a tuxedo" (semantic parallelism abused) and can see dimly that something is wrong with "He likes swimming and to row small boats" (structural parallelism abused), but go on producing comparable bastards in their own prose. As a result, any kind of balanced period of the John Henry Newman type— "The true gentleman is never mean or little in his disputes, never takes unfair advantage, never mistakes personalities or sharp sayings for arguments, or insinuates evil which he dare not say out"—is a very rare bird in a freshman paper. Yet with a little conscious effort the student can prove to himself that complex parallelisms are possible and usable.

A paraphrase that has proved useful in demonstrating balanced sentences governed by careful parallelism of structure and ideas is the following passage from Mark Twain, a description of the Sphinx. At the same time it is a valuable exercise in controlling the reference of pronouns (thus the surprising bracketing of these two items in the subhead). The passage is generously sprinkled with *its*. As the student begins to construct his picture within the Twain frame, he has to consider the reference of each pronoun in turn. There are no structural *its* in the paragraph; each *it* functions as a true pronoun:

After years of waiting, it was before me at last. The great face was so sad, so earnest, so longing, so patient. There was a dignity not of earth in its mien, and in its countenance a benignity such as never anything human wore. It was stone, but it seemed sentient. If ever image of stone thought, it was thinking. It was looking toward the verge of the landscape, yet looking at nothing—nothing but distance

[20] From Phyllis Brooks, "Mimesis: Grammar and the Echoing Voice," *College English* 35 (November 1973): 165–167.

and vacancy. It was looking over and beyond everything of the present, and far into the past. It was gazing out over the ocean of Time — over lines of century-waves which, further and further receding, closed nearer and nearer together, and blended at last into one unbroken tide, away toward the horizon of remote antiquity. It was thinking of the wars of departed ages; of the empires it had seen created and destroyed; of the nations whose birth it had witnessed, whose progress it had watched, whose annihilation it had noted; of the joy and sorrow, the life and death, the grandeur and decay, of five thousand slow revolving years. It was the type of an attribute of man — of a faculty of his heart and brain. It was *memory — retrospection —* wrought into visible, tangible form. All who knew what pathos there is in memories of days that are accomplished and faces that have vanished — albeit only a trifling score of years gone by — will have some appreciation of the pathos that dwells in these grave eyes that look so steadfastly back upon the things they knew before History was born. — *The Innocents Abroad*

In this paraphrase, as in most others, students found themselves earnestly considering the structure of the passage and the progression of thought. From a concrete image Twain moves farther and farther into realms of abstraction — the thoughts suggested by the material object and its meaning for the observer. Only by trying to construct a new paragraph on Twain's model can the beginning student of language become completely aware of and involved in this process. Here is a student's effort:

[A College Dorm] After a lifetime of anticipation, it loomed before me. The tall structure was so cold, so bleak, so lonesome, so much without any personality or character of its own. There was nothing unique in it at all, and inside on the tile floors were heel marks of all the students who had been there before. The building wasn't human, but it wanted to speak. If the appearance of a building was ever trying to give a warning, then it was this building that was philosophizing. It was talking to me, yet also to others — others who would soon enter its halls. It was thinking of all that it had seen from the present to the past. It was fascinated by the movie of its memories — of all the single frames and incidents which, one by one, quickly add up till they produce a moving image. It was thinking of all the people who had come in wanting to make the world better; of all the idealism and romanticism that had once flourished; of the individuals with such questioning minds, whose regression it had watched, whose decay was observed; of the beginning and the end, hope and death, the illusions and reality, of all the people who had ended up as they did not originally want to. It was a lesson to Man — of the meaning of hypocrisy. It was *memory — knowledge —* brought into reality. All those who have a conception of life—who can easily realize what message is being conveyed—will realize what the warning is—for experience has told this college dorm that people who enter with young and optimistic ideas leave with old and rational realizations.—CRAIG WEINTRAUB

Effective plain style

There is no question at all that by this stage of your development as a student-writer you have acquired a distinct style—one your composition instructor can distinguish from those of your classmates by your characteristic choices of subject matter, tone, language, and general rhetorical stance. How satisfied are you with that style?

If you have made it a habit to be *informal, direct,* and *sincere* in your writing stance, you very likely have developed an effective *plain style.* Unlike some of the styles and rhetorical tones so far presented in this chapter, the plain style is always in good taste in almost any circumstance. It appeals by not being pretentious or flashy; it does not talk over the heads of its audience; nor on the contrary does it talk down to them; it does not beat around the bush and waste words; instead, its message is clear and sufficiently complete. Its word choice reflects an intelligent effort to take into consideration the tastes and interests of its readers or listeners; and, finally, it moves at a pace and rhythm natural to the writer who is fluent in his dialect. For these reasons it is a most serviceable style, one we have tried to make characteristic of this book.

Montaigne's "What I Find in My Essays" is an example of one kind of plain style which is rich in its directness and sincerity of tone and yet imaginative and dramatic in many of its expressions, as are these:

> I have no sergeant to whip my ideas into rank—except chance itself. Sometimes they come trooping in a single file, and sometimes by brigades; and as they come I line them up. I want the reader to see my natural and ordinary gait for the stagger it is.

As Montaigne might have advised, "Speak like yourself if you want a good plain style."

If through your varied experiences so far with writing you feel you have steadily been improving, you do not need to be told again the importance of *desiring* to be a skilled writer. Without desire, without self-motivation, no one advances beyond mediocrity in anything. You do not need a textbook to tell you that. Nor by now do you require a reminder that any improvement in your writing style involves also changes in yourself.

It means choosing to learn more about composition, rhetoric, effective language, and sentence syntax, and then being willing to put that knowledge into practice. It means choosing to improve in your ability to think logically about all manner of problems so as not to be ruled by blind emotion or prejudices. It also means becoming more aware of the relationships you have with things and people in your daily life and their possible significance to you.

If you make it a habit to be informal, direct, and sincere in your writing stance, your chances of becoming increasingly effective are good. Striving for those qualities, you will become more self-critical of your own work and even seek further help. This is the method and regime followed by professional players in sports as well as by artists in all arts. In these matters, analysis and criticism, as well as approval from your instructors and classmates are most helpful.

As final evidence of how those qualities of informality, directness, and sincerity help shape personal styles that are distinct in their effectiveness, consider the two selections that follow. The first is by James A. Michener, author of the well-known *Tales of the South Pacific*, *Hawaii*, and 15 other books, and the second is by a student who is a Vietnam war veteran. Both writers are recalling wartime experiences but of different wars and, of course, in totally different kinds of plain style.

Once more you are not asked to "imitate" authors but rather to emulate them, that is, to discover their rhetorical and compositional skills, or their shortcomings, and then resolve to put those skills properly to use yourself in your own writing projects.

THIS I BELIEVE[21]

by JAMES A. MICHENER

I really believe that every man on this earth is my brother. He has a soul like mine, the ability to understand friendship, the capacity to create beauty. In all the continents of this world I have met such men. In the most savage jungles of New Guinea I have met my brother, and in Tokyo I have seen him clearly walking before me.

[21] Copyright 1954 by Help, Inc. Copyright © 1973 by Random House, Inc. and the Reader's Digest Association, Inc. Reprinted from *A Michener Miscellany: 1950–1970*, by James A. Michener, by permission of Random House, Inc.

In my brother's house I have lived without fear. Once in the wildest part of Guadalcanal I had to spend some days with men who still lived and thought in the old Stone Age, but we got along together fine, and I was to see those men in a space of only four weeks ripped from their jungle hideaways and brought down to the airstrips, where some of them learned to drive the ten-ton trucks which carried gasoline to our bombing planes.

Once in India I lived for several days with villagers who didn't know a word of English. But the fact that I couldn't speak their language was no hindrance. Differences in social custom never kept me from getting to know and like savage Melanesians in the New Hebrides. They ate roast dog and I ate army Spam, and if we had wanted to emphasize differences, I am sure each of us could have concluded the other was nuts. But we stressed similarities, and so long as I could snatch a Navy blanket for them now and then, we had a fine old time with no words spoken.

I believe it was only fortunate experience that enabled me to travel among my brothers and to live with them. Therefore I do not believe it is my duty to preach to other people and insist that they also accept all men as their true and immediate brothers. These things come slow. Sometimes it takes lucky breaks to open our eyes. I had to learn gradually, as I believe the world will one day learn.

To my home in rural Pennsylvania come brown men and yellow men and black men from around the world. In their countries I lived and ate with them. In my country they shall live and eat with me. Until the day I die my home must be free to receive these travelers, and it never seems so big a home or so much a place of love as when some man from India or Japan or Mexico or Tahiti or Fiji shares it with me. For on those happy days it reminds me of the wonderful affection I have known throughout the world.

I believe that all men are my brothers. I know it when I see them sharing my home.

THE KILLING OF THE FROGS
by JACK E. ROSS, JR.

THE PLACE:

East of Hue, South Vietnam, on a firebase called Birmingham.

THE PEOPLE

There were three of us. We had spent about 8 of our 12 month tour together. We had flown on the same flight and had through luck been assigned to the same company, which upon our arrival at headquarters had assigned us to the same three-man radar squad. Note: the fact that we had no experience as ground surveillance radar operators did not deter them from assigning us to the squad.

Of the three of us, one, Joe Handy, was given to much boasting and never had doubts as to his ability as a radar operator or his unusual ability (at least in his own eyes) to be absolutely right in all situations. The other, Alvin Korm, had gone through many personal troubles, his wife having run off with a friend of his when he had entered the army, subsequently gotten a divorce and then remarried him while he was on special leave from a hospital in Japan, where he was recuperating from wounds he had received in combat. And me, mixed up in my own identity, being secure enough in my ability to perform a given task, having enough initiative to be recognized, but being an easy going sort of person with the tendency to take a certain amount of abuse, not verbal or physical, but rather mental, not wishing to exert myself and cause bad feelings.

THREE DAYS BEFORE

It was while Korm was standing guard on the radar that we heard a shot from the next bunker. We reacted to the situation rather than thought about it. Then when we were in our fighting positions we realized that the shot had not been caused by any enemy initiated action, but instead had been a case of false instincts on the part of the man on guard. We had to wait until the next morning to find out what had actually occurred.

It seems that the man on guard, having been in the country only three weeks, had turned and faced inward towards the center of the perimeter, where the other four men manning that bunker were sleeping on cots, the cots being spread out directly behind the bunker. His guard being up, he had called the man who was to relieve him. This man started to get up and evidently the man still on duty had momentarily closed his eyes; when he opened them again he saw some movement. Evidently forgetting that he still faced inward, the guard shot one of the other three men, the one on the opposite side from the man getting up for guard. The man shot was killed. He had less than one month left of his tour.

THE NIGHT BEFORE

It was a sleepless night for the three of us, for although the typhoon had passed us several miles out to sea, we were buffeted by high winds and unbelievable amounts of gushing rain. We had two men on guard duty at all times. Because of the rain, we were unable to see more than 10 feet down the hill in front of our bunker. To us it seemed reasonable to expect a visit from Mr. Charlie. The radar was inoperable in high winds as it did not differentiate the movements it was picking up of grass, bushes, and trees being blown by high winds. The deluge of rain also clouded the signal.

ANOTHER RELEVANT FACT

We were constantly being startled while on guard duty by loud rustling noises in the grasses beside and in front of our bunker. We knew that the enemy was out there and perhaps had accidentally made the noise while sneaking up on our bunker. We had given up the idea that the wind was making the noise because we heard the noise even when the wind would let up. It was not so bad around the full of the moon as there was enough light to read a newspaper, but on this night during the dark of the moon it was downright spooky.

THE INCIDENT

We were sitting in the hot sun the next afternoon trying to get a better suntan when Joe said, "I know what's making all those noises at night. It's those damn frogs." Before I realized it, we were all out there searching in the grass trying to find frogs. When one of us would spot one, he would yell and we would all run over there and start throwing our "altered bayonet" throwing knives to see who could be the first to hit it. After the first knife hit one, we would quickly kill it and start looking for another one. We continued in this way for over an hour before we got hot and tired and decided to quit. We had killed twenty-one frogs.

THE SYMBOLISM

First the act of killing itself. To me this symbolized to a certain extent what we had become: blood-and-flesh-killing machines. It was a natural response, something one did without thinking. The Army taught us not to think but just to obey orders. In combat you don't think, you react, you kill. *"The purpose of the bayonet is to kill!"* The Army taught us all kinds of ways to kill: with a weapon, with a natural object (sticks, rocks, etc.), with our bare hands or feet, with piano wire, hatchets, knives, grenades, mines —I could go on but I won't. An example of what comes from this type of training was the shooting of one of our men by the guard.

As to the fact that it was frogs we were killing, it is symbolic in that the killing did not stop the rest of the frogs from making noises at night. Nor did it scare them from the area. In short it accomplished nothing. What did we accomplish in Vietnam?

FOCUS POINT

1. Objective reporting

2. Sentimental narrative

3. The self-assured personal voice

4. The tone of protest

5. The urbane tone

6. The tone of allegory

7. Tones of irony and satire

8. Mannered styles and tones

9. The effective plain style

FINAL EXERCISES

1. As a kind of review and means of trying to bring into clear focus what you consider may yet be most helpful to you as a developing student-writer, study the index of articles appearing in this book and the writing principles each exemplifies.

2. Choose a subject suitable to the practice of those particular principles that interest you the most.

3. Write in a stance suitable to your subject and audience the thoughts and feelings you have regarding the subject.

4. Be your own critic and revise and rewrite as you judge you should.

Author Index

Subject Index